LAW AND THE ARTS

Recent Titles in
Contributions in Legal Studies

LAW AND THE ARTS

Edited by Susan Tiefenbrun

Prepared under the auspices of Hofstra University

Contributions in Legal Studies, Number 87

Greenwood Press
Westport, Connecticut • London

Library of Congress Cataloging-in-Publication Data

Law and the arts / edited by Susan Tiefenbrun ; foreword by Stuart
    Rabinowitz ; prepared under the auspices of Hofstra University.
        p.   cm.—(Contributions in legal studies, ISSN 0147–1074 ;
    no. 87)
        "Based on an . . . interdisciplinary seminar on Law and the Arts
    which was held at Hofstra University School of Law . . . on October
    30, 1996"—Foreword.
        Includes bibliographical references and index.
        ISBN 0–313–30805–5 (alk. paper)
        1. Law and art—United States—Congresses.   2. Arts—Censorship—
    United States—Congresses.   3. Copyright and electronic data
    processing—United States—Congresses.   4. Law and literature—
    Congresses.   5. Critical legal studies—Congresses.
    6. Shakespeare, William, 1564–1616. Merchant of Venice—Congresses.
    I. Tiefenbrun, Susan W.   II. Hofstra University.   III. Series.
    KF4288.A75L374   1999
    344.73′097—dc21   98–14237

British Library Cataloguing in Publication Data is available.

Library of Congress Catalog Card Number: 98–14237
ISBN: 0–313–30805–5
ISSN: 0147–1074

First published in 1999

Greenwood Press, 88 Post Road West, Westport, CT 06881
An imprint of Greenwood Publishing Group, Inc.

Printed in the United States of America

The paper used in this book complies with the
Permanent Paper Standard issued by the National
Information Standards Organization (Z39.48–1984).

10 9 8 7 6 5 4 3 2 1

Copyright Acknowledgments

Every reasonable effort has been made to trace the owners of copyright materials in this book,
but in some instances this has proven impossible. The editor and publisher will be glad to receive
information leading to more complete acknowledgments in subsequent printings of the book
and in the meantime extend their apologies for any omissions.

Contents

Critical Legal Theory

Howard Kissel
Theater Critic, *The Daily News*

Peter J. Alscher
Senior Area Manager
Cleveland Cotton Products

Appellate *Daniel J. Kornstein, Esq.*, for Shylock
Attorneys: *Floyd Abrams, Esq.*, for Antonio
     Kevin Castel, Esq., for Antonio

Foreword

Stuart Rabinowitz

This book is based on an unusual one-day interdisciplinary conference on law and the arts that was held at the Hofstra University School of Law on October 30, 1996.

The Law and the Arts Symposium attracted a large audience of interested people from diverse backgrounds. The relationship between the law and the arts was explored by more than forty distinguished speakers who entertained and informed the audience through a wide variety of media. Well-known scholars, professors, writers, artists, theater critics, actors, judges, and lawyers exchanged ideas with people in diverse fields of law, communications, art, literature, film and theater. Law-related topics discussed included censorship of the media, art and repression during the McCarthy era, indecency on the Internet, copyright infringement and museums in cyberspace, and the status of the critical legal theory movement. The day ended with the reargument of *Shylock v. Antonio* of *The Merchant of Venice* before a distinguished panel of judges. This retrial was so stimulating and thought provoking that it was reargued before the Bar Association of the City of New York almost a year later on September 23, 1997.

The Law and the Arts Symposium was cosponsored by the Hofstra University School of Law, the Hofstra Cultural Center, the Hofstra University School of Communication, and the Law and Humanities Institute. The United States Supreme Court generously lent Hofstra selected works from its permanent art collection which remained on exhibit at the Hofstra Museum for several weeks before and after the conference.

This book provides the opportunity to rethink the law and its intricate relationship to the humanities, to society, and to civilization.

Stuart Rabinowitz, Dean
Hofstra University
School of Law

Preface

Susan Tiefenbrun

Law and the Arts is a venture into interdisciplinarity. These two ancient and complex fields have many points in common, which, when uncovered and applied to specific issues in either field, may result in new insights and rediscoveries. The book represents a collaborative effort between scholars and practitioners in the Hofstra University School of Law, the Hofstra University School of Communication, and the Law and Humanities Institute who are committed to the beneficial effects of an interdisciplinary approach to investigative research and learning.

Interdisciplinarity is an approach, not a solution. The methodology is designed to promote the exchange of ideas among people from diverse but related fields of law, literature, film, theater, communications, art and architecture. The goal of an interdisciplinary approach is to explore relationships between varied disciplines using language as a common tool. The desired effect of such an approach is to inspire readers to think about the laws hidden in the interstices of the arts as well as the artistry of the law.

It is no secret that we have entered a new and challenging era of global communication. In this digital age we are moving forward and faster on the information superhighway in an attempt to determine the impact of the law on technology and the affect of technology on the arts. Great works of literature and the visual arts are now available on computer. Copyright laws must keep up with these technological advances. This book focuses attention on legal restraints in the media, censorship of the arts, copyright protection on the Internet, and artists' rights in the past and in the present cyberspace era.

This book also ventures into the well-traveled crossroads of law and literature. Literature, like the law, has many rules and regulations which, if followed, may or may not lead to a work of art, a masterpiece, like Shakespeare's *Merchant of Venice*, whose trial scene is here revisited. Law, too, has its rules, its constitution, its statutes, treaties, cases, which, if followed, may or may not lead to truth and justice. In this volume, scholars examine the role that interpretation plays in the legal community's response to unjust laws; the critical legal theorists discuss the value of interdisciplinarity, the relationship between legal and literary discourse, and the status of legal and literary theory; and, finally, an art historian examines the architectural design of the U.S. Supreme Court and how its architect fit into a rather unusual political history.

This venture in interdisciplinarity would not be possible if language were not common to both the law and the arts. It has been said that the law is a method of ordering reality through language. Artists order their reality with devices of style just as lawyers use the tools of persuasion, rhetoric, argumentation and legal reasoning. Many will admit the artistic nature of the legal enterprise, but some skeptics continue to shun the very idea of a link between the perceived certainty of the law and the ineffable qualities of the arts. Other skeptics shun the link between law and the arts for different reasons which unfairly disparage the law while ennobling the arts. Montaigne said, "We have in France more laws than all the rest of the world together and more than would be needed to rule all the worlds of Epicurus (Of Experience)." In its search to find relationships between law and the arts in an ever widening international and global arena, this book invites you to think about the law of literature and the literature of law.

I wish to express my deep appreciation to Professor Mitchel Lasser and Daniel J. Kornstein for their assistance in editing the chapters devoted to critical legal theory and to law and Shakespeare, respectively. It is with profound respect that I express my gratitude to Professor Richard Weisberg, my friend and colleague, who inspires me and many other scholars in the field of law and literature. I also wish to thank my editorial assistant, Jeremy Wolk, for his diligent and precise readings of the manuscripts and Sheila Shoob for her devotion to the typing of parts of this book, and Judith D'Angio of the Hofstra Cultural Center for formatting the manuscripts and camera-ready preparation of the volume. I wish to express my profound gratitude to Dean Stuart Rabinowitz of Hofsta Law School and to Hofsta University for making this interdisciplinary venture a reality.

Part I

Law, the Arts, and Censorship

1

Legal Restraints and the TV Channeling Controversy

Sondra M. Rubenstein

INTRODUCTION

In the battle between the two ancient enemies—"Anything Goes" and "Enough Already"[1]—where do *you* stand? The answer probably depends on your view of the First Amendment or on whether you would be willing, as attorney Robert Corn-Revere asks, to take First Amendment advice from Newton Minow. It probably also depends on your perception of the media's role in a free enterprise system and on your definitions of obscenity, profanity, indecency, and "to serve the public interest." The book *Abandoned in the Wasteland* was written by Minow, President Kennedy's Federal Communications Commission (FCC) chairman. Its cover shows a child about a year old, sitting in a type of walker that many consider dangerous, parked about three feet away from a portable TV set that is placed just above eye level, in a kitchen that appears to be unsupervised. The electrical cord to the TV dangles invitingly within reach. On the walker's tray, next to the child's hand, is a hard pretzel, flaking salt. To those who criticize government regulation of television, these TV images are clearly the safest things in this child's life.

Now consider the following: A guest on an afternoon talk show discusses having sex with a dog and others discuss their sexual preferences, perversions, and addictions. Add to the mix radio "shock jocks," sexually explicit performances, raunchy jokes on sitcoms, and "gangsta rap" performers whose lyrics deal with sex, drugs, and gangs and glorify violence toward women, homosexuals, and police officers. Does any of this make you so uncomfortable that you want government to regulate such programming? Well, those who call for government restraints to protect their children from such programming say they have had enough. Since they make no legal distinction between indecency and obscenity, they reject—with ease—First Amendment arguments. Beginning with a historical perspective, this chapter examines recent government attempts to lay pavement in the swampland of subjectivity.

HISTORIC WRESTLING WITH INDECENCY AND OBSCENITY

Three well-known constitutional tests evolved out of societal concern to protect the status quo in terms of threats to national security and social issues, such as obscenity and indecency. The first, the dangerous tendency test, can be seen in the 1868 British *Hicklin* decision,[2] which ruled that if there were a tendency for something to result in a substantive evil, it was appropriate for the government to intervene. Applied to indecent behavior and obscenity, this British decision guided American courts until 1933. The *Hicklin* precedent defined obscene material as that which had a dangerous tendency to provoke prurient thoughts and antisocial behavior among the most vulnerable segments of society (defined as children and those who were mental and social misfits). This meant that even if an isolated passage in a book were deemed to contain prurient thoughts, the whole book was considered obscene. If it wasn't good for children and society's misfits, it wasn't good for you. In 1933, Judge John Woolsey of New York rejected most of the *Hicklin* rule, stating that the work must be taken in its entirety, the author's purpose must be considered, and the standard would be a person with average sexual instincts and not a child or a disturbed individual.[3] Three years later, in 1936, the decision in *U.S. v. Levine*, incorporated Judge Woolsey's provision that the work be considered in its entirety. However, what was troublesome was that the court would continue to consider whether the work in question tended to stir impure or lustful thoughts.[4] Consider that, despite the introduction of the clear-and-present-danger doctrine in 1919, dangerous tendency persevered. The *Schenck* case, which reached the Supreme Court in 1919, involved a perceived Communist threat to our nation on the eve of war. In the new constitutional test derived from this case, Justices Holmes and Brandeis argued that freedom of expression is not absolute. There are limits, the Court said, and we generally accepted that we cannot, at whim, shout "fire" in a crowded theater.[5] Although, to those versed in legal terminology, the clear-and-present-danger doctrine seemed more precise than dangerous tendency; to many constitutionalists, it was still too subjective.

In the 1957 *Roth* case, the Supreme Court wrestled with what Judge Jerome M. Frank, of the U.S. Court of Appeals, had called the "exquisite vagueness" of obscenity laws.[6] The three "tests" approved in *Roth*—"lustful desire," "lustful thoughts," "appeal to prurient interest"[7]—remind us of the old *Hicklin* rule and of dangerous tendency because they all imply that if a work is assumed to induce "improper" sexual thoughts, it can be banned, as Henry Miller discovered. During the late 1950s, the Court turned to the balancing doctrine, weighing the rights to be lost against the potential evil to be prevented. Although the new doctrine helped acquit the Communists,[8] it still didn't let us read Henry Miller.

In the case of *Marvin Miller v. California*,[9] and in its four companion cases[10] decided by the Supreme Court on June 21, 1973, as well as in subsequent cases, the Court continued to struggle with the definition of obscenity and came to reject the notion of setting a national standard. Dissenting in the *Miller* case, Justice Brennan expressed his opinion that obscenity cannot be described precisely enough to give defendants fair notice. He wrote, "I am convinced that the approach initiated 15 years ago in *Roth v. United States* . . . culminating in the Court's decision today, cannot bring stability to this area of the law without jeopardizing First Amendment values."[11]

We still do not have a clear definition of either obscenity or indecency. Therefore, something could still be considered obscene if the average person, applying contemporary community standards, says it is or, some would argue, if the FCC says it is. As we shall see, some two decades later, the same concerns would be raised with regard to the Court's subsequent generic definition of indecency.

FROM ELVIS TO THE "NEW INDECENCY ENFORCEMENT STANDARDS"

Government regulation to prohibit broadcasting indecent language dates to the Radio Act of 1927 and was reinforced by the Federal Communications Act of 1934. Airing obscene, indecent, or profane language was made a federal offense which could lead to a fine or imprisonment or both, as well as license suspension for up to two years.[12] The penal provisions covering obscenity were amended in 1937 to include license suspension for the use of profane or obscene "words, language, or meaning." License suspension was no longer limited to two years and, as television's popularity grew, the word *meaning*, with its subjective taint, became more significant.

Beginning with Elvis Presley's first appearance on the *Ed Sullivan Show* in 1956, there was great concern over lyrics and sexual innuendo on television. TV camera operators were told not to show Elvis below the waist to avoid his bumping, grinding and gyrating hips. In the 1960s, the Rolling Stones had to sing "let's spend some time together" instead of "let's spend the night together." And, when Jim Morrison and the Doors appeared on the *Ed Sullivan Show*, they were told to omit the word *higher* from their 1967 hit "Light My Fire." They didn't comply and were never invited back.

During the 1970s, the FCC became concerned with drug-oriented lyrics and issued a notice requiring broadcasters to be aware of the content of the records they played. In *Yale Broadcasting Co. v. FCC* (1973), the U.S. Court of Appeals ruled that this FCC order did not violate the First Amendment because it did not prohibit stations from playing drug-oriented material. Since a license to broadcast was, in 1973, still considered—as it had been under the 1927 spectrum scarcity principle—to be a privilege that carried with it the obligation to serve the public interest, the Court noted that broadcasters were obliged to have knowledge of what they were broadcasting.[13]

A GENERIC DEFINITION

In the 1978 *Pacifica* case, New York's WBAI aired George Carlin's "Filthy Words," a 12-minute monologue covering the "heavy seven," the seven words you can never use on TV (or at a Hofstra conference). Following a warning, the words were listed and discussed individually in a satiric manner. It was two o'clock in the afternoon. A man and his young son turned on their car radio smack in the middle of Carlin's seven dirty words. The man complained to the FCC, which reviewed this single complaint and sent Pacifica Foundation, owner of WBAI, a warning of administrative sanction. The agency then filed its report. Pacifica, afraid of problems at license renewal time, appealed to the Court of Appeals for the District of Columbia.

When the Court of Appeals overturned the FCC decision in favor of *Pacifica*, the FCC appealed to the Supreme Court, which in a close five-to-four decision upheld the commission's ruling characterizing the Carlin monologue as "patently offensive," though not necessarily obscene. The Supreme Court cited two justifications for the FCC's actions: the uniquely pervasive presence of broadcasting in our everyday lives, and accessibility to children and the difficulty of exercising parental control. Accepting the FCC's first justification, the Court explained that the individual's right to be let alone—not to be confronted with patently offensive, indecent material in the privacy of one's home—outweighs the First Amendment rights of the intruder. For those who argue that on hearing indecent language, one can simply avoid further offense by turning off the radio, Justice John Paul Stevens said that was "like saying . . . the remedy for an assault is to run away after the first blow."[14]

The second rationale focused on societal interest in protecting children from inappropriate language; but, insofar as this affected adult accessibility to adult programming, it raised the issue of using children as a national standard and was reminiscent of the discredited British *Hicklin* rule. Thus, the FCC introduced the new concept of "channeling"—rather than prohibiting—adult programs. Using this rationale, no censorship was considered by the FCC, or by the Court's majority, to have taken place. In other words, if the Carlin monologue had not aired at 2 P.M. (when children may tune in), but rather had it aired after 10 P.M., Pacifica would not have had a problem. Or so it then seemed.

The Supreme Court also affirmed a generic definition of indecent language as that which describes "in terms patently offensive as measured by contemporary community standards for the broadcast medium, sexual or excretory activities and organs." As we shall see, the FCC would soon extend this generic definition to words not included in Carlin's dirty seven, and by doing so would raise further concerns in the minds of its critics.

No other broadcasters were found guilty of indecent programming until 1987, and the FCC reassured broadcasters that they were only concerned with the "seven dirty words" and, specifically, that those words not be used repeatedly. However, in 1987, Pacifica's Los Angeles station, the University of California at Santa Barbara's FM station, and an FM station in Philadelphia all had complaints lodged against them for repeated use of offensive language, which mentioned sexual organs and included descriptive terms for women that the FCC considered indecent, that is, vulgar and offensive.

Those complaints and the results of subsequent research, indicating that a significant number of children were still tuning in to "adult" programming at 10 P.M., led to the FCC's New Indecency Enforcement Standards of 1987.[15] This revised code, went beyond Carlin's seven dirty words. The commission also narrowed the number of hours during which such programs could be aired. The "safe" hours were channeled to the hours between midnight and 6 A.M., but the matter was still unresolved and would occupy the FCC for the next several years.

ACT V. FCC IN THREE ACTS

Enter ACT I: Action for Children's Television (ACT), a coalition of media and public interest groups, brought the matter to court in 1988. The coalition argued that the First Amendment protects indecent expression.[16] Many were surprised by ACT's involvement in this case because ACT has always supported government regulation of broadcast commercials aimed at young children. It seemed a contradiction in ACT's mission to protect youngsters from commercials but not from indecent programming, which explicitly described sexual acts and contained vulgar and offensive language. The D.C. Court of Appeals supported the FCC's policy objective and its right to channel indecent programs to those hours when children were most likely asleep. But, precisely when was that? And was a six-hour allotment for the "safe harbor" for adult programming excessive? The court found that the FCC needed to present additional data on audience composition to support its rationale for its midnight to 6 A.M. allotment. Despite these questions, the court noted that the FCC was not censoring indecent language; it was merely moving it to a later hour. In her opinion for the Court of Appeals, Judge Ruth Bader Ginsburg explained the court's inability to deal with the issue of vagueness of the generic definition of indecency. She wrote: "If acceptance of the FCC's generic definition of 'indecent' as capable of surviving a vagueness challenge is not implicit in Pacifica, we have misunderstood Higher Authority and welcome correction."[17]

In the meantime, in October 1988, Congress passed Public Law 100-459 (608), compelling the FCC to institute a total ban on indecent material. Shortly thereafter, and in compliance with the congressional directive, the FCC announced that as of January 1989 it would enforce a total ban. ACT, by obtaining a court order, was able to stop the FCC from implementing the new rule until the Court could determine its validity. However, the Court gave the FCC provisional permission to enforce its indecency standards until it would return with documentation to support its concept of channeling.

After reviewing the more than six thousand complaints it had received annually since the mid-1980s, the FCC voted unanimously (in July 1990) to support a total ban of indecent programming on radio and television. These complaints detailed explicit, sexually-oriented language broadcast at various times during the day and night.[18] The FCC decision was based on the conclusion that only a total ban would protect children from such fare.

Enter ACT II: Reviewed by the U.S. Court of Appeals in 1991, the FCC's total ban was struck down as unconstitutional, and the commission was again asked to define and establish a "reasonable . . . safe harbor" for indecent content, to "channel" such programs away from those seventeen or younger, and to do so without infringing on the rights of adults to have access to such material.[19]

When Congress passed the Public Telecommunications Act of 1992, dealing with public broadcasting, it included different "safe harbor" provisions for public radio stations that go off the air before midnight and for commercial stations and the remaining public stations. For those stations that sign off before midnight, the safe hours in which to air adult programs would begin at 10 P.M. For the others, the safe hours would begin at midnight and continue to 6 A.M. The FCC then tried to bolster its arguments for the six-hour ban with further research and documentation.

Enter ACT III: Still seeking redress of what the coalition saw as censorship of protected speech, ACT returned to court. Although the Court of Appeals was unimpressed with the commission's new presentation, it called for still another review of the entire issue. On June 30, 1995, in a politically charged seven-to-four decision, the Court of Appeals, ruled that radio and television stations cannot air "indecent" programs between 6 A.M. and 10 P.M. The justices split along political lines with the seven Republican appointees supporting the FCC rules and the four Democratic appointees supporting the ACT coalition, which included broadcasters and civil liberties groups.

Although the decision appeared to expand the number of hours (from six to eight) during which "adult" programming can air (by now being able to begin at 10 P.M.), the court also left "ample room" for the government to extend the prohibition to 10 P.M. Noting the government's "compelling interest" in protecting children from potentially harmful programming, Judge James L. Buckley wrote: "It is fanciful to believe that the vast majority of parents who wish to shield their children from indecent material can effectively do so without meaningful restrictions on the airwaves."[20]

Reacting to the decision, FCC chairman Reed E. Hundt characterized it as a victory for parents and the public, adding: "The court's action serves the goal of confining this material to the hours when minors are less likely to be exposed."[21]

On the other hand, some media experts expressed concern that Congress would, indeed, expand the hours of prohibition. The head of ACT, Peggy Charren, citing the chilling effect of the decision, said: "Too often, we try to protect children by doing in free speech." One of the four dissenting judges, Chief Judge Harry T. Edwards, wrote that the court had made an "utterly irrational distinction" by not applying the indecency rules to cable television," and that government restrictions have gone "too far." Timothy Dyke, the attorney who represented the major networks and who argued the case, expressed his disappointment in the decision, saying that "it is a sharp departure from the approach reflected in earlier court decisions."[22]

Given the ups and downs of the case's history, and the controversial nature of the decision, it was not surprising that the ACT coalition appealed to the U.S. Supreme Court. However, on January 8, 1996, the high Court refused to grant certiorari, effectively upholding the FCC's 6 A.M. to 10 P.M. ban on indecent programming.

RIGHTS VERSUS VALUES

On February 9, 1996, FCC Chairman Reed Hundt addressed the Administrative Law Conference at Duke University School of Law. He noted that in most years the FCC receives over one hundred complaints about violence on television and well over one thousand complaints about indecency. Although the volume was not "great," the controversy level was very high. The commissioner explained that Congress, responding to public pressure, "has continuously asked the FCC to guarantee that indecent broadcasts will not run when children are likely to be in the audience. . . . Yet broadcasters have devoted years of effort and millions of dollars in fees to litigate the right to broadcast indecent shows whenever they wish."[23]

Controversial media content involves balancing the constitutionally guaranteed right of freedom of expression with society's need and concern for its children and the desire to protect them from potentially harmful material that critics claim results in anti-social behavior. Many believe that the passive acceptance of indecent programming and the media's glorification of crime leads to further erosion of societal values and of acceptable standards of behavior. Various social scientists have even claimed that it leads to crime in the street.

While some call for strong governmental regulation, a sort of red light to stop publication, *New York Times* columnist William Safire, a consistent advocate of unrestricted freedom of the press, argues that government regulation offends constitutionally granted freedoms of speech and expression. Safire speaks of the need for citizens' groups and crusading talk show hosts to turn on the white light of publicity, and that those who profit from inciting violence should be "identified, vilified, picketed and ostracized."

Consistent with this approach, in December 1996 two Democratic senators, Joseph Lieberman (Conn.) and Sam Nunn (Ga.) supported former education secretary Bill Bennett's announcement that his conservative public interest group, Empower America, was initiating a $50,000 media campaign naming advertisers that support "trash TV." The targeted shows included those hosted by Jenny Jones, Sally Jessy Rafael, Jerry Springer, Montel Williams, Maury Povich, Geraldo Rivera, Charles Perez, Rolonda, Ricki Lake, and Richard Bey. Among the advertisers named were Warner Lambert, General Mills, Smithkline Beecham, and Finesse shampoo. Although some broadcasters saw Bennett and his congressional backers as "making an end run around the First Amendment rights of broadcasters," not all broadcasters were disturbed, and a number of advertisers withdrew from the targeted shows, saying things like such programs are "inconsistent with our values and are not vehicles with which we want to be associated."[24]

Floyd Abrams[25] and other First Amendment specialists, have expressed concern over further Congressional action in this area, and Robert Corn-Revere, a Washington attorney with Hogan & Hartson and a former legal adviser to FCC Commissioner and former chairman James Quello, has criticized FCC attempts to set a national standard for indecency under the guise of "voluntary" self-regulation. Corn-Revere has written that "censorship does not get much more real than when the government threatens to cancel broadcast licenses if holding them fails to please the Ministry of Education. . . . Large corporations that depend on FCC decisions for their future economic well-being now find themselves becoming volunteer conscripts in the service of broadcast policy debates."[26]

I am sure you noted Corn-Revere's interesting choice of words: "Ministry" of Education and "volunteer conscripts" in the "service of" some government scheme. Quite clearly, Corn-Revere is sounding a warning, tripping the censorship alarm. On the other side of the debate, Reed Hundt has said that he prefers the idea of broadcasters as public trustees as opposed to the recommendation of his predecessor Mark Fowler, who would replace the notion of public trustee with that of broadcasters as market participants who respond only to market forces. Weighing into the debate, a *Wall Street Journal* editorial last fall stated that "[i]t's hard . . . to work up much sympathy for broadcasters." At the same time they're protesting "public interest" programming requirements, the broadcasters are asking Congress for multibillion-dollar handouts in the form of free spectrum allocated to additional broadcasting. The broadcasters' main argument? That they perform a "public service." Responding to Corn-Revere's criticisms, Newton Minow commented: "Most Americans cherish three values: free speech, free markets and protection of our children. . . . Those of us who care about all three will continue to advocate that broadcasters have a special obligation as public trustees to serve our children and grandchildren."[27]

Now, consider the arguments of those media scholars who have argued that indecency may not be as harmful to children as the FCC thinks. They say that there are, apparently, few studies on the effects of indecency on children up to age eighteen, and those who have been examined do not "demonstrate that exposure to indecency had any harmful effects." For example, Donnerstein, Wilson, and Linz found that children under the age of twelve lack the sexual literacy to understand sexual references and innuendo. They, therefore, appear to lack interest in indecent subject matter and do not seem to be affected by exposure to it. Those between the ages of thirteen and seventeen are more apt to understand the material. However, researchers argue that by then they generally have acquired moral standards and the ability to critically evaluate what they experience.[28] The researchers also acknowledged the difficulties involved in conducting studies in such a sensitive area, where parental consent is required. Seeking a compromise, media researchers Samoriski, Huffman, and Trauth have proposed a framework for regulating indecency. Using the Supreme Court's premise articulated in *Miller v. California*, that the United States is "simply too big and too diverse" to articulate a national obscenity standard, they propose that the Court do the following:

- Discard the concept of a national indecency standard and accept a community standard as determined by a jury.

- Make a finding of prurient appeal central to a finding of indecency.

- Accept that certain words, regardless of their context, could not be barred from the airwaves.

- Apply the requirement that the work be taken as a whole when determining indecency, just as it is when a determination of obscenity is being made.

- Provide indecency with the same protection afforded obscenity under the LAPS test, namely the possibility of the work having redeeming literary, artistic, political or scientific value, as determined by using the reasonable-person standard.

- Retain, as a defense against a charge of indecency, the time-of-day defense and the provision that indecency may be aired during the designated safe harbor hours.[29]

ENTER THE V-CHIP

When Congress included the V-chip and an accompanying call for a TV ratings system in the 1996 Telecommunications Act, American parents were told that technology had found a way to permit them to block out objectionable programs so that, as Vice President Al Gore said, they "shouldn't be forced to choose between throwing the TV out of the house and monitoring every second that [their] child watches."[30] Jack Valenti, head of the Motion Picture Association and the man credited with devising the code used by the film industry for almost thirty years, was selected to lead the coalition of broadcasting, cable, and production companies that will create a TV ratings system. Interviewed by Don West and Chris Stern of *Broadcasting & Cable*, Valenti was asked about his testimony in Congress against the V-chip. He said that, with the passage of the V-chip provision, he had to confront reality.

But I also know . . . that the law does not command this industry to do anything. Not a thing. But I think if you're going to be a responsible industry, you ought to do what you can to give parents more information. . . . The First Amendment is the least ambiguous clause in the Constitution . . . it says precisely what it means. Therefore, I don't think that any attempt by the Congress or the FCC to invade this fragile, brittle area of content will ever pass muster in the courts.[31]

When reminded by his interviewers that "these are the same courts that just passed the indecency decision, with a safe harbor," Valenti responded, "This Supreme Court will not allow anyone to intrude on the First Amendment." He continued, "Any time Congress or the FCC goes beyond that well-marked line . . . we have judicial remedies for that, and we will seek solace in the courts."

CONCLUSION

Now that the courts and a proactive FCC have given our children a safe harbor from 6 A.M. to 10 P.M., does that mean that they will no longer be exposed to adult programs? Now that Congress has given us the V-chip, does that mean that our children will no longer be able to see violence on television? And now that we will have an industry-created TV ratings system, does that mean that we won't have to, as Al Gore said, throw out our TV sets to ensure that our children won't ever again hear sexual innuendo or experience? The answer to the above is no, no, and no. Broadcasters will channel adult programs to those designated late night hours when responsible parents have seen their children to bed, and they may even control the daytime "topless" radio shock jocks, the Howard Sterns, who use explicit sexual language to attract larger audiences and to test the boundaries of free speech. But, in the end, we must take responsibility for what our children listen to and watch.

Television images will remain the great seducer, and the creative process will continue to be nurtured by both the beautiful and the ugly—the conflict, passion, and, yes, even violence that is part of our lives. However, we must remember that in a free enterprise system, the marketplace still determines the success or failure of any product. Media consumers do have some recourse. Complaining by letter or phone to those who advertise on unsavory programs has shown results. The implied threat of a consumer boycott has worked without weakening our First Amendment.

So where do you stand on this issue? Is it "enough is enough," or is it "anything goes?" Of course, there is a middle ground. That is where you will find socially responsible media gatekeepers, conscientious parents, the absence of government interference by politically-motivated politicians and an untarnished and untrampled First Amendment. While that is where I hope we will meet, I do have my doubts.

NOTES

1. Skywalker Records Inc. v. Navarro, 17 MED.L.RPTR. 2073 (DC So. Fla., 1990). Quoted from remarks by Justice J. Gonzalez of the District Court of South Florida.

2. Regina v. Hicklin, L.R. 3 Q.B. 360 (1868).

3. U.S. v. One Book Called "Ulysses," 5 F.Supp. 182, 184 (S.D.N.Y. 1933).

4. U.S. v. Levine, 83 F.2d 156 (2d Cir. 1936).

5. Schenck v. U.S., 249 U.S. 47, 52 (1919).

6. Roth v. U.S., 237 F.2d 796, 825-827 (2nd Cir. 1956). See Stanley Fleishman, *Witchcraft and Obscenity: Twin Superstitions*, WILSON LIBRARY BULLETIN, Apr. 1965, at p. 4.

7. Roth v. U.S., 354 U.S. 476, 487 (1957). The source of the "appeal to prurient interest" test can be found in the MODEL PENAL CODE, Tentative Draft No. 6 (Philadelphia, American Law Institute, May 6, 1957).

8. Yates v. U.S., 354 U.S. 298 (1957).

9. Miller v. California, 413 U.S. 15 (1973).

10. See Paris Adult Theatre I v. Slaton, 413 U.S. 49 (1973); United States v. Orito, 413 U.S. 139 (1973); Kaplan v. California, 413 U.S. 115 (1973); U.S. v. Twelve 200-ft. Reels of Super 8 mm Film, 413 U.S. 123 (1973).

11. Paris Adult Theatre I v. Slaton, 413 U.S. 49, 90 (1973) (Brennan, J., dissenting).

12. U.S. code dealing with the broadcasting of obscene language. 18 U.S.C.A. Section 1464.

13. Yale Broadcasting Co. v. FCC, 478 F.2d 594 (D.C. Cir.), *cert. denied*, 414 U.S. 914 (1973).

14. FCC v. Pacifica Foundation, 438 U.S. 748 (1978).

15. 62 RR2d 1218 (1987).

16. Action for Children's Televison v. FCC (ACT I), 852 F.2d 1332, (D.C. Cir. 1988).

17. *Id.* at 1339.

18. ACT v. FCC, 67 RR2d 1714, 1990.

19. ACT v. FCC (ACT II), 932 F.2d 1504 (D.C. Cir. 1991), *cert. denied*, 112 S.Ct. 1281 (1992).

20. N.Y. TIMES, July 1, 1995, at p. 7.

21. *Id.*

22. *Id.*

23. Reed Hundt, An Address to Duke Law Journal's Twenty-seventh Annual Administrative Law Conference on the subject of Television, Kids, Indecency, Violence and the Public Interest *delivered on* February 9, 1996.

24. *See* Christopher Stern, *Talk Targeters Names Names*, BROADCASTING & CABLE, Dec. 11, 1995, at 17. *See also* Cynthia Littleton, *A Question of Content*, BROADCASTING & CABLE, Dec. 11, 1995, at 17.

25. *See* e.g., Floyd Abrams, *The Press Is Different: Reflections on Justice Stewart and the Autonomous Press*, 7 HOFSTRA LAW REVIEW 563 (1979). *See also* Floyd Abrams, *NY Times v. Sullivan*, 10 MED.L.RPTR. 17, Apr. 24, 1984; Floyd Abrams, *Afterword*, *in* ESSENTIAL LIBERTY: FIRST AMENDMENT BATTLES FOR A FREE PRESS (Francis Wilkinson 1992).

26. Robert Corn-Revere, *Would You Take First Amendment Advice from Newton Minow*? BROADCASTING & CABLE, Nov. 27, 1995, at 24, 116.

27. Newton N. Minow, *Open Mike: The Author's Answer*, BROADCASTING & CABLE, Dec. 4, 1995, at 96. *See also* Robert Corn-Revere, *Would You Take First Amendment Advice from Newton Minow*? BROADCASTING & CABLE, Nov. 27, 1995, at 109.

28. E. Donnerstein, B. Wilson, & D. Linz, *On the Regulation of Broadcast Indecency to Protect Children*, 36 JOURNAL OF BROADCASTING AND ELECTRONIC MEDIA 111 (1992).

29. Jan H. Samoriski, John L. Huffman, & Denise M. Trauth, *Indecency, the Federal Communications Commission, and the Post-Sikes Era: A Framework for Regulation*, 39 JOURNAL OF BROADCASTING & ELECTRONIC MEDIA 51 (1995).

30. Heather Fleming, *TV Gored in Chicago*, BROADCASTING & CABLE, Sept. 2, 1996, at 6.

31. Don West & Chris Stern, *Jack of All Trades: The Man in the Middle on the V-Chip*, BROADCASTING & CABLE, Mar. 18, 1996, at 26.

REFERENCES

Broadcasting Obscene Language. Title 18 of U.S.C.A. 1464.

Corn-Revere, Robert. *Would You Take First Amendment Advice from Newton Minow*? BROADCASTING & CABLE, Nov. 27, 1995.

Corn-Revere, Robert. *Rebuttal*, BROADCASTING & CABLE, Dec. 11, 1995.

Donnerstein, E., Wilson, B., & Linz, D. *On the Regulation of Broadcast Indecency to Protect Children*, JOURNAL OF BROADCASTING AND ELECTRONIC MEDIA, Vol. 36, 1992.

Fleishman, Stanley. *Witchcraft and Obscenity: Twin Superstitions*, WILSON LIBRARY BULLETIN, Apr. 1965.

Fleming, Heather. *TV Gored in Chicago*, BROADCASTING & CABLE, Sept. 2, 1996.

Hundt, Reed. *Television, Kids, Indecency, Violence and the Public Interest*, Duke Law Journal's Twenty-seventh Annual Admin. Law Conference, Feb. 9, 1996.

Littleton, Cynthia. *A Question of Content*, BROADCASTING & CABLE, Dec. 11, 1995.

Minow, Newton N. *Open Mike: The Author's Answer*, BROADCASTING & CABLE, Dec. 4, 1995.

Samoriski, Jan H., Huffman, John L., and Trauth, Denise M. *Indecency, the Federal Communications Commission, and the Post-Sikes Era: A Framework for Regulation*, JOURNAL OF BROADCASTING & ELECTRONIC MEDIA, Vol. 39, 1995.

Stern, Christopher. *Talk Targeters Name Names*, BROADCASTING & CABLE, Dec. 11, 1995.

West, Don & Stern, Chris. *Jack of All Trades: The Man in the Middle on the V-Chip*,

BROADCASTING & CABLE, Mar. 18, 1996.

New York Times Articles

Abrams, Floyd & Hollings, Ernest F. *TV Violence: Survival vs. Censorship, a Dialogue* op. ed., N.Y. TIMES, Nov. 23, 1993.

Andrews, Edmund L. *Court Upholds a Ban on 'Indecent' Broadcast Programming*, Jul. 1, 1995, at A1.

Cleaning Up Violence on Radio, ed., Dec. 11, 1993, at A1.

Lewis, Anthony. *Law and Politics*, op. ed., N.Y. TIMES, Nov. 29, 1993.

Lewis, Neil A. *U.S. Restrictions on Adult TV Fare Are Struck Down—Constitutional Question*, Nov. 24, 1993, at C1.

Janet Reno's Heavy Hand, ed., Oct. 22, 1993, at A1.

Myers, Steven Lee. *WBLS-FM to Stop Playing Violent Songs*, Dec. 5, 1993, at A4.

Pareles, Jon. *Parody, Not Smut, Has Rappers in Court*, Nov. 13, 1993, at A1.

Quindlen, Anna. *Public and Private*, TV GUIDE, op. ed., N.Y. TIMES, Oct. 28, 1993.

Sims, Calvin. *Gangster Rappers: The Lives, The Lyrics,* Nov. 28, 1993.

Wines, Michael. *Reno Chastises TV Networks on Violence in Programming*, Oct. 21, 1993, at A1.

Cases

ACT v. FCC (ACT I), 852 F.2d 1332, D.C. Cir. (1988).

ACT v. FCC 67 RR2d 1714 (1990).

ACT v. FCC (ACT II), 932 F.2d 1504, D.C. Cir. 1991, *cert. denied*, 112 S.Ct. 1281 (1992).

FCC v. Pacifica Foundation, 438 U.S. 748 (1978).

Miller v. California, 413 U.S. 15, 93 S.Ct. 2607 (1973).

Paris Adult Theatre I v. Slaton, 413 U.S. 49, 93 S.Ct. 2628 (1973).

Regina v. Hicklin, L.R. 3 Q.B. 360 (1868).

Roth v. U.S., 354 U.S. 476, 487, 77 S.Ct. 1304, 1310 (1957).

Schenck v. U.S., 249 U.S. 47, 52, 39 S.Ct. 247, 249 (1919).

Skywalker Records Inc. v. Navarro, 17 MED.L.RPTR. 2073 (DC So. Fla., 1990).

U.S. v. One Book Called "Ulysses," 5 F.Supp. 182, 184 (S.D.N.Y., 1933).

U.S. v. Levine, 83 F.2d 156 (2d Cir., 1936).

Yale Broadcastng Co. v. FCC, U.S. Ct. App. DC, 478 F.2d 594 (1973), *cert. denied*, 414 U.S. 914 (1973), 128.

Yates v. U.S., 354 U.S. 298, 77 S.Ct. 1064 (1957).

2

Censorship and the Arts
in the United States Today

Leanne Katz

Remember the old *New Yorker* cartoon where the fellow at a party is saying, "So what if we lose the First Amendment? We still have 25 more." Since 1980, there has been an ominous and steadily worsening shift in the climate for the arts in this country. It is commonplace today to scapegoat expression and the arts and to designate them as the causes of many of our problems, whether the problems are real or imagined. This climate affects all the arts. The volume, nature, and consequences of the attacks on expression and the arts are little recognized but alarming.

Pro-censorship activists have helped create and exploit this climate, with horrendous results. Although the work of my organization, the National Coalition Against Censorship, is about censorship in the United States, early on we widely publicized a Canadian case. The Canadian Supreme Court in its *Butler* decision on obscenity demonstrated the inevitable real-life consequences of Catherine MacKinnon's arguments for restrictions on her expression. The ruling produced an explosion of censorship, including the banning of much art and literature (e.g., books by Andrea Dworkin). Many people were appalled—but not surprised—when the effects of the Canadian decision fell most heavily on feminist bookstores and on lesbian-and gay-related expression.

All of us live in this climate of censorship. Legal scholars may be affected by and even contribute to it. Some legal academics—who do not appear to consider themselves followers of Robert Bork—have suggested, in theorizing about First Amendment protections, that political expression should be privileged; however, artistic expression falls into a different, inferior, category. But as the Second Circuit Court of Appeals said a few weeks ago in the Art-On-NYC-Streets case, *Berg v. City of New York*, 97 F.3d 689, 695 (2d Cir.) (1996) in language which certainly applies to all the arts: "Visual art is as wide-ranging in its depiction of ideas, concepts and emotions as any book, treatise, pamphlet or other writing, and is similarly entitled to First Amendment protection."

It tells us something about the national level of art appreciation and understanding if at the Philadelphia hearings on the constitutionality of the Communications Decency Act of 1996 (Pub.L. 104, Title V, Feb. 8, 1996, 110 Stat. 133), an expert witness for the government answered "yes" when asked by one of the judges whether an image of a nude statue of Aphrodite from the University of Philadelphia Museum of Archeology and Anthropology could be blocked under the law from the Internet. (It is seen in the museum by 40,000 children each year.)

Most of the attacks on the arts take place on a local level and scholars need to consider the broader implications of these local cases. The demands for censorship of artistic expression take place everywhere. Recently, right here in Long Island close to Hofstra, the Manhasset Public Library canceled an art exhibit of Robyn Bellospirito's work because three of the paintings included abstractions of nudes. That was against library policy.

Libraries often have policies stating that nude works cannot be part of any exhibit. A measure of the chill such restrictions place on creativity is that many artists don't consider this censorship at all, but self-censor their own work so that it can be shown. It's a source of continuing astonishment to me—quite apart from the prurient nature of so much in our culture to which we are all exposed so much of the time—that representations of nudity, by themselves, have become a no-no in so many places in our society. And that this should be so in the very institutions that presumably specialize in the free exchange of ideas—libraries, colleges, public spaces—is even more appalling.

Bellospirito, as spirited as her name befits, ignored the advice of one constitutional expert and sued the library for violating her First Amendment rights. She won a victory for artists and for all of us. Federal district court judge Thomas Platt ruled that the library had created a display area which constituted a "limited public forum," and that the state lacked a compelling interest in suppressing all nudity.

Imagine being a twenty-four-year-old person in Pinellas County, Florida, and found guilty of obscenity for drawings in your homemade comic books. Mike Diana was convicted for drawings in his zine, *Boiled Angel*. Despite good representation and testimony on his behalf by professional artists, Mike Diana was not only convicted but given an outrageous and humiliating sentence, which included psychological evaluation, participation in an ethics in journalism class, three years' probation during which time the artist was to avoid contact with anyone under eighteen, and the subjection of his art and other personal papers to unscheduled, warrantless searches.

Diana's case has been supported by the Comic Book Legal Defense Fund. His conviction has just been upheld by a Florida Circuit Court, and further appeals are contemplated. Many prosecutors today use obscenity prosecutions to curry voter favor, and to exploit fears about crime, and very often to exploit homophobia.

In today's climate, complicity can come from disheartening sources. For example, last year in Charlotte, North Carolina, a forthcoming production of Tony Kushner's *Angels in America* was attacked because a religious right group opposed its homosexual themes. No news there: the real news was the role of the prestigious Blumenthal Performing Arts Center, where the local theater company was to put on the play. Instead of assuming the role of defender and protector of the Pulitzer Prize–winning play, the arts center demanded that the theater company either modify the production by eliminating a nude scene that has a character demonstrating the ravages of AIDS, or go to court beforehand to guarantee that a local "indecent exposure" law (conceded by the arts center to be "almost certainly unconstitutional") would not be invoked against the play. At the last minute, the company did successfully go to court but that certainly shouldn't have been required of them. And when the National Coalition Against Censorship criticized the arts center, its head replied indignantly that the center had asked the theater company to go to court about the issue a year ago and that the theater company was publicizing the controversy to sell tickets!

In Orlando, Florida, the police tossed an original Picasso onto a "pornography" pyre. It was rescued from a pile of confiscated materials about to be burned when a city property manager admired the frame. The aquatint etching of a nude woman posing for a bearded artist was done by Picasso in 1966, and hangs today in the Orlando Museum of Art.

Everyone knows Cincinnati is the place where the police stormed into and shut down the gallery with the Mapplethorpe exhibit and brought obscenity charges against the gallery and its director. More recently in Cincinnati, the owner and the manager of a small lesbian and gay bookstore were prosecuted for obscenity and faced jail charges for renting a videotape of Pier Paolo Pasolini's antifascist film *Salò* to an undercover member of the city's vice squad.

Pasolini was described by Alberto Moravia as "one of the most important intellectuals of post-war Europe." Prosecutors pursued the case through the courts for two years despite an amicus brief signed by film experts including Martin Scorsese, the Film Society of Lincoln Center, and an array of film critics and scholars. They attested to the work's serious artistic merit and argued that it was disqualified from obscenity prosecution as a matter of law. The Ohio courts apparently preferred to rely on the artistic judgment of the Cincinnati police officer who wrote about *Salò* in his deposition that "it appears to be foreign." In an August 1996 settlement, just before a court-ordered trial, the defendants pled no contest and paid a $500 fine for attempted pandering because one customer told another (actually the vice squad member), that it was a film "with everything in it."

When touching on attacks on literature today, one hardly knows where to begin. It is notable that most of the demands for censorship of literature take place in the schools: children's books, Shakespeare, contemporary novels, and, still, *Catcher in the Rye*. No book worthy of the name of literature is immune from attack. The National Coalition Against Censorship works on more and more incidents where books found to be "guilty" are taken from students while they are actually using them in the classroom. And that a book is not compulsory reading never satisfies the would-be censor. Copies of *Annie on My Mind*, by Nancy Garden, a novel about Annie and Liza, who fall in love and struggle with declaring their homosexuality to family and friends, were burned in 1993 on the steps of the Kansas City school district headquarters because it was in school libraries. A federal judge later, at the end of last year, ruled that the school system had violated students' First Amendment rights when it ordered that all copies of the book—which contains no sexual references—be removed from school libraries.

In an Illinois town recently, the school board ordered English teachers to suspend the use of *The Canterbury Tales* so the board could decide which portions were appropriate. Then the board voted to ban the book and substitute an expurgated version, which they call "annotated."

Good teachers and librarians complain that our schools and libraries contain many bowdlerized editions of books, such as the dangerous *Romeo and Juliet*, which have been "edited" but do not even say so.

In a Florida controversy that finally was defeated in the federal courts, a school board banned a humanities textbook for containing passages from Chaucer and *Lysistrata*, by Aristophanes, the latter because it taught "women's lib." Did they have an informant about the play? Or—for once—did they actually read the work?

Each of these incidents represents thousands of others. We constantly need to reiterate the idea that the lessons of censorship do not belong in our schools. What does censorship teach children? That reading is dangerous, that adults do not trust young people, and that the way to respond to controversy is by suppression.

Even young children understand that the presence of a word, an act, or an idea in a book does not imply endorsement of that idea or word or act. And even young children learn that one value of literature is that through it we explore ideas, character, acts, and consequences, often profoundly, without actually ourselves cheating, cursing, or stealing. Does the last scene of *Hamlet*, with the stage strewn with dead bodies, advocate mass murder?

But in spite of repeated court decisions that exposure to books or other expression is not the same as inculcation, the other side may be winning. They are by various means raising questions in many minds: Why do children need to do all this reading, anyway, with all the violence, the negativity, the questioning, the bad language of literature? Why are children being taught this stuff? This thinking is really based on what the would-be censor considers teaching: simple indoctrination, instead of nurturing independent minds.

Indeed, right-wing activists have made it clear that the campaign to purge public schools and libraries of "filthy" books and "objectionable" ideas is part of a larger crusade to control—or even eliminate—our public schools and libraries, institutions where it is essential that there be access to a wide range of ideas. This year the right wing has spawned a national campaign called Family Friendly Libraries. Their strategy is designed to apply pressure to elected library trustees and professional librarians to create restricted areas in libraries where all patrons would need to request so-called controversial materials, including any literature with sexual references.

In thinking about the law and arts censorship, three points are important:

1. *We must not slide into habits of using the censors' vocabulary, and thereby letting the arguments end before they even take place.* Contested and unclear terms, such as "pornography," "obscenity," "sexually explicit," and "harmful to minors," are constantly used today with devastating effect against literature and the other arts. We urge use of the neutral term *sexually related expression*, elaborated where necessary with careful specifics. Always go toward the concrete.

2. *We must dispel the myths that censorship is good for women,* that women want censorship, and that those who support censorship speak for women. Restrictions on sexually related expression have always been used against women's interests; they can never enhance women's freedom, equality or safety.

3. *We must discredit the "spin" that it's desirable for different standards to apply in different communities* and that students in any of the places where there are efforts to style professional educators as enemies of families don't need access to—or aren't entitled to—the same array of books and ideas as young people elsewhere.

The fallout from these battles goes beyond the arts and culture. Nearly every one of the censorship cases is full of extraordinary human drama and emotion; many have elements of real anguish including shattered lives. And nearly every case involves courageous and talented people who often risk reputation and livelihood to oppose suppression.

These are many rationales for opposing censorship, but for me it's simple: Who decides? And how do the would-be censors deny that it is only dedication to the free interchange of ideas that gives them a hearing in the first place?

Over a hundred years ago, Mark Twain said, "In this country, we have three unspeakably precious things: freedom of speech, freedom of conscience, and the good sense never to practice either." We can probably agree that what Twain meant was that we need to give a little more reality to the ideas behind the First Amendment. I hope you'll want to explore how the law can help that great endeavor, particularly as it applies to freedom of artistic expression.

3
Art and Repression in the McCarthy Era

Howard Fast

Censorship is an enormous subject. Even the small part of censorship that I will cover here is difficult to convey in the few minutes I have to speak. But I will try.

You know, every writer lives with the burden of censorship; every human being does too. You censor yourself. You look at someone and think, "God only knows what a fool he is." But you don't say it, and all the thoughts that we don't speak are also censored. A newspaper writer censors his writing to the view of the newspaper. A novelist censors his novel to the taste of his publisher. Censorship is, you might say, a normal part of the process of writing.

Here in America, during the first hundred and forty years or so of its history, censorship was always based on the writer's use of prurience. This is not too different from television and film today. Murder was palatable, but sex was in a different category. Through our history starting with Hawthorne's *Scarlet Letter*, book after book was censored because it touched on the fact that a man or a woman comes into this world and because a man and a woman do something to each other that was unprintable and unspeakable in those days. You can search from Melville to Mark Twain, up and down the ranks of the American writers of the Victorian and the Civil War period, and never, never does anyone dare speak about the way of conception.

But suddenly in our time a different kind of censorship came into being. The libraries of America, since the time of Andrew Carnegie, have been filled with all the works of Karl Marx, many of the works of Lenin, works of an assortment of left wing writers from Jack London to myself. No one ever dreamed of censoring them or objecting to them. That was because there was no Soviet Union in those days. But once the Soviet Union came into being, the United States found an ideology, and the ideology was anti-Russian and anti-

Communist. This ideology became overwhelming during the years (that I am sure all of you here remember, at least in part from 1945 to 1960). The ideological war, when it came to books, was not carried on by people who read books. And so as I say the works of Karl Marx were never censored right up to today. The works of Lenin were never censored.

But another kind of a mess was brewing. There were people, certain very special people from Washington's point of view, who slipped messages into books and films. These messages were going to undermine and destroy the United States. In Hollywood it was easier because all these people who were the defenders of the United States, mainly the House Un-American Activities Committee, never read very much. This is still a prevailing habit of our Congress. But they watch movies, and thus the movement of censorship against writers and directors and actors in Hollywood developed. As enforcer, Congress enrolled the producers. This was achieved easily with a simple threat to profits. Once under way, censorship rolled on with results that I am sure you know about, but which is not in my province today.

The case of the Holly Ten red-baiting and imprisonment—this has been told again and again. But when the same people led by John Rankin and Parnell Thomas of the House committee turned to books, they were in a quandary. There was an interesting historical reason for this quandary. In 1936, when Bucharan and other Russian Communists were put on trial and tried by the Stalinites, most of them were condemned to death. A horrible series of unjust convictions took place, which the Soviets denied. The members of the U.S. Communist Party accepted the Soviet denial. A group of people led by Trotsky, who knew the truth, denounced these trials. A group of serious writers—perhaps the most well remembered one being James T. Farrel, condemned the Soviet Union. As a result, the intellectuals and the writers in the Communist Party split.

The split happened here in the East Coast for historical reasons that I don't have time to go into. It did not happen on the West Coast. The Communist Party intellectuals on the West Coast remained pro-Soviet, united, and together, and therefore the campaign against them was relatively simple. But the campaign against the intellectuals in the East drove the House committee and the Senate committee, which was then called the McCarthy Committee, to distraction precisely because of that split. And the only writer, I must confess, who had a national reputation and a very wide readership that remained loyal to the Communist Party was myself. Myself because I was the kind of kid who said "No sir, you're not gonna move me. I am committed to this, and I'm going to stay with this, and I don't believe all those lies about the Soviet Union."

So an extraordinary thing happened. I will try to spell out how it happened. I trust that you remember Clark Clifford, although you're all younger than I am. Clifford was the legal counsel for President Truman, a very estimable lawyer. In his older years he got into a variety of trouble, but this was before then. Being a good American, when it came to doing his Christmas shopping, he went out and bought books. He bought fifty copies—"five-zero" copies—of *Citizen Tom Paine*, by Howard Fast, and he gave them to his friends. He sent them out to all his friends, and for this he was subpoenaed to appear before the House Un-American Activities Committee. He groveled before the committee. This was the beginning of the era of groveling in America. That this man, who was a presidential attorney and a presidential assistant, should abase himself before an ignorant and illiterate group of congressmen was shameful. But he did it. He begged them to forgive him. He said he had read the book twice and he over-looked somehow, due to his own deficiencies, the Communist passages. But he explained that he had given them as gifts and he couldn't get them back again. So much for Clark Clifford.

They went on to make sure that this would not happen again. They took measures. But before they took the measures, Scarsdale, a rather strange community between Connecticut and New York, had a reputation for foolish censorship—and Scarsdale obediently banned *Citizen Tom Paine*. The Scarsdale Public Library had well over 50,000 books, but they chose *Citizen Tom Paine* to ban. This was the first time, insofar as I know, that an American novel was banned for any other reason than its use of a four-letter word or a sexual reference.

When challenged by the attorneys, civil liberties attorneys, they said it had "purple passages." What was purple and what wasn't? A cartoon in the *New Yorker* pictured one of Stamity's little kids with a sly expression on his face. A copy of *Citizen Tom Paine* faces him and behind it a larger book says American History. All the other kids are reading American History. And he, with this sly look, is reading *Citizen Tom Paine*.

J. Edgar Hoover now began a personal vendetta against me. He would not tolerate this, and he did an extraordinary thing. He sent a form letter to every neighborhood librarian, and to all the Carnegie libraries scattered around New York, Brooklyn, and Queens. He told them that every book by Howard Fast was to be removed from their shelves and burned. "Burned!" He apparently had no idea of the historical impact of the term he used.

J. Edgar Hoover marched on. He got in touch with a man called Kurt Enoch. I'll have to take a sidebar and explain about Kurt Enoch, and then I'll get back to Mr. Hoover. Enoch's line of paperbound books was called Signet, and he was the publisher. He was an interesting man. He published in Germany. Before Hitler, he published the Panther Books in Germany which were printed in English and sold all over the European continent, except England. Here and there I had picked up three or four Panther Books, and it was through them that I got in touch with Kurt Enoch who now published in America. All of his warehouse had been confiscated and burned by Hitler. I sent him the three books. We met, and he told me what these three books meant to him. He said, "For years I have been trying to find my books, books that people saved from Hitler and to reassemble my publishing history." Well, Enoch unfortunately selected Howard Fast and Eric Ambler for his line of American paperbacks. J.

Edgar Hoover learned of this, and he learned that Eric Ambler was a British Communist. Ambler was the only Communist novelist, excepting myself, Hoover could pin down and identify, so Hoover sent a notice to Kurt Enoch to destroy all of these books. I don't know whether Hoover used the term *burn* in that case or *destroy*. Someone in Kurt Enoch's office tipped off the *Compass* newspaper. If any of you remember the *Compass*—and I am sure many of you do—they ran a story about it. Then Kurt Enoch called me. He was in tears. What could he do?

I said, "Kurt sell the books to me. How many do you have?"

He said, "I have 330,000 of yours, and I have 60,000 of Eric Amblers."

I said, "Sell them all to me."

He said, "I'm not going to hurt you with this. Send me $200 and we've got a deal."

So I sent him the $200 for 400,000 books which was a nice buy. I had a father-in-law then who was very kind to me—I better put it that way considering everything—and very dear to his daughter. He was a newspaper distributor, and he had a fleet of trucks. So I took 400,000 books.

He said, "Howard you must hire a trailer truck."

So I hired a trailer truck and brought the 400,000 books from Michigan, and my father-in-law gave them storage space in Jersey. He sold them to his dealers for ten cents a book, and they sold them for fifteen cents a book. Believe it or not, I made money on the deal.

But this is only one detail in my crazy conflict with J. Edgar Hoover. And please do not consider me a victim. Never in my life have I looked at myself as a victim. I was not a victim. I was a contender, and I think, in the end, I won.

What was his next step? I told you about the branch libraries and all the letters to every branch library. The librarians called a meeting in the central library on Forty-second Street, and, believe me, my respect for librarians increased. They are wonderful, good people, and all these women—there must have been about 300 of them—defied Hoover and came to the meeting. I was the designated speaker. There was a small, white-haired lady who was the chairwoman, and when she introduced me, she said, "But we have not burned the books. We are not Nazis. We will not do what Mr. J. Edgar Hoover says we should do. We have put them in the basement, and when the time is right, we'll bring them up again."

Well, now I found myself the focus of Hoover's campaign against the elite, as he put it, against the intellectual monsters who were out to destroy America. A dear friend of mine, Angus Cameron, had become editor-in-chief of Little, Brown and Company. I said, "Angus I've got to have another name because I will be in the same boat as all those people in Hollywood who can't work. They have no income. They have families to support. So have I. I want to establish another name." I sent him a book which was called *The Fallen Angel*, and he agreed to publish it under another name. It was made into a film in due time. However, one of the people who worked at Little, Brown in Boston informed the FBI, and J. Edgar Hoover sent an FBI man to warn Little, Brown that the book was not to be published under a pseudonym. It would have to be published under my name. Even if they used a pseudonym, the book must explain who the real writer is. Well, you might say this was an exercise in censorship the likes of which had never before taken place in the United States.

Well, then, I went to jail. I went to jail for contempt of Congress, refusing to name names for the House Un-American Activities Committee. I won't go into that because that's much too long a story for the time I have left. But jail was a fascinating experience, and I got the whole idea for *Spartacus* there. As soon as I got out of jail, I began work on *Spartacus* which remains one of my favorite books. Some people have been kind enough to say that it ranks as a great novel. When I finished *Spartacus* about a year later, I sent the manuscript to Angus Cameron, and I said that this I wanted published under my own name—not under a pseudonym.

He loved the book. He said, "This is the best novel we've received since I've been here. Of course, we'll publish it. It will be our major book of the season." And so forth and so on. And then a G-man came. I remember the men of the Justice Department then. Thank God they're all too old to be in there anymore. It was not the Justice Department of today. Whatever failings the Justice Department has today, compared to the Justice Department of forty years ago, they're a set of white knights. So J. Edgar Hoover sent one of his G-men to Boston, and he spoke to the president of Little Brown.

He said, "Under no circumstances are you to publish this book which we understand is called *Spartacus*. It's about a revolution."

And they said, "But it's about a revolution that happened 2,000 years ago!"

"You are not to publish it."

Whereupon they called a meeting of the board, and they discussed the matter. They decided that they would accede to J. Edgar Hoover's wishes and not publish it. The only one who refused to go along with them was Angus Cameron, the vice president of the company.

He said, "If you don't publish this book then I must resign." He did.

Now the interesting thing is that this aura of fear—and it was very pervasive—this fear saturated an area of the United States. There are people who lived through those times and had little notion of it. But I remember, on more than one occasion, walking into a restaurant where there were people I knew, and they would turn their heads immediately so they wouldn't catch my eye and have to speak to me. Someone might see them speaking to me and report it. This is what I always called the miniterror, and it was a small but very real terror indeed.

Well, Little, Brown wouldn't publish *Spartacus*. Angus Cameron said it was a great book, and I decided to go to other publishers. I went to seven other publishers. Alfred E. Knopf, who was then alive and head of the firm (this was before Random House absorbed Knopf), refused to open the package of the manuscript. In a letter to me, he wrote, "I will not read the words of a dirty traitor."

It was a time of lunacy. Now remember, at that time you would go into any library and find *Das Kapital*, find everything Marx wrote, everything Lenin wrote. Everything was there. Jack London's forthright calls to revolution; they were all there. Edward Bellamy was there. Of course, none of them knew there was ever such a man as Bellamy.

Well, I sent the book to seven publishers. I sent it to Houghton Mifflin, Harcourt Brace, Doubleday, Knopf, of course, Random House. Random House was then owned by Bennett Cerf, still his company. He had put three of my books into his modern library. Finally, I sent it to Doubleday, and then I got a call from the man who ran the Doubleday bookstores. He said, "Mr. Fast, I've been at the worst and most disgusting editorial meeting of my life. I was with all the Doubleday editors. They discussed your book and said it was the finest book they had received in the year. But because J. Edgar Hoover prohibited its publication, they could not publish it. This bunch of wretched cowards is beyond description. So I'll tell you what to do. You publish the damn book, and I'll buy 600 copies right now for the Doubleday Book Shop."

This had never occurred to me, but I said to myself, "Well, who knows? Why not?" Then I got together with an editor who helped me edit it. I had a book designer, a friend of mine, design it. A man who worked for the American Book Company manufactured it. Another company's salesman picked it up, and I sold 45,000 copies in hard cover within a matter of weeks. So *Spartacus* got published. But this is the story of, I think, the most amazing and ridiculous piece of censorship carried out in the entire history of the United States. It was based not on sex, not on violence, but simply on a political invention of J. Edgar Hoover, who probably never read a book in his life.

So, there is my contribution to the story of censorship in America, and I'll be happy to answer any questions you wish to ask me if I have any time left.

4

The Old Problem of
New Communications Technologies:
Can We Do Better This Time?

Eric M. Freedman

One important contribution to the maintenance of artistic freedom in this country would be the enforcement of a First Amendment rule of technology neutrality:[1] a rule that the existence or extent of First Amendment coverage is independent of the method by which the expression may be conveyed.[2] Technology neutrality has at least two major advantages.

First, the rapid proliferation of new communications media—a development that shows every sign of accelerating for the foreseeable future[3]—means that tying the degree of permissible regulation to the identity of the medium will necessarily promote *ad hoc* fragmentation in the law.[4] The view that such a development would be undesirable is not based on its untidiness, but upon a long record demonstrating that permitting technological discrimination is inimical to freedom of expression. Historical experience—with, among others, printing presses,[5] secular dramatic troupes,[6] photographs,[7] movies,[8] rock music,[9] broadcasting,[10] sexually explicit telephone services,[11] and video games[12]— shows that each new medium is seen at first as uniquely threatening,[13] because uniquely influential,[14] and therefore a uniquely appropriate target of censorship. This is the backdrop against which we currently find governments reacting with near hysteria to the possibility of the creation, dissemination and viewing through the use of computer technology of messages even vaguely related to sexuality.[15] To be sure, computers are already covered by the existing statutory prohibition on the interstate distribution of obscene materials;[16] 18 U.S.C. §2252 (a)(2) already specifically criminalizes computer dissemination of depictions of minors engaging in sexually explicit conduct;[17] the existing general federal prohibition on the possession of child pornography already extends to one's home computer; [18] and prosecutions in computer-related cases are already regularly brought under such statutes.[19]

But unfamiliarity makes this new medium seem particularly dangerous,[20] and governments are haunted by the fear that the mechanisms of communications may be outrunning those of control.[21] Hence there arises a widespread view that neither the doctrinal categories nor the substantive content of current First Amendment law are adequate to deal with emerging problems.[22] This common pattern reflects the reality that new media achieve their initial marketplace success precisely because they are for some purposes a more effective form of communication than preexisting ones.[23]

As long as the courts enforce the First Amendment in the context of new media just as they do in the context of old ones—with an awareness that, historically, erring on the side of freedom of speech under conditions of uncertainty, whether technological, political (as during World War I or the Cold War), or empirical (as in the case of the Pentagon Papers) has proven in retrospect to be the wiser course—the damage that such fears may do to public discourse will be minimized. Assuming that ordinary First Amendment standards are applicable, for example, the Communications Decency Act of 1996 is patently unconstitutional.[24] And, in time, a consensus will arise that the first reaction to the perceived threat of cyberspace was as overblown as with other new media.[25]

As in all of First Amendment law, though, the danger is in the meantime[26] —when the ability to declare certain technologically defined categories of speech "outside" the First Amendment provides the courts an ever-available escape hatch from the need to provide coherent justifications for imposing otherwise impermissible regulations on just those communications formats in which the public has the liveliest interest.[27]

This is not only unjustifiable, but unnecessary. For the second consideration in favor of a single standard is that the marketplace will tend to do effectively— perhaps too effectively[28]—that which would be a threat to civil liberties if done by the government.[29] Today, for example, as all consumers know, standards for sexual explicitness differ among the commercial broadcast, cable, and movie industries, and, within the movie industry, between productions designed to be seen in movie theaters and in hotel rooms.[30] So too, there was greater reluctance among the long distance telephone carriers than the local ones to carry "dial-a-porn" services, even though the latter were subject to more stringent legal regulations.[31] In all of these cases, marketplace considerations, not legal ones, have determined the outcomes.

However distressing those outcomes may be to some aesthetic or political tastes,[32] this process represents the First Amendment working as it usually does in fact.[33] Just as the Constitution provides a quite lax outer framework within which ordinary politics operates to produce results that, whatever one may think of their substance, have been determined after a generally unimpeded contest between political groups of varying power,[34] so does it provide very broad limits within which the marketplace operates to disseminate that which the public wishes to obtain.[35] The key constitutional concern is that control rest with the people, not the government.

To be sure, there is implicit in this view the realization (which one may, according to taste, label realistic or cynical) that the political and economic marketplace, not the legal system, will determine the ultimate extent of speech regulation,[36] a conclusion that may initially cause all of those sparring over First Amendment standards to wonder why they are bothering.[37] The Supreme Court does not exist apart from the culture that it both shapes and reflects,[38] and, as we should have learned long ago from Learned Hand, Americans will in the long run have just as much freedom of speech as the majority desires.[39]

But "in the long run we are all dead."[40] As the now-vanished flag-burning uproar illustrates, First Amendment doctrine makes a difference in keeping the channels of discourse—and hence the possibilities of change—open during the interval that elapses between the initial urge towards suppression and the time, if ever, that the majority overcomes the constitutional obstacles to the exercise of its will. As the rapid pace of modern communications works to shorten that interval, the importance of robust First Amendment standards increases.

NOTES

1. I have made this argument in somewhat more detail, and within a broader theoretical context, in Part IV of Eric M. Freedman, *A Lot More Comes into Focus When You Remove the Lens Cap: Why Proliferating New Communications Technologies Make It Particularly Urgent for the Supreme Court to Abandon Its Inside-Out Approach to Freedom of Speech and Bring Obscenity, Fighting Words, and Group Libel within the First Amendment*, 81 IOWA L.R. 883 (1996).

2. *See generally* Laurence H. Tribe, *The Constitution in Cyberspace*, THE HUMANIST, Sept./Oct., 1991, at 15, 20, 39 (arguing that "the Constitution's norms, at their deepest level, must be invariant under merely *technological* transformations"); Note, Terri A. Cutrera, *Computer Networks, Libel and the First Amendment*, 11 COMPUTER/LAW J. 555, 580–82 (1992) (criticizing differential First Amendment standards based on technology by which message is carried).

3. *See generally* Robert L. Pettit & Christopher J. McGuire, *Video Dialtone: Reflections on Changing Perspectives in Telecommunications Regulation*, 6 HARV. J.L. & TECH. 343 (1993); James Gleick, *The Telephone Transformed—Into Almost Everything*, N.Y. TIMES MAG., May 16, 1993, at 26.

4. *See, e.g.*, John V. Edwards, Note, *Obscenity in the Age of Direct Broadcast Satellite: A Final Burial for* Stanley v. Georgia *(?), A National Obscenity Standard, and Other Miscellany*, 33 WM. & MARY L. REV. 949, 993 (1992) ("Direct broadcast satellite transmission is unique among media forms for obscenity analysis"); Karl A. Groskaufmanis, Note, *What Films We May Watch: Videotape Distribution and the First Amendment*, 136 U. PA. L. REV. 1263 (1988) (unique characteristics of videocassette medium warrant extensive First Amendment protection, particularly with regard to sexually explicit images); Randolph Stuart Sergent, Note, *Sex Candor and Computers: Obscenity and Indecency on the Electronic Frontier*, 10 J.L. & POL. 703, 705 (1994) ("The approach to regulation of sexual speech taken by the Supreme Court does not translate well to the new medium of computer networks").

There has been for the past several years a broad accord among policy makers in

Washington that uniform legislative and regulatory treatment of the various newer communications technologies is appropriate, *see* Edmund L. Andrews, *New Tack on Technology*, N.Y. TIMES, Jan. 12, 1994, at A1, and the Telecommunications Act of 1996 represents movement in this direction, *see* Edmund L. Andrews, *A Measure's Long Reach*, N.Y. TIMES, Feb. 2, 1996, at A1; Richard E. Wiley, *Communications Law*, NATL. L.J., March 11, 1996, at B4.

5. *See* WILLIAM E. RINGEL, OBSCENITY LAW TODAY 148–49 (1970) (English system requiring prior licensing of publications was a response to the arrival of the printing press and resulting fear on the part "of the King, members of the church hierarchy, and other members of the 'Establishment'" of dissemination of undesirable publications); ROBERT SHACKLETON, CENSURE AND CENSORSHIP: IMPEDIMENTS TO FREE PUBLICATION IN THE AGE OF ENLIGHTENMENT 11 (1975) (describing how invention of printing intensified the French regime of censorship); *see also* VINCENT BLASI, MILTON'S *AREOPAGITICA* AND THE MODERN FIRST AMENDMENT 16–17 (1995). *Cf.* Walter Kendrick, *Increasing Our Dirty Word Power: Why Yesterday's Smut is Today's Erotica*, N.Y. TIMES BOOK REV., May 31, 1992 (reviewing NICHOLSON BAKER, VOX (1992) (America today is divided into "a two-class culture, the top that reads and the bottom that does not or cannot. Even alarmists hardly fear the corrupting effect of pornography on literate adults; danger looms when it falls into the hands of the subliterate, and of course children. The subliterate avoid bookshops—they prefer video stores—and today's children read only under compulsion. Pictureless books can say what they please; they are impotent.") The broader implications of this latter trend are the subject of NEIL POSTMAN, AMUSING OURSELVES TO DEATH (1985).

6. *See generally* Margot Heinemann, *Drama and Opinion in the 1620s: Middleton and Massinger*, *in* THEATRE AND GOVERNMENT UNDER THE EARLY STUARTS, 237 (J. R. Mulryne & Margaret Shewring eds., 1993) (describing the impact of censorship on the political content of the English drama of the 1620s).

7. "Photography became a frequent censorship target in the late nineteenth century because it was supposedly more graphic and realistic than painting." Carlin Mayer, *Sex, Sin, and Women's Liberation: Against Porn-Suppression*, 72 TEX. L. REV. 1097, 1189–90 (1994). *See generally* Sam Roberts, *Giving Hardship and Poverty a Human Face*, N.Y. TIMES, Jan. 19, 1995, at H28 (nineteenth-century audiences, confronted with the novelty of "magic lantern" shows, "'were often so shocked by the portrayal of this new and terrifying world that they fainted, cried, or talked back to the lantern-slide screen,' according to Peter Bacon Hales, a historian of photography"); *infra* note 11 (quoting similar account of history).

8. *See* Mutual Film Corp. v. Industrial Commn. of Ohio, 236 U.S. 230 (1915) (no constitutional violation in the censorship system for movies because they are not part of the "press"). This case is analyzed at length in John Wertheimer, *Mutual Film Reviewed: The Movies, Censorship, and Free Speech in Progressive America*, 37 AM. J. LEGAL HIST. 158 (1993). *See also* DANIEL J. PIVAR, PURITY CRUSADE: SEXUAL MORALITY AND SOCIAL CONTROL, 1868–1900, at 234–35 (describing attempts at motion picture censorship in the late 1890s); *infra* note 25 (describing the overruling of *Mutual Film*).

9. *See* Robert N. Houser, Note, *Alleged Inciteful Rock Lyrics—A Look at Legal Censorship and Inapplicability of First Amendment Standards*, 17 OHIO N.U.L. REV. 323, 325–327 (1990) (sketching the history of attempts to censor rock and roll); Trent Hill, *The Enemy Within: Censorship in Rock Music in the 1950s*, 90 S. ATLANTIC Q. 675 (1991) (comprehensive account); *see also Record Labelling: Hearing Before the Senate Committee on Commerce, Science, and Transportation*, 99th Cong., 1st Sess. (1985) (hearing inspired by Tipper Gore and others, to see if, in the words of Senator Hollings, *id.* at 3, "there is . . . an approach that can be used by Congress to limit this outrageous filth, suggestive violence, suicide, and everything else in this Lord's world that . . . the writers and framers of our first amendment never perhaps heard . . . in their time"); Jon Pareles, *Should Rock Lyrics be Sanitized?*, N.Y. TIMES, Oct. 13, 1985, at H1; Calvin Sims, *Gangster Rappers: The Lives, the Lyrics*, N.Y. TIMES, Nov. 28, 1993, at E3 ("From Mozart to Frank Sinatra to Michael Jackson, popular music has had a long history of run-ins with the law. But the recent arrests of three major hip-hop artists on charges including sexual assault and murder have heightened concerns that some of these performers, particularly the stars of gangster rap, have become dangerous emblems for an immensely popular, primarily black musical genre that celebrates violence, gangs, guns, and sexual conquest"). *See generally* Richard Greener, *It's the Same Old Cry about Black Music*, N.Y. TIMES, Sept. 17, 1993, at A28 (letter to the editor arguing that attempts to censor popular music have long had a racist component).

Martha Bayles has addressed the area comprehensively in her book, THE HOLE IN OUR SOUL: THE LOSS OF BEAUTY AND MEANING IN AMERICAN POPULAR MUSIC (1994), which argues that although much of the music of the last decade lacks the social worth of the dissenting voices of earlier years, the answer lies in the aesthetic judgment of the public rather than government censorship. *Cf. Song Lyric Ratings Are Backed by A.M.A.*, N.Y. TIMES, June 23, 1995, at A20 (AMA calls upon the recording industry to develop a comprehensive system for rating song lyrics for violent content).

10. In *F.C.C. v. Pacifica Foundation*, 438 U.S. 726 (1978), the Court held that the particular pervasiveness of the broadcast media permitted the government to suppress "indecent" speech there—and only there. *See* Turner Broadcasting Sys., Inc. v. F.C.C., 114 S. Ct. 2445, 2457–59 (1994) (the relaxed First Amendment scrutiny of restraints on broadcasters is due to "the special physical characteristics of broadcast transmission," and is inapplicable to cable); Sable Communications v. F.C.C., 109 S. Ct. 2829, 2836–37 (1989) (striking down restraints on "indecent" messages offered by "dial-a-porn" services). For a comprehensive analysis, *see* Lili Levi, *The Hard Case of Broadcast Indecency*, 20 N.Y.U. REV. L. & SOC. CHANGE 49 (1992–93). *See also* Michael I. Meyerson, *The Right to Speak, the Right to Hear, and the Right Not to Hear: The Technological Resolution to the Cable/Pornography Debate*, 21 MICH. J.L. REFORM 137, 138–39 (1987–88) (concluding that, even presuming correctness of all relevant Supreme Court decisions and rationales, "the power of government to regulate cable pornography is limited to that which is legally obscene"); Theresa M. Sheehan, Note, *A Post-Sable Look at Indecent Speech on the Airwaves and over the Telephone Lines*, 15 W. NEW ENG. L. REV. 347 (1993); Edmund L. Andrews, *2 Views of Decency*, N.Y. TIMES, Dec. 28, 1992, at A12 (reviewing current regulatory predicaments). As I discuss in greater detail in Part II.C.2 of Freedman, *supra* note 1, the First Amendment ordinarily prohibits speech regulations based on the premise that the content being communicated is offensive to community taste.

In his persuasive opinion in *Telecommunications Research and Action Center v.*

F.C.C., 801 F.2d 501, 507–09 (D.C. Cir. 1986), *cert. denied*, 482 U.S. 919 (1987), Judge Bork showed that neither a rationale resting upon the alleged greater impact of the medium nor one resting upon considerations of spectrum scarcity could justify imposing greater restrictions on broadcasters than on newspaper publishers, *see* Tribe, *supra* note 2, at 21 (making same point), and invited the Supreme Court to extend to the former the freedoms now enjoyed by the latter. The Court should take an early opportunity to accept this invitation, and overrule *Pacifica, supra. See* Matthew L. Spitzer, SEVEN DIRTY WORDS AND SIX OTHER STORIES 131 (1986) (full-length presentation of same argument); Seth T. Goldsamt, Note, *"Crucified by the FCC"? Howard Stern, the FCC, and Selective Prosecution*, 28 COLUM. J. L. & SOC. PROBS. 203, 250–52 (1995) (describing recent efforts at enforcing the indecency standard as constituting selective prosecution and suggesting a re-examination of *Pacifica*); Tara Phelan, Note, *Selective Hearing: A Challenge to the FCC's Indecency Policy*, 12 N.Y.L. SCH. J. HUM. RTS. 347, 390–92 (1995) (both *Pacifica* and FCC's implementation of it are "in total contradiction to the preservation of a meaningful First Amendment").

Among other desirable effects of this development would be an end to the pattern in which legislators repeatedly test the limits of *Pacifica* by imposing indecency regulations on new media (like dial-a-porn services or computer networks, *see infra* note 24 and accompanying text) and then waiting to see whether the medium is or is not held to be within the boundaries of that decision. Even when the ultimate result is—as it invariably has been in all post-*Pacifica* cases—that such broad suppression is impermissible, there have been serious chilling effects in the meanwhile, and new technologies have been discriminatorily targeted.

11. *See* Christian A. Davis, Comment, *Revisiting the Lurid World of Telephones, Sex, and the First Amendment: Is This the End of Dial-A-Porn?* 2 WIDENER J. PUB. L. 621 (1993) (arguing that unique nature of pre-recorded message services warrants regulating them on the basis of indecency, either because they are like radio or because they constitute a separate medium for First Amendment purposes); Brian D. Woolfall, Comment, *Implications of a Bond Requirement for 900-Number Dial-A-Porn Providers: Exploring the Need for Tighter Restrictions on Obscenity and Indecency*, 30 CAL. WEST. L. REV. 297, 310–11 (1994). (Because "dial-a-porn has been linked to an increase in sexual violence and sexually deviant thought," providers of indecent phone messages that are not legally obscene should be required to post bonds to compensate potential victims of crimes committed by those who listen to the messages.)

12. After legislation was introduced in Congress to require the video game industry to implement a rating system, it agreed to do so voluntarily. *See* John Burgess, *Video Game Industry Plans Rating System; Move Is Response to Congressional Pressure*, WASH. POST, Dec. 8, 1993, at F1; *see also* 1994 ANN. SURV. AM. L. 461–69 (setting forth rating system eventually adopted). The producer of one of the video games attacked at Senate hearings commented, "[I]f my name were Steven Spielberg or Francis Coppola, they wouldn't be criticizing me. . . . Much of the reaction to "Night Trap" is the shock of the new. When Thomas Edison started making short films around the turn of the century, patrons ran from theaters in horror when they saw a steam engine barreling directly toward the front-row seats. . . . Interactive TV is here, and like rock-and roll it's here to stay." Tom Zito, *Senate Demagoguery: Leave My Company's Video Game Alone*, WASH. POST, Dec. 17, 1993, at A25.

13. For a good historic overview of this phenomenon in modern times, together with a well-reasoned discussion of the appropriate judicial approach to such problems, *see* Philip H. Miller, Note, *New Technology, Old Problem: Determining the First Amendment Status of Electronic Information Services*, 61 FORDHAM L. REV. 1147 (1993). It is commonly the case that one of the first experimental uses of a new medium involves the transmission of sexual imagery, *see* Anne Wells Branscomb, *Internet Babylon? Does the Carnegie Mellon Study of Pornography on the Information Superhighway Reveal a Threat to the Stability of Society?*, 83 GEO. L.J. 1935, 1935–37 (1995); John Tierney, *Porn, the Low-Slung Engine of Progress*, N.Y. TIMES, Jan. 9, 1994, at H1; PC MAGAZINE, Aug., 1993, at 525–26, 535–36, 545 (advertisements for sexually-oriented material in numerous formats obtainable by computer modem), which tends to reinforce the perceived threat.

14. *See generally* United States v. Roth, 237 F.2d 796, 799 n.5 (2d Cir. 1956) (noting special concern of authorities with "the perversion of young minds through the mass media of the movies, television, radio, and the press, especially so-called comics"), *aff'd*, 354 U.S. 476 (1957); JOSEPH T. KLAPPER, THE EFFECTS OF MASS COMMUNICATIONS 143–59 (1960) (reviewing 1950s studies exploring this concern); Gail Johnston, Note, *It's All in the Cards: Serial Killers, Trading Cards, and the First Amendment*, 39 N.Y.L. SCH. L. REV. 549, 552–53, 555–57 (1994) (noting that 1950s concern about comic books had been preceded by campaign against dime novels in the late 1800s); Dorothy Rabinowitz, *The Attorney General as Scriptwriter*, WALL ST. J., Nov. 1, 1993, at A14 (comparing the recent campaign against TV violence, discussed *infra* note 35, with the congressional hearings of the 1950s on the dangers of comic books). The longer-term cultural impact of the fears of the 1950s about the influence of new commercial media is explored in TOM ENGLERHARDT, THE END OF VICTORY CULTURE: COLD WAS AMERICA AND THE DISSILLUSIONING OF A GENERATION (1995), *reviewed in* N.Y. TIMES, Jan. 16, 1995, at C16.

15. *See* Peter H. Lewis, *About Freedom of the Virtual Press*, N.Y. TIMES, Jan. 2, 1996, at B14; David L. Wilson, *Restricting the Networks*, CHRON. HIGHER EDUC., June 30, 1995, at A17; *infra* note 22.

16. 28 U.S.C. § 1465 (1988). *See* United States v. Thomas, 74 F. 3d 701 (6th Cir. 1996). But, lest there be any doubt, Section 507 of Title V of the Telecommunications Act of 1996, Pub. L. 104–104 (1996), so provides explicitly.

17. The statutory penalties were drastically increased by the Sexual Crimes Against Children Prevention Act of 1995, Pub. L. 104–71 (1995), which President Clinton signed into law on December 23, 1995. *See Child-Sex Bill Is Signed*, N.Y. TIMES, Dec. 24, 1995, at A14. On the presidential campaign trail five months later, Senator Bob Dole denounced these new sentences as insufficiently harsh, and promised that they would be increased if he were elected. *See* Katherine Q. Seelye, *Revisiting the Issue of Crime, Dole Offers Test of Remedies*, N.Y. TIMES, May 29, 1996, at A1.

18. *See Sentenced for Cyber Porn*, NATL. L. J., Dec. 26, 1994-Jan. 2, 1995, at A10.

19. *See, e.g.*, Glenn R. Simpson, *U.S. Arrests Three in Customs Probe of Computer Porn*, WALL ST. J., Jan 12, 1996, at B7; Peter H. Lewis, *Computer Stings Gain Favor as Arrests for Smut Increase*, N.Y. TIMES, Sept. 16, 1995, at A1; David Johnston, *Use of Computer Network for Child Sex Sets Off Raids*, N.Y. TIMES, Sept. 14, 1996, at A1; *Jail for Couple Over Computer Pornography*, N.Y. TIMES, Dec. 3, 1994, at A9. *See generally* Thomas J. DeLoughry, *Existing Laws Called Adequate to Bar Children's*

Access to On-Line Pornography, CHRON. HIGHER EDUC., Aug. 4, 1995, at A17.

20. For a brief summary of the primary forms of computer-based communications technologies in current use, see Robert F. Goldman, Note, *Put Another Log on the Fire, There's a Chill on the Internet: The Effect of Applying Current Anti-Obscenity Laws to Online Communications*, 29 GA. L. REV. 1075, 1079–88 (1995). *Cf.* James Gleick, *This is Sex?* N.Y. TIMES MAG., June 11, 1995, at 26. (Legislation to control access to on-line sexual imagery "reflects a mental picture of how the on-line world works that does not match the reality.") Once these technologies are understood, it can be plausibly argued that—contrary to current fears—their spread will have a positive effect on children, by teaching "complex analytical skills similar to those required of a fully literate person," and thereby tending to overcome the negative effects caused by the substitution of television and videocassettes for books, *see* Neil Postman, THE DISAPPEARANCE OF CHILDHOOD 149 (1982), and by providing access to beneficial sexual education that would otherwise be unavailable, *see* Carlin Mayer, *Reclaiming Sex From the Pornographers: Cybersexual Possibilities*, 83 GEO. L.J. 1969, 1974–76 (1995).

The pervasive misperceptions were exacerbated by the publication in mid-1995 of Marty Rimm, *Marketing Pornography on the Information Superhighway: A Survey of 917,410 Images, Descriptions, Short Stories and Animations Downloaded 8.5 Million Times by Consumers in Over 2000 Cities in Forty Countries, Provinces, and Territories*, 83 GEO. L.J. 1849 (1995), which was featured on the front cover of the TIME MAGAZINE of July 3, 1995. The article's depiction of major portions of cyberspace as awash in sexual imagery was quickly exploded, *see* Mike Godwin, *Villains and Heroes*, INTERNET WORLD, Jan. 1996, at 32; *Senator Grassley's Surf Police*, N.Y. TIMES, July 28, 1995, at A26; Philip Elmer-De Witt, *Fire Storm on the Computer Nets*, TIME, July 24, 1995, at 57; Peter H. Lewis, *New Concerns Raised Over a Computer Smut Study*, N.Y. TIMES, July 16, 1995, at A22; Peter H. Lewis, *Critics Troubled by Computer Study on Pornography*, N.Y. TIMES, July 3, 1995, at B37, but doubtless lingers in the official mind.

21. Among the many examples of this concern are the sudden awakening of countries around the world to the potential of computers to assist in the spread of the two phenomena "authoritarian government most dreads political dissent and pornography," *Beijing Seeks to Build Version of the Internet that Can be Censored*, WALL ST. J., Jan. 31, 1996, at A1; *see* Amy Knoll, Comment, *Any Which Way but Loose: Nations Regulate the Internet*, 4 TUL. J. INT. & COMP. L. 275 (1996); HUMAN RIGHTS WATCH, SILENCING THE NET (1996) (documenting recent worldwide trend towards governmental censorship of the Internet); Charles Platt, *Americans Are Not as Free as We Think We Are*, WIRED, April, 1996, at 82 (describing current campaigns by state and local authorities to suppress erotic on-line speech), *see also* Nadine Strossen, *Hate Speech and Pornography: Do We Have to Choose Between Freedom of Speech and Equality?* 46 CASE WEST. RES. L. REV. 449, 473–76 (1996) (explicating link between sexual and political repression), and the long-running obsession of the American government with maintaining controls on encryption technology, *see* Denise Caruso, *Digital Commerce*, N.Y. TIMES, March 25, 1996, at D5 ("The key issue for the Net is not smut, it is the use of encryption," since "Big Brother legislation that would give law enforcement the ability and rationale to monitor all the electronic messages of citizens" could "suffocate the Internet"); James P. Lucier, Jr., *The Government Would Like a Key to Your Computer Files*, WASH. TIMES, March 5, 1996, at A15.

Although the governments' perceptions may well be correct—computer technologies may empower ordinary citizens to bypass both governmental and private gatekeepers, effectively enabling everyman to be a publisher, *see* Mike Godwin, *Witness against Net Prosecution*, INTERNET WORLD, Dec. 1995, at 102; Jim Hoagland, *Around the World on a Modem*, WASH. POST, April 4, 1996, at A31; *infra* note 28—the First Amendment requires our government at least to embrace rather than suppress this potential. *See, e.g.*, Jeremy Stone Weber, Note, *Defining Cyberlibel: A First Amendment Limit for Libel Suits Against Individuals Arising From Computer Bulletin Board Speech*, 46 CASE W. RES. L. REV. 235 (1995) (proposing that when a private libel plaintiff has been defamed on a computer bulletin board to which she has access to post a reply, the First Amendment requires her to prove actual malice).

22. Thus, in an effort at thought control that flatly defies the First Amendment as understood to date—and that would never attain serious consideration in any other context—Congress is diligently at work on S. 1237, 104th Cong., 1st Sess. (1995). Introduced by Senator Orrin G. Hatch of Utah as the Child Pornography Protection Act of 1995, this legislation would broadly criminalize dissemination of all visual images of children engaging in "sexually explicit" conduct, notwithstanding that the images were generated purely electronically, without the use of any children (or adult actors, for that matter) at all. The committee report in support of this proposal explains that it "is needed due to technological advances" in the creation of visual images, "particularly through the use of computers," that have "made possible the production of visual depictions that appear to be of minors engaging in sexually explicit conduct." S. Rep. No. 104-358, 104th Cong., 2d Sess., pt. I, at 7 (1996). *See* David B. Johnson, Comment, *Why the Possession of Computer-Generated Child Pornography Can be Constitutionally Prohibited*, 4 ALBANY L.J. SCI. & TECH. 311, 326, 331 (images of child pornography made with animation software are indistinguishable as a policy matter from depictions involving real children, and new legislation should outlaw their sale, transportation or possession). The issues arising under such a statute were the subject of the thirteenth annual John Marshall Law School National Moot Court competition in Information Technology and Privacy Law, whose bench memorandum and party briefs have been published as *Sysop, User and Programmer Liability: The Constitutionality of Computer Generated Child Pornography*, 13 J. COMPUTER & INFO. L. 881 (1995). *See also* Henry J. Reske, *Computer Porn a Prosecutorial Challenge*, A.B.A.J., Dec. 1994, at 40 ("computer porn prosecutions are likely to continue, perhaps forcing a reevaluation of First Amendment law on obscenity," in light of the mutability of computer images and the difficulty of defining community standards); Andrea Gerlin, *Electronic Smut Is Drawing Fire of Prosecutors, Raising Questions*, WALL ST. J., May 27, 1994, at B3; *Future Watch* (CNN Cablecast, Sept. 7, 1993) (summarizing issues). *See also* Clyde H. Farnsworth, *Canadian Test Case: "Pornography" vs. Imagination*, N.Y. TIMES, Jan. 7, 1994, at A10 (reporting case of Eli Langer, artist arrested in Toronto for displaying images of child sexuality that were painted from imagination; statute prohibits depictions of sexual acts by those under 18 unless defendant demonstrates artistic merit); Richard Huntington, *Conjuring Up the Fears of Childhood*, BUFF. NEWS, Sept. 28, 1995, at 4B (reviewing show of Langer's drawings). ("Langer is the Canadian artist who had his work confiscated by Toronto authorities for alleged obscenity. He subsequently won the case, and justly so: These are powerful statements of the horrors and guilty pleasures of childhood. Though they depict forbidden sex acts, they never titillate or exploit. They have a harrowing honesty, and they give voice to a segment of the population that seldom is allowed to speak.")

23. *Cf.* Superior Films, Inc. v. Dep't of Educ., 346 U.S. 587, 589 (1954) (Douglas, J., concurring). ("[T]he First Amendment draws no distinction between the various methods of communicating ideas. On occasion one may be more powerful or effective than another. . . . Which medium will give the most excitement and have the most enduring effect will vary. . . . It is not for the censor to determine in any case.")

24. The Act, which is Title V of the Telecommunications Act of 1996, Pub. L. 104–104 (1996), subjects to fines and imprisonment for up to two years:

(a) the knowing transmission of "any comment, request, suggestion, proposal, image, or other communication which is obscene or indecent, knowing that the recipient of the communication is under 18 years of age, regardless of whether the maker of such communication placed the call or initiated the communication," *id.* § 502(1)(a)(1)(B); and

(b) the knowing use of "any interactive computer service to display in a manner available to a person under 18 years of age, any comment, request, suggestion, proposal, image, or other communication that, in context, depicts or describes, in terms patently offensive as measured by contemporary community standards, sexual or excretory activities or organs, regardless of whether the user of such service placed the call or initiated the communication," *id.* § 502(1)(d).

In accordance with the special judicial review provisions contained in § 561, these restrictions (along with related ones imposing vicarious liability on information service providers, *see* Daniel G. Bernstein & Michelle W. Cohen, *Federal Legislation Confronts Cybersmut*, N.Y.L.J., April 22, 1996, at S8, and ones on abortion-related speech that the government immediately conceded were invalid, *see* Letter from Janet Reno to Newt Gingrich, Feb. 9, 1996, *reprinted* in 142 CONG. REC. S1599 (daily ed. March 6, 1996) were challenged in two major actions, American Civil Liberties Union v. Reno, No. 96–963, and American Library Association v. United States Department of Justice, No. 96–1458, that were consolidated before a three-judge court in the Eastern District of Pennsylvania. As a result of a combination of a temporary restraining order issued by District Judge Ronald Buckwalter on February 15, 1996, *see* American Civil Liberties Union v. Reno, 24 MED. L. REP. 1379 (E.D. Pa. 1996), and a subsequent agreement between counsel, neither provision took effect *pendente lite, see U.S. Will Not Prosecute for "Offensive" Internet Material*, CHRON. HIGH. EDUC., March 1, 1996, at A29. *See also infra* note 27 (noting subsequent grant of preliminary injunction).

Both restrictions are manifestly invalid. The principal reasons are:

(1) As described *supra* note 10, regulation on the basis of indecency has been pointedly limited by the Court to the broadcast media, a context in which it has been justified on the basis of spectrum scarcity and the special intrusiveness of those media. *See* Joanna H. Kim, Comment, *Cyber-Porn Obscenity: The Viability of Local Community Standards and the Federal Venue Rules in the Computer Network Age*, 15 LOY. L.A. ENT. L.J. 415, 435–38 (1995). The Internet is not a physically limited medium; on the contrary, it is infinitely expandable as people set up additional nodes. *See* Jerry Berman & Daniel J. Weitzner, *Abundance and User Control: Renewing the Democratic Heart of the First Amendment in the Age of Interactive Media*, 104 YALE L.J. 1619, 1623–24 (1995). Nor is the medium intrusive; on the contrary, one has to search with considerable diligence to find what one is seeking. *See* Joan E. Rigdon, *For Some, the Web Is Just a Slow Crawl to a Splattered Cat*, WALL ST. J., Jan. 25, 1996, at A1; Gleick, *supra* note 20. *See also Cybertech in Philadelphia*, WASH. POST, May 18, 1996, at A18. (Editorializing that the "Internet is not a broadcast medium, where the basis for regulation is that transmissions can be 'pervasive' and viewers can't avoid being exposed

to them. It's something entirely new—a medium where you choose at every step what you want to see or read.")

(2) Assuming regulation on the basis of indecency were permissible, the term is not defined in the provision quoted in paragraph (a) above, while the definition quoted in paragraph (b) above does no more than reiterate that of the FCC in the broadcast context, *see* Richard Raysman & Peter Brown, *Liability of Internet Access Provider under Decency Act*, N.Y.L.J., March 12, 1996, at 3, 31; both thus suffer from the same vices of vagueness, overbreadth and potential for selective enforcement that have led to the universal condemnation of those standards, *see supra* note 10.

(3) In any event, in contrast to the broadcast media (and analogously to the case of dial-a-porn), there are less restrictive alternatives to a total ban available, in the form of a variety of access control and content-labelling systems. *See* Peter H. Lewis, *Microsoft Backs Ratings System for the Internet*, N.Y. TIMES, March 1, 1996, at D1; John Markoff, *New Internet Feature Will Make Voluntary Ratings Possible*, N.Y. TIMES, July 3, 1995, at D40; Frank Rich, *Newt to the Rescue*, N.Y. TIMES, July 1, 1995, at A19; *see also Cyber-Regs*, NATL. L.J., June 26, 1995, at A20 (editorial urging that an appropriate method of protecting children from Internet threats is "encouraging service providers to devise virtual lockboxes, as cable TV companies have done.")

(4) Technical considerations make the statute so extremely unlikely to achieve its stated purpose—while so extremely likely to suppress speech that is protected by any standard, *see* Mayer, *supra* note 20, at 1979–94; Anna G. Eshoo, *Nanny on the Net*, WASH. POST, Jan. 31, 1996, at A15—as to render it invalid under the First Amendment on the grounds of simple irrationality. *See* Rubin v. Coors Brewing Co., 115 S.Ct. 1585, 1592 (1995) (the prohibition against stating the alcohol content on beer labels is unconstitutional because, although the asserted goal of the statute is valid, "the irrationality of this unique and puzzling regulatory framework ensures that the labeling ban will fail to achieve that end.")

This challenge is particularly strong in a context where pursuit of the unattainable goal of keeping the targeted material out of the hands of minors will necessarily "restrict all communications on the Internet to a level suitable for children," Harvey A. Silverglate, *Cyber Speech at Risk*, NATL. L.J., March 4, 1996, at A19. *See* Virginia v. American Booksellers Association, 484 U.S. 383, 389 (1988); Butler v. Michigan, 352 U.S. 380, 383–84 (1957) (statutes having this effect violate the First Amendment).

25. *See, e.g.*, Joseph Burstyn, Inc. v. Wilson, 343 U.S. 495, 502 (1952) (overruling *Mutual Film, supra* note 8; rejecting the argument "that motion pictures should be disqualified from First Amendment protection" because they "possess a greater capacity for evil, particularly among the youth of a community, than other modes of expression"; such considerations are relevant only to a permissible scope of controls); ZECHARIAH CHAFFEE, JR., FREE SPEECH IN THE UNITED STATES 542–48 (2d ed. 1941) (arguing that *Mutual Film* should be overruled in light of the economic power of audiences to determine the film content, and the importance of art in furthering a discussion of social issues); Wertheimer, *supra* note 8, at 160 (summarizing the history of the professional reaction to *Mutual Film*); *see also supra* note 5 (noting a change in the perceived power of print media); *see generally* Robert Corn-Revere, *New Technology and the First Amendment: Breaking the Cycle of Repression*, 17 HASTINGS COMM/ENT L.J. 247, 252 (1994). ("Initially, new technologies are given little or no First Amendment protection. As each medium gains cultural penetration and becomes more mainstream, courts are increasingly willing to recognize its First Amendment

status.")

26. See *infra* text accompanying note 40.

27. There are a number of sound reasons—including the overwhelming factual record assembled by the wide range of plaintiffs challenging the Communications Decency Act—to believe that the Court will not utilize the escape hatch in that particular instance, and will instead apply its well-established jurisprudence to strike down the law. Indeed, two separate three-judge District Courts, in powerful opinions, have recently granted preliminary injunctions against enforcement of the key provisions of the Act. *See* Shea v. Reno, 930 F. Supp. 916 (E.D.N.Y. 1996); American Civil Liberties Union v. Reno, 929 F. Supp. 824 (E.D. Pa. 1996). But, as the example of movies demonstrates, until the escape hatch is bolted tight, the temptation to use it will always exist. Moreover, a technology-based definition of speech "outside" the First Amendment may interact perniciously with a content-based one. *Cf.* Peter F. Lewis, *Group Urges an Internet Ban on Hate Groups' Messages*, N.Y. TIMES, Jan. 10, 1996, at A10. (In urging Internet service providers not to provide access to hate groups' World Wide Web sites, the Simon Wiesenthal Center explains that the "unprecedented potential and scope of the Internet" gives it "incredible power to promote violence, threaten women, denigrate minorities, promote homophobia and conspire against democracy.")

28. *Compare* Owen Fiss, *Why the State?* 100 HARV. L. REV. 81 (1987); Owen Fiss, *Free Speech and Social Structure*, 71 IOWA L. REV. 1405 (1986); Jerome A. Barron, *Access to the Press—A New First Amendment Right*, 80 HARV. L. REV. 1641 (1967) *with* L.A. Powe, Jr., *Scholarship and Markets*, 56 GEO. WASH. L. REV. 172 (1987). *See generally* C. EDWIN BAKER, ADVERTISING AND A DEMOCRATIC PROCESS (1994), *reviewed in* 108 HARV. L. REV. 489 (1994).

For the suggestion that the expansion of new information technologies will reduce speakers' distribution costs and hence make it more difficult for private gatekeepers to stifle speech, *see* Eugene Volokh, *Cheap Speech and What It Will Do*, 104 Yale L.J. 1805 (1995).

Quite apart from the problem that the effect may be to "compound our current social divisions, given that men, whites, the young and the affluent so far tend to be the information 'haves' while women, blacks, the old and the poor are the have-nots," Frank Rich, *Gates Goes Public*, N.Y. TIMES, Dec. 2, 1995, at A21, it remains to be seen whether and to what extent this development may counter a trend favoring private censorship: the increasing consolidation of businesses in such a way that the financial interests of the entity as a whole are adversely impacted if the speech-related sub-unit is aggressive in the defense of First Amendment rights, *see* Frank Rich, *Media Amok*, N.Y. TIMES, May 18, 1996, at A19; Ken Auletta, *The Wages of Synergy*, THE NEW YORKER, Nov. 27, 1995, at 8; Leon Friedman, *The Scary Shift Towards Corporate News*, NEWSDAY, Nov. 27, 1995, at A21; Max Frankel, *Couplings*, N.Y. TIMES MAG., Sept. 24, 1995, at 30. *See also* Jane E. Kirtley, *Media Cave Despite High Court Support*, NATL. L.J., Dec. 4, 1995, at A19.

29. *Compare* Frank I. Michelman, *Conceptions of Democracy in American Constitutional Argument: The Case of Pornography Regulation*, 56 TENN. L. REV. 291, 310–11 (1989) (questioning whether this distinction makes sense) *with* Kathleen M. Sullivan, *Free Speech and Unfree Markets*, 42 UCLA L. REV. 949 (1995) (arguing that it does). *See also* Jonathan Weinberg, *Broadcasting and Speech*, 81 CAL. L. REV. 1101, 1193–1204 (1993) (arguing that deficiencies of the present system of broadcast regulation reflect a contradiction between underlying goals: keeping government out of

the marketplace of ideas, and regulating that marketplace to eliminate distortions caused by private censorship).

30. *See* Nick Ravo, *A Fact of Life: Sex-Video Rentals*, N.Y. TIMES, May 16, 1990, at C1. ("One factor cited by industry officials for the increased popularity of adult videotapes is that more people are seeing them—and discovering they enjoy them—in hotel rooms and on home televisions, via satellite dish antennas and on some cable channels. But most of the broadcast versions are less explicit than those available on videocassette.") Similarly, "[v]iewers—especially parents—have known for years" that "premium cable channels like HBO and Showtime are more violent than broadcast and basic cable," Hal Boedeker, *TV Violence: Latest Study is a Rerun*, ORLANDO SENTINEL, Feb. 15, 1996, at E1.

31. There is a complete discussion in Jerome A. Barron, *The Telco, the Common Carrier Model and the First Amendment—The "Dial-A-Porn" Precedent*, 19 RUTGERS COMPUTER & TECH. L.J. 371 (1993) (arguing on the basis of this experience that local phone companies should remain subject to common carrier regulation as they move into the provision of information services). The content and regulatory environment of the remaining long distance providers of sexually oriented messages are described in Jack Glasock & Robert LaRose, *Dial-A-Porn Recordings: The Role of the Female Participant in Male Sexual Fantasies*, 37 J. BROADCASTING & ELECTRONIC MEDIA 313 (1993).

32. *See, e.g.*, Mary E. Becker, *The Politics of Women's Wrongs and the Bill of "Rights": A Bicentennial Perspective*, 59 U. CHI. L. REV. 453, 486-94 (1992) (criticizing messages that are heard when "a 'free' market in speech means that the market, governed by ability to pay, determines who can speak," and suggesting that the Free Speech Clause be reinterpreted or amended to permit government intervention to correct the situation).

33. *See* Telecommunications Research and Action Center v. F.C.C., 801 F.2d 501, 508 & n.3 (D.C. Cir. 1986), *cert. denied*, 482 U.S. 919 (1987); WILLIAM ERNST HOCKING, FREEDOM OF THE PRESS: A FRAMEWORK OF PRINCIPLE 13-15 (1947) (tracing the rising influence of market forces on press content in early national years; "what in other times and places the king's censor might have done, the 'gentle bribery of one's own pocket book' accomplished silently in the New World"); CATHARINE A. MACKINNON, ONLY WORDS 77-78 (1993); Ronald K. L. Collins & David M. Skover, *Pissing in the Snow: A Cultural Approach to the First Amendment*, 45 STAN. L. REV. 783 (1993); *see also* Lawrie Mifflin, *Talk-Show Critics Urge Boycott of Programs by Advertisers*, N.Y. TIMES, Dec. 8, 1995, at A22 (two Senators and former Secretary of Education urge advertisers to "take the trash out" of daytime talk shows by refusing to sponsor ones that broadcast "degrading material" with offensive sexual themes; as a result, six such shows expected to be canceled, *see* John Elvin, *Talk Shows Damaged by Publicity Barrage*, WASH. TIMES, Jan. 22, 1996, at 28); John J. O'Connor, *Is the BBC Too Adult for American Viewers?* N.Y. TIMES, Dec. 29, 1994, at C11 ("It's hardly news that America is inhabited by large numbers of Puritanical hysterics. A week rarely goes by without some watchdog group railing against four-letter words, nudity and—the all-purpose smear—pornography . . . all of which is having an accelerated impact on what viewers can or, more precisely, cannot see at home"); Vernon Silver, *Loss of Gay TV Shows Stirs a Key West Debate*, N.Y. TIMES, Feb. 28, 1994, at D6 (producers of two gay television programs say the owner of a small station in Key West canceled their shows because of pressure from a Christian network that buys

time on the channel); Armistead Maupin, *A Line That Commercial TV Won't Cross*, N.Y. TIMES, Jan. 9, 1994, at H29 (commercial television will not permit gay couples to be shown kissing, on the basis that the audience wouldn't stand for it); Tom Redburn, *Toys 'R' Us Stops Selling a Violent Video Game*, N.Y. TIMES, Dec. 17, 1993, at B1 (the nation's largest toy seller announces it has stopped selling the video game "Night Trap" because it is too violent for children, but will continue selling "Mortal Kombat," a much more widely available game that has also generated protests over violence; only a few hundred thousand machines able to play "Night Trap" have been sold, in contrast to the more than 15 million able to play "Mortal Kombat"); Kevin Goldman, *"Beavis and Butt-Head" Stirs Advertisers*, WALL ST. J., Oct. 28, 1993, at B12 (under pressure from American Family Association, some major advertisers are abandoning the show); Elizabeth Jensen, *Crusade Against ABC's "NYPD Blue" Goes Local*, WALL ST. J., Oct. 6, 1993, at B1 (tactics of groups supporting or opposing particular shows "have become increasingly sophisticated"); Brent Staples, *The Politics of Gangster Rap*, N.Y. TIMES, Aug. 27, 1993, at A28 (consumers should boycott gangster rap music because it perpetuates negative stereotypes); N.Y. TIMES, Aug. 23, 1993, §4, at 16 (advertisement by American Family Association urging a boycott of companies that "are the leading sponsors of sex, violence and profanity on primetime, network television"); Michael Marriott, *Hard-Core Rap Lyrics Stir Backlash*, N.Y. TIMES, Aug. 15, 1993, at A1 (segments of the Black community protesting rap lyrics with socially negative messages); Fred Cohen, *The Tabloid Press Abuses Children*, N.Y. TIMES, March 13, 1993, at 21 (if press insufficiently restrained in reporting sensational stories involving school children, the public should respond with advertiser boycotts).

34. *See generally* New York City Transit Authority v. Beazer, 440 U.S. 568 (1979); Williamson v. Lee Optical of Oklahoma, 348 U.S. 483 (1955).

35. *See* Monroe E. Price, *The Market for Loyalties: Electronic Media and the Global Competition for Allegiances*, 104 YALE L.J. 667, 691–94 (1994); Ronald K. L. Collins & David M. Skover, *Commerce & Communication*, 71 TEX. L. REV. 697 (1993).

Broadcasters, however, because of the flaccid regime of First Amendment protections applicable to them, *see supra* note 10; *compare* Red Lion Broadcasting Co. v. F.C.C., 395 U.S. 367 (1969) (the government could require the radio station to allow a reply by the individual attacked) *with* Miami Herald Pub. Co. v. Tornillo, 418 U.S. 241 (1974) (the government could not impose such a requirement on the newspaper) are to some extent more easily intimidated by the possibility of government regulation than other media of equal economic power *and* Turner Broadcasting Sys., Inc. v. F.C.C., 114 S. Ct. 2445, 2457–64 (1994) (applying the standards of United States v. O'Brien, 391 U.S. 367, 377 (1968) to cable television). *See generally* Daniel Pearl, *Broadcasters Ready to Fight Clinton Plan*, WALL ST. J., Jan 30, 1995, at A4 ("[P]oliticians in both parties may use the threat of spectrum auctions to browbeat broadcasters over content issues"); Edmund L. Andrews, *Employer of Howard Stern Wins F.C.C. Purchase Vote*, N.Y. TIMES, Feb. 1, 1994, at D1 (in an effort to punish the employer of disc jockey Howard Stern for his "crude commentaries," the F.C.C. blocks it for a month from the acquisition of new stations, costing the company approximately $1 million, and then reluctantly permits consummation of the deal on constraint of Action for Children's Television v. FCC, 11 F.3d 170 (D.C. Cir. 1993); Stan Soocher, *Stern's Radio Flap: FCC Indecency Rules*, N.Y.L.J., Aug. 6, 1993, at 9.

This is the background against which the second half of 1993 saw a number of federal officials engage in one of the campaigns against violence on television that have taken place regularly since the 1950s. *See* Stephen J. Kim, Comment, *"Viewer Discretion is Advised": A Structural Approach to the Issue of Television Violence*, 142 U. PA. L. REV. 1383, 1385 (1994); Elizabeth Jensen & Ellen Graham, *Stamping Out TV Violence: A Losing Fight*, WALL ST. J., Oct. 26, 1993, at B1 (recounting history); Bernard Weinrub, *Despite Clinton, Hollywood is Still Trading in Violence*, N.Y. TIMES, Dec. 28, 1993, at A1 (attempts at pressuring TV into showing less violence take place in a period when "[e]ven critics of violence acknowledge that the major television networks . . . have generally curbed violent programs," while "[v]iolence in films . . . seems to have gone in the opposite direction.") *See also* Edmund L. Andrews, *Mild Slap at TV Violence*, N.Y. TIMES, July 1, 1993, at A1; Mark Conrad, *Violence on Television: What Congress Is Doing*, N.Y.L.J., Aug. 27, 1993, at 5; Peggy Charren, *It's 8 P.M. Where Are Your Parents?* N.Y. TIMES, July 7, 1993, at A15; *Clinton Takes on Film, TV Violence*, NEWSDAY, Dec. 6, 1993, at 6; Patrick Cooke, *TV Causes Violence? Says Who?* N.Y. TIMES, Aug. 14, 1993, at A19; Elizabeth Kolbert, *Entertainment Values vs. Social Concerns in TV-Violence Debate*, N.Y. TIMES, Aug. 3, 1993, at C13. *See generally* Frank Rich, *Crime Crusaders on Parade*, N.Y. TIMES, Jan, 27, 1994, at A21; Ronald Slaby, *Combating Television Violence*, CHRON. HIGH. ED., Jan. 5, 1994, at B1 (summarizing research findings on the effect of TV violence).

The campaign continued into the run-up to the 1996 Presidential election, with candidates Pete Wilson, Bob Dole, and Bill Clinton all issuing denunciations. *See* Todd S. Purdum, *Clinton Takes on Violent Television*, N.Y. TIMES, July 11, 1995, at A1; *Gov. Wilson Joins Attack on Movies*, N.Y. TIMES, June 15, 1995, at A18; Gerald F. Seib, *Time Warner Is Assailed by Sen. Dole for Sex and Violence in Entertainment*, WALL ST. J., June 1, 1995, at B7. The eventual result was that Section 551 of Title V (B) of the Telecommunications Act of 1996, Pub. L. No. 104–104 (1996) provided for the so-called V-chip. Under its provisions, manufacturers were required to equip newly made television sets with microchips capable of detecting ratings codes contained in broadcast programs so that viewers could choose not to receive unacceptable programs. The ratings system was to be formulated by the industry, or, failing that, one would be established by the FCC. On February 29, 1996, the broadcasters announced at a White House ceremony that they had agreed to set up their own system. *See* Alison Mitchell, *TV Executives Promise Clinton a Violence Ratings System by '97*, N.Y. TIMES, March 1, 1996, at A1. *See generally* Kevin W. Saunders, *Media Self-Regulation of Depictions of Violence: A Last Opportunity*, 47 OKLA. L. REV. 445 (1994).

Although—in light of the power of market forces, *see* Jon Pareles, *Rapping and Politicking: Show Time on the Stump*, N.Y. TIMES, June 11, 1995, at H32, and the likelihood that children are more technologically sophisticated than their parents, *see* Walter Goodman, *Fixing TV Violence With a Gizmo*, N.Y. TIMES, Dec. 19, 1995, at C15—there is reason to doubt how effective this system will ultimately prove; there is tentative research indicating that "[v]iewer discretion notices on films during the 1987-1992 television seasons did have a negative and statistically significant impact on ratings for children 2-11, while the ratings had no impact on the ratings among teens and adults," JAMES T. HAMILTON, MARKETING VIOLENCE: THE IMPACT OF LABELING VIOLENT TELEVISION CONTENT 17 (1995).

36. *See* Ronald K. L. Collins & David M. Skover, *The Pornographic State*, 107 HARV. L. REV. 1374, 1398 (1994) (drawing this conclusion with respect to pornography regulation).

37. *Cf.* Eric M. Freedman, Book Review, 48 BROOK. L. REV. 391, 393 (1982) (liberals and conservatives share the central problem of how much faith is to be placed in democracy); David Post, *New Rules for the Net?* AM. LAW., July-August, 1995, at 112 (the ultimate problem in the application of the First Amendment to cyberspace may arise not from the need to adapt legal doctrines, but from the discovery "that many among us are in fact less interested in speech that is truly free than we might have previously believed").

38. *See* Thomas R. Marshall & Joseph Ignagni, *Supreme Court and Public Support for Rights Claims*, 78 JUDICATURE 146, 151 (1994) (presenting empirical data showing a close relationship between Supreme Court civil liberties rulings and public opinion on the same issues).

39. *See* Learned Hand, *The Spirit of Liberty*, *in* THE SPIRIT OF LIBERTY: PAPERS AND ADDRESSES OF LEARNED HAND 189-90 (Irving Dilliard ed., 3d ed. 1963); *see also* GERALD GUNTHER, LEARNED HAND: THE MAN AND THE JUDGE 547-52 (1994).

40. JOHN MAYNARD KEYES, A TRACT ON MONETARY REFORM 80 (1923).

Part II

Law and Cyberspace

5

Museums Without Walls: Property Rights and Reproduction in the World of Cyberspace

Susan J. Drucker and Gary Gumpert

There has always been something special about visiting the museum. It usually involved a stroll into the unexpected—a nonprogrammed gambol into a room that you had not visited before. Do you remember your first encounter with Degas? Or that sudden realization that you have stumbled onto a Monet, Renoir, or a Chagall? Do you remember the place as well as the experience? The museum has always been something special, because it was the venue for the aesthetic moment and the place where loneliness could be transcended because every beautiful person next to you was a potential lover. Every visit to the museum was punctuated by the purchase of postcard or poster reproduction of some new discovery. Relatively cheap reproductions of art substituted for expensive interior designers.

Instead of a train, plane, bus, or car trip, the computer and the virtual museum beckon. How different is that finger-tapping, mouse-pointing sojourn into the virtual realm? What an extraordinary experience! On to the Internet, and the Alta Vista search engine reveals a listing of the virtual museums around the world. The decision is difficult—whether to visit the Pompidou in Paris, the National Archaeological Museum of Athens, or the Hungarian National Museum in Budapest. Eventually we choose the Diego Rivera Virtual Museum, located somewhere in Mexico (the URL address does not reveal the actual address). Metaphorically wandering through the gallery we see an unfamiliar work, *Los Viejos* (The Old Ones), painted by him in 1912. It's lovely and the subject and treatment appeal to us. The image of *Los Viejos* is downloaded and printed through a colorless laser jet printer and then enlarged on the photocopy machine so that a slide can be taken of it to be used in an upcoming lecture on "communication and public space."

Time on the Internet is measured not by the price of admission but by the cost of telephone connection. Besides that, the fax machine is being tied up and so one of two new CD-ROM discs is slipped into the computer tower of magic in order to visit the Louvre and the Orsay in Paris. The interactive visit is advertised as the "plus grand musée du monde" and accompanied by a baroque fanfare and the disembodied voice of an electronic docent as we enter the Richelieu wing. A floor plan of the Richelieu is chosen rather than an index of available works. Using the mouse one can select where in the wing the virtual visitor would like to go. Each room in the Louvre is generally devoted to a theme, artist, or period. Room 21, devoted to the work of Rubens, is selected, and eventually we click on a small frame of *La Bohémienne* by Frans Hals who painted the lusty individual some time between 1628 and 1630. A number of options are available. We are given the choice of enlarging details of the particular work, and can examine about 25 percent of the frame at a time. We can also place that work on a comparative scale that provides an idea of its actual size (measured in meters and centimeters) and juxtaposes it along other works and human figures.

This new experience is phenomenal and initially exciting, but it raises complex issues of qualitative and legal dimensions. On a qualitative level, the nature of the museum and its intrinsic aesthetic experience and relationship to the public become a matter of importance. From the moment that museums became public institutions of import, economic and legal factors played an important role. It is somewhat easy to get sidetracked in examining the implication of the virtual museum, because a number of other factors need to be considered, particularly, the early development of the museum concept and later the impact of technology upon the nature of art.

Museums began as private collections "formed for reasons of prestige or out of genuine interest,"[1] but sometime during the eighteenth century they evolved into institutions whose works would be accessible to the public. Thus, in 1793 the Louvre was opened as the national showcase of France. "The fact that it existed was the consequence of the Revolution, which had nationalized the property of the Church and religious establishments, and of Napoleon's campaigns, which swept the artistic treasures of Europe into the booty-wagons of the conquerors."[2] The nature of the museum, originally derived from the Greek temple of the Muses,[3] would be altered by the access of individuals to works of art. The shift from the private to the public collection becomes a fundamental factor in changing the economic identity of the museum. The second factor that would alter and transform the relationship of art and public would be the reproducibility of the work. The technologies of duplication including printing, the casting of molds, etching, lithography, photography and now digitized multimedia transmission would potentially transform the artistic experience—once based on the economics of scarcity. In *The Work of Art in the Age of Mechanical Reproduction*,[4] Walter Benjamin noted that works of art were always "reproducible" and the "artifacts could always be imitated," but mechanical reproductions of a work of art represent a new development. Before copies used to be restricted by efforts to repeat the same process of creation as that which was originally used and each copy contained unavoidable variation, each copy being somewhat unique.[5] Such variations could now be avoidable.

The questions raised by a jaunt through a virtual museum concern the relationship between a physical object and the experience that is derived from it. A communication perspective accounts for the influence of the medium utilized, the sensory engagement and the qualitative relationship of art and audience in context. Corporeal communication is now but one option with many of our communicative experiences shifting into more controllable, safe confines of electronic landscapes in which information and potential contacts abound. But do not confuse quality and function. Viewing and listening on the Internet or on CD-ROM may be functionally equivalent but quite distinct experientially. Although the possibilities of museums without walls are dizzying, they must also raise the specter of an element of personal loss of connection, of sensory displacement, of the loss of civic engagement in the physical public space in which that work is situated.[6]

At times communication and legal perspectives coalesce providing a more complete and realistic understanding and approach to the legal implications.[7] Privacy rights and the nature of communication experiences are among those areas particularly intertwined with psychological and functional anticipation in using a given medium or instrument forming the basis of legal standards such as the "reasonable expectation of privacy" (*Katz v. United States*, 1967). In 1967, the Supreme Court enunciated this point in *Katz v. United States* at which time the Court expectations of privacy were limited to the use of particular media technologies in specific locations. Constitutional protections of the fourth amendment were found to protect people from unwarranted government use of electronic devices as in this case in which FBI agents bugged a public telephone without a warrant. In isolating key legal concerns raised by multimedia productions such as the virtual museum, there is a need to isolate the "work," to reference it as a physical entity situated in a particular place and time. We refer to that entity as the "primary base point." Rights and liabilities are then derived from the nature of the physical "primary base point" with economic and property rights of paramount importance.

The extension and creation of legal rules applicable to new means of distribution and interaction raise questions as to whether technological advances require "rethinking legal principles that have existed for previous modalities."[8] The one consistency found in the evolutionary development of media law is that technologies develop more rapidly than legal approaches which often results in falling back on first preexisting principles and analogies to other media.[9] This chapter provides a survey of issues introduced by the creation of virtual museums while suggesting an approach that can meld the communication and legal perspectives.

COPYRIGHTS AND LICENSING AGREEMENTS

When approaching electronic reproduction, the legal implication that emerges most prominently is that of intellectual property, most significantly copyright interests in the object to be digitalized.[10] Museums acquire materials for their collections in a variety of ways ranging from purchase or loan to gift or bequest *but title does not determine* copyright, trademark rights or the interests reserved to the creator or seller.[11] Most copyright systems in the world sever ownership of an object and copyright so that completeness of title held by the museum cannot be assumed.[12] Copyright[13] may be held by museums, individual artists, or their estates, but museums do hold the copyright to photographic images of many works of art in their collections as well as to those works in the public domain. Even the use of works in the public domain[14] are not automatically free from proprietary rights since these works may be covered by trademark protections, so publishers would have to negotiate and pay a fee for the use of the title alone.[15]

The traditional method of acquiring rights for reproduction has been a onetime use (license) for a fee payable to the holder of the copyright.[16] Compliance with licensing agreements comes through contract theory backed by international copyright protections and U.S. copyright law.[17] Exclusive and nonexclusive licensing agreements are each options. In one of the earliest attempts to enter into an exclusive licensing agreement in order to furnish images to be digitalized, Corbis, the publishing subsidiary of Microsoft, negotiated digital rights licenses with the Seattle Art Museum, the Barnes Foundation, and the National Gallery in London but failed in their efforts to purchase an exclusive agreement.[18] Presently, there are several ongoing projects to launch a licensing organization for collective administration of licenses[19] which would ensure full benefit to owners of copyrighted artworks similar to those organizations created for composers and lyricists.[20] In the Spring 1995 issue of the *Indiana International & Comparative Law Review*, Kim Milone argued that standard language used in licensing agreements may require some revision within the context of the "intersection of international copyright and contract in multimedia licensing agreements,"[21] a position which clearly recognizes that the acquisition of images from museums raises complex questions for museums and artists.

For multimedia producers of both online and CD-ROM products the initial challenge is the acquisition of images. New media publishers faced with acquiring massive numbers of images as content for one compilation realize the limits of traditional one time use licenses and favor dealing with museums because they are single entities holding the reproduction rights to thousands of items.[22]

Museums also possess works in the public domain that are valuable sources of content for a publisher providing the publisher with a less expensive option in gathering material for new media products. Some museums use on-site computer work stations, others provide material to online networks, and some develop CD-ROMs which may be sold to off site users.[23] Another variation occurs when museums themselves establish an Internet presence, an approach gaining in popularity among museums large and small all over the world. The Smithsonian, the Louvre, the Whitney, Vatican Museums, the Peggy Guggenheim collection in Venice, the National Museum of Modern Art in Tokyo, Carillo Gil Museum of Contemporary Art in Mexico City, the Warhol, Dallas Art Museum, Montreal's Museum of Fine Arts, and the National Gallery of Australia to name but a few have taken this approach.[24] Not only are actual museums going digital, but in addition collections gathered together only in electronic form without physical counterparts are springing up such as the Interactive People's Museum on the Internet from Austria, the Tina Modotti Museum from Mexico, the Auckland Web Museum, and Le Web Museum from Paris, which collected images from galleries around the world and sends out over 3 million pages of electronic information weekly.[25] The relationship between museums going online and the creation of virtual museums that exist nowhere but online or in disk form is problematic. Le Web was originally called Le Web Louvre but had to change its name based on action taken by lawyers for the Louvre in which laws similar to U.S. trademark laws were invoked.[26]

Although the lure of electronic public access (and potential profits) may be great, digital reproduction imposes a dilemma of conflicting duties upon a museum. Both public and private museums share a mission to preserve and display the artworks they hold which is accompanied by fiduciary duties to the public and to the artists they represent.[27] Electronic technology will allow the display of the fine arts to a greater number of people in what may be asserted to be a more *educationally rewarding* manner creating an obligation on the part of the museum to explore this new technology. The museum functions as an educational forum, making works accessible to the public in *appropriate* displays. A spokesperson for the Louvre states: "We think that electronic reproductions are just the next step in the history of reproducing art works which started in the 18th century with the engravings of famous paintings, then photography etc. We think that we should take part in this evolution in the same way as we did with other 'more traditional' reproductions."[28] What is significant here is the distinction that is made between the work itself and electronic copies of such a work. The position that is taken by the Louvre is that what is seen on the Web are not works of art but reproductions of works of art.[29] But if the technology that will allow for greater public exposure to artwork will put the integrity of the artwork at risk, then the path to follow in fulfilling that duty is uncertain.[30]

Although much in this realm is undecided, the principle that copyrights apply to cyberspace (i.e. electronic digitalized media) was established in a U.S. District Court in Florida's ruling in *Playboy Enterprises Inc. v. Frena*.[31] In this case, the magazine brought suit against the operator of a subscription computer billboard's use of copyrighted photographs. The court found the "display right" of copyrighted material includes the unauthorized transmission of display from one place to another, for example, by computer system.[32] However, the application of copyright law to digitalized images is complex.

Copying

The complexity of copyright in virtual museums reveals itself with a very elementary question with regard to a fundamental right of copyright holders, the right to control copying. But what constitutes copying in the digital realm?

The language in a typical license specifies that the artwork is furnished "for the purpose of one time reproduction but must not be loaned, syndicated or used for advertising or other purpose without prior written permission from the artists . . . but once a piece of art becomes part of a new media compilation, however, neither the grantor nor the licensee can guarantee that unauthorized duplication or alteration will not occur in the hands of home, library, or museum users."[33]

In her four-part series entitled, "From Virtual Gallery to the Legal Web," which appeared in the *New York Law Journal* early in 1996, Barbara Hoffman raised the following questions with regard to what constitutes copying: "Is the mere display of an image on a video monitor a technical violation of the copyright law? Is the transitory storage of an image in a computer memory a copy? What rights of adaptation and reproduction exist for users who download images? Does the right to display accompany transmission of a digital image?"[34] One answer to when digitalized artwork has been copied was offered by the authors of the recent White Paper issued by the Working Group on Intellectual Property Rights in the National Information Infrastructure (NII), chaired by Bruce A. Lehman, Assistant Secretary of Commerce and Commissioner of Patents and Trademarks. Their conclusion is that temporary storage of a computer file in memory constitutes copying for the purposes of copyright, as does "browsing," "scanning," "uploading," and "downloading." The proposed amendment to Sec. 106(3) of the U.S. copyright law, which creates a right of distribution by transmission, blurs the distinction between the right of display, reproduction and performance. Thus, the copyright owner's exclusive rights to reproduce the work, to display a work publicly and to distribute the work by transmission, are implicated on the basis of NII interpretation.[35]

Alteration, Adaptation and Moral Rights

Alteration of the art is a special consideration with multimedia works, simply because the digital nature of the work lends itself to modification. "The computer's ability to break a work down into digital fragments and to recombine these fragments with bits and pieces from other works and databases means that an author who commits his work to a digital database exposes it irretrievably to a potentially indeterminate degree of sampling, rearrangement, and recombination."[36]

Terms like "interactivity" and "non-linearity" which mean that the end user may determine the sequence, timing and repetitions of the work . . . to complicate this factor further, concepts such as "scalability" or "manipulability" suggest how images can [be] changed in size and modified by the end user or consumer who is interacting with the work.[37]

Some museums are reticent to grant a publisher a license to use copyrighted images because of the ease with which they can be reproduced, with and without alterations, thereby creating a conflict with their fiduciary duty to the artwork and the artists or their estates.[38]

Various technological responses to a technologically created dilemma have been explored in response to copying and modifications. A watermark can be encoded on the image to provide copyright information during home printing.[39] Printing of an image could be prevented entirely, or prevention of printing only those images that have been distorted is another option. Yet another approach is that of using audit trail devices with data on the exact number of copies of each individual work reported back to the producer. One suggestion with regard to such an audit device would establish a per use charge for each copyrighted image downloaded, with tracking and billing for each copy printed.[40] However, it should be kept in mind that each technological attempt at protection may prove unreliable or surmountable.[41]

Moral rights have been recognized as a means by which artists may guarantee the integrity of their works after they have been sold and provide protection so that artists will be accurately identified with their works. Countries belonging to the Berne Convention for the Protection of Literary and Artistic Works are required to protect artists' "moral rights"[42] in their work.[43] These rights include the right to be known as the creator of one's work, the right to withdraw the work from distribution, and the right to allow the creator of works to prevent others from deforming a work or using it in a way that reflects poorly on the creator. In the United States, eleven states have enacted moral rights legislation in recent years.[44] On the federal level, the Visual Artists Rights Act (VARA), which was enacted on December 1, 1990, as an amendment to the copyright law (and took effect on June 1, 1991), constitutes landmark legislation creating moral rights for artists in the United States. This law is analogous to the moral rights protected in the Berne Convention by protecting artists' rights of attribution and integrity in paintings, drawings, photographs produced for exhibition, prints, and sculpture. Remedies for an artist whose work is violated include suit to stop the violation as well as monetary damages.[45] The law prohibits intentional distortion, mutilation or other modification of an artist's work if changes "would be prejudicial to his or her honor or reputation" but it is not a violation of the Visual Artists' Rights Act to modify a work of art in an effort to preserve it. The term of protection for works created after the effective date of VARA is the artist's life,[46] which suggests that the inability to bring an action for copyright infringement might lead to seeking a remedy under VARA.[47] The enactment of VARA at a time when digital technologies are rapidly evolving reflects concern for potential abuses created by the technology.

Fair Use and the Public/Private Dilemma

The fair use doctrine has been said to provide a safety valve[48] allowing copying of copyrighted materials if done for commendable purposes such as new reports, education, criticism and comment. According to *Nimmer on Copyright*,[49] for copying to be of fair use, the copier should be "engaged in creating a work of authorship whereby he adds his own original contribution to that which is copied."[50] The design of a virtual museum involves the selection and placement of images, choices as to which works receive commentary, and which may be scrutinized through successive points and clicks of the mouse. Although most CD-ROMs are produced for commercial purposes, many Internet sites are created for informational or public relations purposes rather than as profit-seeking enterprises,[51] so these sites may well fall within the fair use privilege with regard to its creators. Users of portions of both CD-ROM and Internet virtual museums may also fall under the fair use privilege if they make use of the images for teaching, criticism, comment, or noncommercial research.

The fair use doctrine is at the heart of the issue as to whether private use of copyrighted materials is fair use. Museums are public places, environments in which public display and contact with others (both wanted and unwanted) are essential components of the experience. "Copyright has been primarily a doctrine of *public places*."[52]

Every American copyright act since 1790 has clung to the idea that copyright is a law of public places and commercial interest...[T]his idea has dominated some of copyright law's central doctrines: only public, not private, performances infringe copyright, noncommercial uses are more likely to be held fair use than commercial ones; to prevail against a fair use defense, a copyright owner must often show that it has suffered economic harm.[53]

"Historically, Congress has declined to extend copyright to protect against private uses because transaction costs—the costs to copyright owners and users of locating and negotiating with each other as a practical matter—prevent them from entering into a copyright license."[54] Television and radio broadcasts come within the U.S. Copyright Act's definition of public performance, but the question unanswered by courts to date is whether broadcasting on demand in which a broadcast is not simultaneous but transmitted one performance at a time will be considered a public or private event for purposes of copyright.[55] Although the European approach to copyright has tended to extend rights in any direction which might have economic value, the U.S. approach has been reticent to extend copyright into private use situations. Enjoying the beauty of the *Mona Lisa* from one's bedroom, or wherever the laptop is taken, may not only serve teaching and noncommercial research functions which fall under the fair use doctrine but may also be used for personal entertainment. Private (personal entertainment) was at the very heart of *Sony Corporation of America v. Universal City Studios, Inc.*,[56] in which the U.S. Supreme Court ruled that homeowners may record complete copyrighted television shows off the air for their personal, noncommercial use.[57] Although efforts were made in Congress to impose a statutory royalty on recording equipment and blank tapes, this measure was never passed into law. The *Sony* decision did not deal with other forms of home electronic copying such as audiotape recording.[58]

Current developments and the quest for privacy have been inextricably linked to the swift evolution of media technology.[59] From the 1970s onward, there has been a consistent increase in the value placed on privacy by Americans.[60] Public life (time spent in public places and public amusements and cultural activities) has declined as the ability to transcend place alters the importance we attribute to the nature of privacy and publicness. Evidence of the decline of public social life is revealed in "time budget" studies.[61] Laws protecting rights and creating liability reflect changing societal values, and the relationship between private life (and uses) and copyright is no exception with Congress continuing to refrain from extending liability against private uses of copyrighted materials.

The private use of copies made by downloading or printing images from a virtual museum appear to avoid copyright liability. However, one of the justifications for this approach to protect private use may be eroding. Congress and courts have excused the otherwise infringing use of copyrighted material, in large part, because of pragmatic considerations (e.g., when it would be too cumbersome or costly for each private user to negotiate a license). But just as technology has made private use more accessible and attractive, technological advances could reopen the issue of private use of virtual museums for example. In *Copyright's Highway: The Law and Lore of Copyright from Gutenberg to the Celestial Jukebox*, Paul Goldstein notes:

Technologies exist today to enable copyright owners and users to negotiate individual licenses for electronically stored works at a cost lower even than the cost of administering a blanket license. When a copyright owner deposits its works into some electronic retrieval system, it will be able to attach a price tag to each work, listing its rates for different uses of the work. If the user decides to make a copy at the posted rate, the system will print it out and charge.[62]

THE VIRTUAL MUSEUM AS A DISTINCT ENTITY

As one surfs the net entering virtual museum after virtual museum or replaces one CD-ROM from a disk drive with another, the uniqueness of packaging, marketing and selections become apparent. Virtual museums gather, organize, adapt, and reconfigure to yield a whole that may be quite distinct from the sum of the parts alone. Intellectual property rights issues may belong not only to those holding rights to the physical works but to the creators of virtual museums themselves.[63] Thus, the Musée d'Orsay and Editions Assouline package *Livre d'Art & CD-ROM*. What constitutes the work in question, the primary base point, is something other than the work found within the Musée d'Orsay and includes a gestalt of music, narration, and treatment found within the CD and the rendering of a print volume inexorably linked to the CD.

Is the treatment given to create the new product, the virtual museum, copyrightable? Copyrights can be placed on compilations formed by collecting and assembling preexisting materials that are "selected, coordinated, or arranged in such a way as to create an original work."[64] The original authorship that the law protects in compilations[65] is the selection, coordination, or arrangement of items which is copyrightable as distinct from any of the materials in the collection. Virtual museums often include biographical text and commentary along with the digitalized images of works of art. Technically, the copyright in the editorial text is separate from the copyright in the collective work, although they are rarely separated in practice.[66] In the creation of a compilation of digitalized artworks there is a good deal of editorial judgment exercised in the selection and organization of collected works. Trademark issues concerning a CD-ROM or name of a Web site may also become a relevant issue.[67]

Virtual museums raise a rather unique question with regard to their distinct copyrightability. The nomenclature of space and architecture have been transformed into metaphors of cyberspace. Thus, the user is linked to bulletin boards, malls, rooms through ports, highways, exits, gateways, bridges, and routers. The vocabulary surrounding these new technologies and multimedia creations shapes the perception of the reality being named. In the creation of a virtual museum, some tours are linked directly to the arrangement of rooms in physical museums, others create their own aspatial rooms. Floor plans may be provided so that to access an image, the electronic visitor to the museum clicks on the desired "room." If one were to create a CD-ROM version of a collection of Monet's, would there be a copyright infringement for a digital "room" in which all of the works gathered in one room of the Marmottan Museum were also placed together in similar digital arrangement? Should virtual spatial arrangement of art works be treated like physical spatial arrangements and some architectural designs receive copyright protection or may they fall under fair use? The issue would be settled by the degree of creativity or originality in terms of selection and arrangement in order for the spatial arrangement of display to be copyrightable.[68] The Copyright Act defines compilation as a work in which separate elements are selected, coordinated, or arranged in a way that meets the standard of originality. The Court has not established any guidelines as to what specific type of coordination or arrangement is required.[69]

Beyond the issues of what constitutes a copyright infringement and what is fair use, beyond the queries as to who retains intellectual property rights for a work of art and the nature and duration of those rights lies a fundamental question as to who may infringe on those rights. Although attention has been focused on the producer of a virtual museum or the end user there lies another potential candidate for liability in an area of law not settled. When dealing with online virtual museums what is the responsibility of information service providers? Service providers have argued that they function like common carriers and do not make "individualized decisions" that determine what is transmitted or carried, thereby avoiding liability.[70] Common carriers[71] avoid liability when they merely make equipment available.[72] In the United States, Congress is taking steps toward passing legislation which attempts to preserve existing theories of copyright liability for online infringements but would limit copyright-owner recovery against "service providers."[73] The broadest exemption from copyright liability would be provided for "mere conduit services and private or real-time electronic communication" which would cover On-line service providers as well as Internet access providers.[74] The resolution of this issue will be in large part determined by how courts view the nature of the medium and the expectations and experiences of those utilizing that medium.

JURISDICTION WITHIN THE BORDERS OF CYBERSPACE

Virtual museum in online or CD-ROM formats are made available by delivery systems that can easily flow across national boundaries thereby requiring a reexamination of fundamental legal issues including jurisdiction and conflict of laws. In an age when signals are beamed and borders crossed via keyboard strokes, geography becomes irrelevant. Global Information Infrastructure relies on disintegrating concepts of territory and sector while ignoring the new network and technological borders that transcend national boundaries.[75] Although copyright is intrinsically a creature of national law, there are now few countries that do not have treaty arrangements for the international protection of copyrights with most of these countries being members of either or both of the two great conventions: the Berne Convention for the Protection of Literary and Artistic Works[76] and the Universal Copyright Convention (UCC). These conventions are essentially multilateral agreements to give certain recognition to copyrights that arise in other member countries.[77] The treaties require that nations conform their laws to international standards, but there is little to no effective enforcement mechanism to compel compliance, although other member states could pursue a claim in the International Court of Justice for infringement on the agreement.[78] There is clearly potential for conflict of laws, a situation foreseen by the European Union, which has tried to establish a rule of interpretation to prevent incompatibility of convention law with European law. Member states of the European Union[79] signed revised convention agreements with the knowledge of community law. Member states should seek to balance the convention requirements with community law.[80]

The United States was a founding member of the UCC in the early 1950s but did not join the Berne Convention until 1989. Both Berne and the UCC deal with "national treatment" and the setting of minimum standards of protection by which all treaty members must abide. National treatment mandates that each member nation extend the protection of its laws to works that originate in other member nations. Most nations impose their own rules on the validity of copyright transfers that allocate rights within their borders. The setting of standards is also addressed by these two conventions. Berne requires longer terms of protection than the UCC.

The clear trend has been toward the internationalization of copyright, but computer-mediated communication complicates the situation because its electronic nature need not recognize borders. As technical obstacles are disappearing, regulatory barriers are easily circumvented. In December of 1996, 160 countries reached agreement in Geneva on "the most sweeping extension of international copyright law in 25 years."[81] Negotiators met under the auspices of the World Intellectual Property Organization of the United Nations and agreed on two treaties. These treaties, upon ratification, will cover two distinct types of works—one covering literary and artistic works including films and computer software, the other covering recorded music. These treaties would grant copyright owners protection for distributing their work in digital form.[82]

One author explores the challenges of redefining jurisdiction in a borderless, aspatial realm, stating:

With the Global Information Infrastructure [GII], however, territorial borders and substantive borders as key paradigms for regulatory governance disintegrate . . . . International law grants legitimacy to a governing authority if it exercises sovereignty over a physical territory and its people. Constitutional governance predicates sovereignty on the existence of geographically distinct political and social units. Regulatory power has always been defined in terms of national borders restricted. Transnational information flows on the GII undermine these foundational borders and erode state sovereignty over regulatory policy and enforcement. Geographic limits have diminishing value. Physical borders become transparent and foreign legal systems have local relevance.[83]

Over time, changes in social and business practices revealed that jurisdiction limited to geography required reevaluation.

Before cyberspace challenged notions of jurisdiction, it was decided that jurisdiction over nonresidents would lie wherever minimum contacts could be established such that the maintenance of the suit does not offend traditional notions of fair play and substantial justice. In fact, courts have found jurisdictional authority in contacts by telephone and mail alone.[84] Most recently, jurisdiction by computer-mediated contact has been asserted by several states including New York and Minnesota.[85] In 1994, Zimmerman, a nationally known cryptographer, was informed that he was the subject of a grand jury investigation being conducted by the U.S. Customs Office in San Jose, California, looking into the international distribution of an encryption program called Pretty Good Privacy (PGP). Zimmerman drafted the PGP program, making it available free of charge to computer users in the United States. Sometime in mid-1991, someone else posted the program on Internet, making it available throughout the world and bringing Zimmerman himself under criminal investigation. In January 1996, the investigation was dropped, but questions remain as to the degree of "knowing participation" required for culpability in the realm of cyberspace.[86] Whose law applies and how one defines the scope of jurisdiction have become increasingly murky issues. One approach to the jurisdictional chaos that is emerging is a move toward entering into enforcement treaties of interstate and international scope.

CONCLUSIONS

"The technological de-monopolization of the arts requires a distinction between object and experience."[87] Clearly aesthetic responses, environmental contexts and economic worth require reevaluation of what Walter Benjamin might have called "The Work of Art in the Age of Digital Reproduction and Aspatial Environments."

Copyright was technology's child from the start. There was no need for copyrights before the printing press. But as movable type brought literature within the reach of everyone, and as the preferences of a few royal, aristocratic, or simply wealthy patrons were supplanted by the accumulated demands of mass consumers, a legal mechanism was needed to connect consumers to authors and commercial publishers. Copyright was the answer. Centuries later, photographs, sound recordings, motion pictures, videocassette recorders, compact discs, and digital computers have dramatically expanded the markets for mechanically reproduced entertainment and information, and increased copyright's function in ordering these markets.[88]

The language of the law, particularly the use of metaphors, has been of concern.[89] It has been argued that the metaphors found within judicial opinions have shaped the substance of laws themselves.[90] Cyberspace in general, and museums without walls more specifically, reflect the adoption of spatial terminology and introduce the economics of a newly emerging commercial realm. These metaphors are useful mechanisms for dealing with the revolutionary changes of the information age making the new territory more familiar, less intimidating, and more manageable within existing legal frames of reference. However, such metaphors are based on the economics of *place* rather than on the economics of the *digital electronic realm*. For example, the entrance fee at a museum is quite different from the purchase price of a CD-ROM, access fee to an online service or the cost of a telephone connection.

The technology of communications challenges developments in applicable laws governing rights of privacy, free expression, liability in such areas as libel,[91] hate speech,[92] and obscenity[93] as well as sexual harassment, jurisdictional issues as well as copyright. In an effort to keep pace with technological developments in "cyberlaw," the legal perspective should be joined with the communication perspective to adequately address changing conceptions of space, control, the significance of nation status, economic valuation, and the ever-changing relationship between publicness and privateness. A museum without walls is also an environment posing issues of significance without end.

NOTES

1. KENNETH HUDSON, MUSEUMS OF INFLUENCE (1987).

2. *Id.* at 41.

3. ERIC PARTRIDGE, ORIGINS: A SHORT ETYMOLOGICAL DICTIONARY OF MODERN ENGLISH (1958).

4. WALTER BENJAMIN, THE WORK OF ART IN THE AGE OF MECHANICAL REPRODUCTION, *reprinted in* FILM, THEORY AND CRITICISM (1974).

5. GARY GUMPERT, TALKING TOMBSTONES AND OTHER TALES OF THE MEDIA AGE (1987).

6. The loss of an opportunity to directly experience a work of art and the public place in which it is located along with eliminating the experience of being with others on a fully sensory level are significant dimensions to be considered in the examination of the virtual museum. *Id.*

7. This may be illustrated by privacy issues. Privacy rights and the nature of communication experiences are amongst those areas particularly intertwined with psychological and functional anticipation in using a given medium or instrument forming the basis of legal standards such as the "reasonable expectation of privacy." Dating back to 1967, the Supreme Court enunciated this point in *Katz v. United States*, 389 U.S. 347 (1967).

8. Daniel v. Dow Jones & Co., 520 N.Y.S. 2d 334, 335 (N.Y.C. Civ. Ct., 1987).

9. Kent D. Stuckey, *Rights and Responsibilities of Information Service Providers, in* BUSINESS AND LEGAL ASPECTS OF THE INTERNET AND ONLINE SERVICES 409-449 (Lance Rose & Shari Steele eds., 1994).

10. PAUL GOLDSTEIN, COPYRIGHT HIGHWAY: THE LAW AND LORE OF COPYRIGHT FROM GUTTENBERG TO THE CELESTIAL JUKEBOX (1994). Goldstein notes widespread confusion even from within the legal profession as to the distinctions and nature of intellectual property rights. He notes that copyright is the law of authorship, patent the law of invention and technology, and trademark the law of consumer marketing and the protection of names. *Id.* at 10.

11. Kim L. Milone, *Dithering over Digitization: International Copyright and Licensing Agreements between Museums, Artists, and New Media Publishers* 5 IND. INT'L & COMP. L. REV. 393, 396 (1995) [hereinafter Milone].

12. Ownership of an object must be conceived of as separate from ownership of copyrights even if the museum owns a painting, bought at great expense, it does not hold the copyright on the painting unless it is specifically transferred by the artists. Rhoda L. Berkowitz & Marshall A. Leaffer, *Copyright and the Art Museum*, 8 COLUM.-VLA J.L. & ARTS 249, 258 (1984). However, if an object was acquired before January 1, 1978 without mention of copyright interests, the U.S. Copyright Code presumes that the copyright was transferred along with the object. *See* Sherri I. Burr, *Introducing Art Law*, COPYRIGHT WORLD, Feb. 1995, at 22.

13. *See* MELVILLE B. NIMMER, NIMMER ON COPYRIGHT (1980). Copyright owners control a bundle of rights including the right to distribute their work, create derivative works, and perform, display, and coy their work.

14. Works enter the public domain in one of two ways: 1) copyright has expired or 2) under the 1909 U.S. Copyright statute, the artist failed to copyright the object, and with the first publication, the work entered the public domain. Milone, *supra* note 12, at 395.

15. Thomas F. Smegal, Jr., *By Taking Precautions, Sellers of CD-ROMs and Multimedia Products Can Minimize the Liability Risks involved in Using Public-Domain Works*, THE NAT. L.J., July 4, 1994, at B5.

16. Allen R. Grogen, *Licensing for Next Generation New Media Technology*, THE COMPUTER LAW, Nov. 1993, at 4. Many such agreements do not adequately define the rights of each party with respect to new technologies emerging today. *Id.*

17. Richard Raysman & Peter Brown, *Multimedia Licensing*, N.Y.L.J., July 13, 1993, at 3.

18. Bill Gates and Microsoft aim to compile a massive archive of images including fine art. In October 1995, publishing subsidiary Corbis purchased the Bettmann photo archive which included purchase of the archive's proprietary rights including copyrights, Barbara Hoffman, *From Virtual Gallery to the Legal Web*, N.Y.L.J., Mar. 15, 1996, at 11.

19. Many concerns that should be addressed in license agreements apply in traditional as well as multimedia contexts. Addressing issues such as a guarantee that the grantor of the license is a rightful holder of the rights and that the work does not infringe on the copyrights of others, indemnification clauses, and term limits of the license may include a reversion clause for the return of the rights to the grantor if the licensee does not produce the product within a set time period. Raysman & Brown, *supra* note 17, at 3.

20. Janet Ibbotson & Nainan Shah, *Interactive Multimedia and Electronic Publishing*, COPYRIGHT WORLD, Oct. 1993, at 31. Several projects are underway including the Getty Museum Site Licensing Project and the DACS licensing scheme in England.

21. Milone, *supra* note 11, at 417. The author notes five key rights which could be addressed in multimedia licensing: initialization, multiplication, public display, printout, and online access. *Id.*

22. Milone, *supra* note 11, at 395.

23. See *id.* at 403.

24. Jonathan P. Bowen, *Museums around the World* (visited September 25, 1996), <http://www.comlab.ox.a...eumus/world.html>.

25. Barbara Hoffman, *From Virtual Gallery to the Legal Web*, N.Y.L.J., March 22, 1996, at 5.

26. Most of the images used by Le Web were in the public domain. Hoffman, *supra* note 18, at 11.

27. Milone, *supra* note 11, at 394.

28. Electronic letter from Marijke Naber, Service de la Communication, Relations Internationales, Louvre, Paris (October 1, 1996).

29. *Id.*

30. *Id.* Interestingly, the position taken by the Louvre assumes personal use of reproductions. It has been noted that there have been requests for links to the Louvre site on the Web but not for use of separate electronic artifacts.

31. Playboy Enterprises, Inc. v. Frena, 839 F. Supp. 1552 (1993).

32. *Id.* In *Playboy Enterprise, Inc. v. Frena*, the court noted that in the United States, the Copyright Act of 1976 gives copyright owners control over most, if not all, activities of conceivable commercial value including public distribution and display. Further, the concept of display was considered to be broad and would cover the projection of an image on a screen or other surface by any method, the transmission of an image by electronic or other means, and the showing of an image on a cathode ray tube or similar viewing apparatus connected with any sort of information storage and retrieval system.

33. Milone, *supra* note 11, at 398.

34. Hoffmann, *supra* note 25, at 11.

35. *Id.*

36. Goldstein, *supra* note 10, at 31.

37. TAD CRAWFORD, LEGAL GUIDE FOR THE VISUAL ARTISTS REVISED 3rd EDITION; THE PROFESSIONAL HANDBOOK 8 (1995).

38. Milone, *supra* note 11, at 405.

39. Jennifer D. Choe, Note, *Interactive Multimedia: A New Technology Tests the Limits of Copyright Law*, 46 RUTGERS L. REV. 929, 987 (Winter 1994).

40. Ibbotson & Nainan, *supra* note 20, at 34.

41. Hoffman, *supra* note 25, at 11.

42. Moral rights derive from codes of civil law countries where they have been recognized including *droit d'auteur* in France and the *derecho de autor* in Spain and Mexico. This approach recognizes an artist's work as an extension of personality and the personal act of creation. These moral rights are perpetual. *See* Crawford, *supra* note 37, at 62.

43. The Berne Convention for the Protection of Literary and Artistic Works of September 9, 1886, completed in Paris, revised in Berlin, Nov. 1908, completed at Berne in March 1914, revised in Rome, June 1928, Brussels, June 1948, Stockholm, July 1967, Paris, July 1971, and amended Oct. 1979.

44. Crawford, *supra* note 37, at 62. The eleven states with moral rights laws in force are California, Connecticut, Massachusetts, Louisiana, Maine, Nevada, New Jersey, New Mexico, New York, Pennsylvania, and Rhode Island. Utah enacted a law dealing with commissioned works. *Id.*

45. VARA covers unique works and consecutively numbered limited editions of 200 fewer copies of either prints or sculptures, as long as the artist has done the numbering and signed the edition. The limited edition provision also applies to still photographic images (must also be an edition of 200 copies or less consecutively numbered and signed by the artists). This is a narrow definition eluding from protection posters, applied art, motion pictures, databases, election information services, electronic publication, merchandising items, packaging materials, and any work made for hire and any work not copyrightable. *See* 17 U.S.C.A. § 106A.

46. *Id.* VARA allows an artist to waive these rights in a written, signed instrument but the waiver does not transfer any right of ownership nor does the sale or transfer of ownership of a work or of a copyright transfer the artist's moral rights.

47. Crawford, *supra*, note 37, at 62.

48. Goldstein, *supra* note 10, at 20. The fair use doctrine has been said to be a significant buffer for copyright from charges that copyright violates First Amendment guarantees of free speech and press.

49. Nimmer, *supra* note 13, at § 13.05[A], at 13-102.11.

50. The factors considered by a court when determining if copying is to be regarded as fair use are (1) the purpose and character of the use, including whether such use is of a commercial nature or is for nonprofit educational purposes; (2) The nature of the copyrighted work; (3) The amount and substantiality of the portion used in relating to the copyrighted work as a whole; and (4) The effect of the use upon the potential market for, or value of, the copyrighted work. 17 U.S.C.A. § 107.

51. Commercial copying is not a fair use. When considering the issue of commercial copying in broadcast media, the U.S. Circuit Court of Appeals for the Eleventh Circuit

ruled that clipping services, such as those which copy portions of broadcasts for profit by selling segments of broadcasts, was not a fair use. *See* Pacific & Southern Co. v. Duncan, 744 F.2d 1490 (11th Cir. 1984).

52. Goldstein, *supra* note 10, at 201.

53. *Id*. at 131.

54. *Id*. at 217.

55. *Id*.

56. Sony Corporation of America v. Universal City Studios, Inc. 464 U.S. 417 (1984).

57. Justice Stevens addressed the issue of private copies as a matter of statutory interpretation rather than fair use. Quite remarkably, in the detailed revision of the entire law, Congress studiously avoided any direct comment on the single-copy private-use question, Stevens observed. Stevens argued for statutory exemption of private copying based on: (1) the privacy interests implicated whenever the law seeks to control conduct within the home; (2) the principle of fair warning that should counsel hesitation in branding literally millions of persons as law breakers; and (3) the economic interest in not imposing a substantial retroactive penalty on an entrepreneur who has successfully developed and marketed a new and useful product, particularly when there is not evidence of actual harm. Goldstein, *supra* note 10, at 150.

58. The Audio Home Recording Act of 1992, signed into law by President Bush in October of that year, required the incorporation of Serial Copy Management System (SCMS) controls in digital audio equipment sold in the U.S. SCMS allows copying from an original prerecorded work but blocks making a copy of a copy. This was agreed upon as a standard sought in legislatures around the world. The Audio Home Recording Act of 1992 also a statutory levy to be paid by the producers of blank digital audiotapes and digital audiotape equipment (three percent of the sales price for tapes and two percent of the sales price of equipment). These sums were to be deposited in the Copyright Office and divided into two funds distributed annually with two-thirds going to the Sound Recordings Fund, and one-third to the Musical Works Funds. *See*: Goldstein, *supra* note 10, at 160.

59. PRISCILLA M. REAGAN, LEGISLATING PRIVACY: TECHNOLOGY, SOCIAL VALUES, AND PUBLIC POLICY 48 (1995).

60. *Id*. During the past several decades, public opinion polls indicate that Americans consider privacy a genuine value "not as a means of concealing improper activities or avoiding punishment or detection." Further, there has been an increase in the concern for privacy protection.

61. Time budget studies indicate that since 1965 time spent on informal socializing and visiting has gone down by as much as 25 percent and time devoted to organizations and clubs has dropped by 50 percent. Surveys show sharp declines in collective participation and sites of civic engagement from political parties to bowling leagues. *See* Robert Putnam, *The Strange Death of Civic America*. THE INDEPENDENT, Mar. 11, 1996, at 13.

62. *See* Goldstein, *supra* note 10.

63. For purposes of this discussion, property interests are being confined to the substance of the digitalized work rather than underlying computer software required in the creation of the virtual museum online or in CD-ROM form.

64. Eckes v. Card Prices Update, 736 F.2d 859 (2d Cir. 1984). Compilations such as data bases and stocklists have been copyrightable compilations even though the individual items in them are not copyrightable. *See* Dow Jónes & Co. v. Board of Trade of

Chicago, 546 F. Supp. 113 (S.D.N.Y. 1982).

65. Compilations are distinct from derivative works which are created when copyright owners or licensees recast, transform or adapt a work. The potential for derivative works in the realm of digitalized art is clear but outside the scope of this treatment. For more on derivative works, *see* 17 U.S.C.A. § 101.

66. WILLIAM STRONG, THE COPYRIGHT BOOK: A PRACTICAL GUIDE 11 (1981).

67. *See* Thomas F. Smegal Jr., *By Taking Precautions, Sellers of CD-ROMs and Multimedia Products Can Minimize the Liability Risks Involved in Using Public-Domain Works*, THE NAT. L.J., July 4, 1994, at B5 & B8.

68. In *Feist Publications, Inc. v. Rural Telephone Service Co.*, 111 S. Ct. 1282 (1991) the issue of arrangement of a compilation, in this case the organization of the "white pages" of a telephone book, was addressed by the U.S. Supreme Court which held that industrious labor alone would not create copyrightable work but "some spark of creativity" is needed for arrangement of a compilation to be copyrightable, However, shortly after *Feist* was decided, a lower court upheld copyright in telephone yellow pages noting whoever compiles a yellow pages directory exercises some arbitrary selection process and categorization requiring some degree of originality. *See* Bellsouth Advertising and Publishing Corp. v. Donnelley Information Publishing, Inc., 933 F.2d 952 (11th cir. 1991).

69. Strong, *supra* note 66, at 12. A compilation that includes *all* the facts, and arranges them by a principle as obvious as the alphabet, is not going to qualify [for copyright protection]. *Id.*

70. *See* David Johnson and Kevin Marks, *Mapping Electronic Data Communication onto Existing Legal Metaphors: Should We Let Our Conscience (and our Contracts) Be Our Guide?* 38 VILL. L. REV., 487-516 (1993). The authors explore the approach to regulating cyberspace which seeks to find the "best fit" between existing law and a new medium as reflected by looking to see if actions in cyberspace are most similar to publishing, common carrier status or distribution.

71. RESTATEMENT (SECOND) OF TORTS § 581, cmt.B (1976).

72. H.R. 2441/S.1284, 104th Cong., 1st Sess. (1995). This legislation would clarify when royalties are due for books and videos transmitted over the Internet. In 1995, Congress began to addresss issues of digital transmissions by enacting legislation to clarify that the Copyright Act does cover digital, as well as physical distribution of phono records. (*See* The Digital Performance Right in Sound Recordings Act of 1995, Pub. L. No. 104-39, 109 Stat. 336 1995).

73. *See* Carey R. Ramos & Carl W. Hempe, *"Mere Conduit" Exemption Stirs Debate*, N.Y.L.J., Sept. 30, 1996, at 1–9.

74. *See id.* at 8. Online service providers argue they cannot and should not be required to police millions of transmissions, whereas copyright owners counter that online service providers would only encounter copyright liability in cases of contributory infringement or vicarious liability, both of which requires either the ability to control the infringement or knowledge of the infringement. The Intellectual Property Subcommittee of the House Judiciary Committee responded by proposing an exemption for service providers from copyright liability when they "(i) provided local exchange, trunk line, or backbone services (ii) carried material over their systems on behalf of another user, did not generate or alter the content carried, and the user committed an act of infringement (iii) provided material contained in private electronic communications which an OSP/IAP

[online service provider/internet access providers] lacked either the technical ability, or authority under law, to access or to disclose to any third party in the normal course of business; or (iv) provided real-time conversation formats, including voice messaging or electronic mail services."

75. Joel Reidenberg, *Governing Networks and Cyberspace Rule-making*, 45 EMORY L.J. 911 (1996).

76. The Berne Convention was established to further uniformity of copyright protection. Under Berne, copyright protect extends over the life of the author plus fifty years unlike U.S. copyright protection of fifty-six years untl 1976, and the revisions of U.S. Copyright Code which harmonized the two standards. Protection applies to nationals of Berne Convention signatory countries and to authors who either publish their works first in a Berne nation. *See* Burr, *supra* note 12, at 3(1)(a)-(b).

77. These conventions do not protect copyright in sound recordings which are the subject of a separate treaty, the Convention for the Protection of Producers of Phonograms against Unauthorized Duplication of Their Phonograms. *See* Strong, *supra* note 62, at 227.

78. Milone, *supra* note 11, at 409.

79. WILHELM NORDEMANND ET AL., INTERNATIONAL COPYRIGHT AND NEIGHBORING RIGHTS LAW: COMMENTARY WITH SPECIAL EMPHASIS ON THE EUROPEAN COMMUNITY 16-26 (1990).

80. *Id.* at 21. Many conflicts of law between convention and country's domestic regulation arise but contracting nations must adopt domestic law. In the case of conflicts if domestic law differs from subsequent convention law, the later statute removes the effect of the prior one but the subsequent statute must expressly repeal the earlier one. But more recent domestic law, which differs from prior convention law, may lead to the domestic law being interpreted in light of convention law or different law may apply to nationals or convention law could be interpreted in light of domestic law. *Id.*

81. Seth Schisel, *Global Agreement Reached to Widen Copyright Law*, N.Y. TIMES, Dec. 21, 1996, at 1.

82. *Id.* A third proposal, which would have extended copyright protecton to computerized data bases that provide sports scores, telephone listings, and so on, was abandoned over objections from other countries. Additionally, wording was deleted which treated even temporary computer copies automatically created to view graphics from the Internet as possible violations of international copyright law.

83. Reidenberg, *supra* note 75, at 914.

84. Quill Corp. v. North Dakota, 112 S.Ct. 1904 (1992).

85. In New York State, on Sept. 4, 1996, Governor George Pataki signed into law Senate Bill S.210-E/ Assembly Bill A. 3967-C, known as the Cybersex Law or the Pedophile Law. The law amends the Penal code to create Class D and Class E felonies for attempting to lure minors to contact with adults who knowingly and intentionally use any computer communication system allowing input and output. Section 235 of the Penal law was amended to address long-distance, high-tech sexual abuse. *See* New York State Senate Introducer's Memorandum in Support of Senate Bill #: S. 210-E. Sponsored by Senator William R. Sears. Other states have claimed jurisdiction based upon Internet contact. The Attorney General of Minnesota, for example, has asserted Internet jurisdiction over persons outside of Minnesota who transmit information via the Internet knowing that information will be disseminated in Minnesota. The question of what constitutes "knowing" that information posted on a home page will be accessed in a

jurisdiction has not been addressed.

86. *See* NETSURFER DIGEST FOCUS ON CRYPTOGRAPHY AND PRIVACY (1995).

87. Gumpert, *supra* note 5, at 37.

88. Goldstein, *supra* note 10, at 27–28.

89. Haig Bosmakian, *Fire, Snakes and Poisons: Metaphors and Analogues in Some Landmark Free Speech Cases*, 20 FREE SPEECH YEARBOOK 16–22.

90. HAIG BOSMAKIAN, METAPHOR AND REASON IN JUDICIAL OPINION (1992).

91. *Cubby v. CompuServe Incorporated*, 776 F.Supp. 135 (S.D.N.Y. 1991) is the sole case to date in which a libel action was reportedly brought against an information service provider. In this case a plaintiff sued CompuServe on the basis of allegedly false and defamatory statements contained in an electronic newsletter available in CompuServe's Journalism Forum. The newsletter was published by a third party (not CompuServe). The Court granted CompuServe's motion for summary judgment relying on CompuServe's actions as distributor, exercising no editorial control and acting as an electronic library.

92. Hate speech has become an issue faced by information providers. The Anti-Defamation League of B'nai B'rith cited anti-Semitic notes sent via e-mail but rejected for public posting by Prodigy as an example of electronically networked hate speech. *See* M. W. Miller, *Prodigy Network Defends Display of Anti-Semitic Notes*, WALL ST. J., Oct. 22, 1991, at B1. *See* C. Leroux, *Speech Enters Computer Age*, CHI. TRI., Oct. 27, 1991, at C4.

93. Obscenity has received a good deal of attention within the context of cyberspace. *See* D. S. Jackson, *Battle for the Soul of Internet*, TIME MAG., July 25, 1994, at 50 & 56. In a prominent case the operators of "Amateur Action" electronic bulletin board service were convicted under the federal law criminalizing transmitting obscene images electronically from California to Tennessee. *See* C. Landis, *Regulating Porn: Does It Compute*? USA TODAY, August 9, 1994, at D1.

6

Copyright and Cyberspace: Functioning in a Digitally Networked Environment

Donald Fishman

At a recent lunch in a busy shopping mall in suburban Boston, a colleague began talking about the impressive growth of communication as an academic discipline, as an industry, and as a perspective for looking at the world. This tripartite analysis—academic discipline, industry, and worldview—presented a flattering view which all of us sitting at the table wanted to believe. It is a saga of a discipline that once was a backwater area in the academy that could now march proudly and triumphantly into the twenty-first century. Media dinosaurs "please stand aside" was our dominant thesis. All who sat at the table added observations to this highly congenial and self-serving portrait until someone blurted out, "Yes, and if Karl Marx were alive today, his great work would not be *Das Kapital,* but *Das Information.*"

This line abruptly stopped the giddy conversation. Everyone was shocked at the boldness of the statement. Had "information" really replaced "capital" as the pivotal force of power? Had "information" really become the twenty-first century's equivalent of geopolitics with its predicted struggles over control of scarce resources? Several members at the table offered modest challenges to correct the hyperbolic observation, but the more the issue was discussed, the more credence was given to the central role that transmitting and receiving information would play in the years ahead.

We live in an era of rapid and widespread change in information technologies. There are many blue-sky predictions of what changes will likely occur. Some of these changes have already begun. It is an era when digitized information allows for the convergence of data, voice, and video. In addition, it is an era that offers cheaper information transmission costs, lower storage costs, quicker speed in retrieving and organizing data files, and easier access to networks of information than one could not have envisioned in an earlier period. The most popular metaphors for this information cornucopia are "the information super highway," "the digital age," and "the electronic marketplace."

The most widely used term to characterize the paradigmatic shift from a

print-and-broadcast-based society to a digital and electronic era is "cyberspace."
The term was first used in 1984 by William Gibson in his science fiction novel
Neuromancer. In Gibson's futuristic account of society, individuals would be
able to place themselves in new environments with electronic machines that
would create sights, sounds, and images, and thus would experience a version
of reality in "cyberspace" that would be analogous to physical reality, a virtual
reality.[1] Katsh argues that:

[t]he power of cyberspace is that it can overcome, or appear to overcome, the limits of
the physical environment. We can process information in novel ways because nothing is
fixed to anything else. Words and images can be moved, edited, lifted off the screen, and
put back down. Humpty Dumpty, as a physical entity, falls and permanently shatters, but
an electronic Humpty Dumpty can be put back together again by clicking on some
magical "undo button."[2]

As it has unfolded, the term *cyberspace* has acquired many connotations,
most of which include a sophisticated collection of networks of electronic
transmission of information where instantaneous interactions between an
individual and databases occur. Some of this technology already exists. The
Internet is a collection of networks—multiple networks—linked by a communication protocol. Like the Internet that was largely unknown in 1989
but now has over 30 million users, most of this technology is only in an
embryonic state. It is fair to conclude that the "communications revolution is
only in its infancy."[3]

One of the pressure points for all of this evolving technology is copyright
law. Over a decade ago, the late Ithiel de Sola Pool argued that the massive
changes in the transmission of information would have a profound consequence
on the field of copyright:

For copyright the implications are fundamental. Established notions about copyright
become obsolete, rooted as they are in the in the technology of print. The recognition of
a copyright and the practice of paying royalties emerged with the printing press. With
the arrival of electronic reproduction, these practices become unworkable. Electronic
publishing is analogous not so much to the print shop of the eighteenth century as to the
word-of-mouth communication to which copyright was never applied.[4]

If Pool is correct, then copyright law, which was born out of a desire to regulate
a new technology (the printing press), may fittingly be sent to its death because
of the emergence of still newer technologies (the information superhighway).
These new technologies will allow us to receive and reproduce information without concern for its source. "Totally new concepts," writes Pool, "will have to
be invented to compensate creative works."[5] Unfortunately, this pessimistic
scenario overlooks the positive incentives that copyright has provided in
encouraging new and creative works and the agility of copyright principles to
adapt to new technologies.

The thesis of this chapter is that copyright principles can be transformed to define and enforce proprietary rights even in an age of digital communication. There are, of course, areas that pose special problems such as protecting fact-oriented databases, but copyright law can evolve so that information may be broadly disseminated to users while still protecting the intellectual property rights of owners. The first section of this chapter examines the contours of copyright. The second section discusses the fair use doctrine and how it has been used to adapt to changing standards of copyright. The final section advances six propositions to suggest that proprietary rights will persist in cyberspace.

THE CONTOURS OF COPYRIGHT

Article I, section 8, clause 8 of the Constitution empowers Congress "to promote the Progress of Science and the useful Arts, by securing for Limited Times to Authors and Inventors the exclusive Right to their respective Writings and Discoveries."[6] This clause is one of the few instances where the term "right" is explicitly used in the Constitution. The premise underlying the copyright clause is that an economic incentive should be provided to encourage authors and inventors to produce, and that society as a whole will benefit because the writings and inventions will create new ideas and new products. The emphasis is placed upon providing incentives to individuals that will lead to a public benefit. In *Mazer v. Stein*, the Court wrote that "[E]ncouragement of individual effort by personal gain is the best way to advance public welfare through the talents of authors."[7]

The notion that the copyright system should provide incentives to innovators sanctioned the legitimacy of proprietary rights, and these rights allow information to be privately owned and selectively distributed. The rationale for excluding others from copying, distributing, or displaying information was to foster attractive incentives for individuals to produce creative works and to allow them to reap the benefits of such creations. But these proprietary rights did not exist in perpetuity and were limited by the Constitution.

In fact, the actual language of the Constitution provides a framework for the copyright statutes that subsequently were enacted. One key phrase in the Constitution that guided statutory construction was "limited times." An individual was granted a monopoly, whether it be a copyright or a patent, for a limited amount of time. The first copyright statute used two terms of fourteen years. The more widely known 1909 Copyright Act used two terms of twenty-eight years. The current 1976 Copyright Act extends the duration to the life of an author plus seventy years. The concept of a monopoly usually carries with it a pejorative status in American law. In copyright law, however, the author or creator is given a monopoly for a limited period in order to encourage him or her to produce. According to the Constitution, authors and creators are thus guaranteed a period when they have an "exclusive right" to control the product in order to reap a profit. The Constitution probably would not permit a "perpetual right" to copyrighted materials. But it does allow Congress the latitude to develop a time frame in order to optimize the benefits of copyright protection. The word "*writings*" in the Constitution has been interpreted by Congress and the courts in an expansive way to include sculpture, videotapes, graphics, maps, paintings, and even makeup designs for clowns.

A copyright thus provides a monopoly to authors, artists, and creators for their respective writings and works. The author has the exclusive right to control the work and can deny authorization to use, reproduce, perform, or display the work for the statutory life of the copyright. This is the trade-off that Congress makes in order to promote intellectual, artistic, and creative work. The monopoly privileges have predetermined goals:

The monopoly privileges that Congress may authorize are neither unlimited nor primarily designed to provide a special private benefit. Rather, the limited grant is a means by which an important public purpose may be achieved. It is intended to motivate the creative activity of authors and inventors by the provision of a special reward, and to allow the public access to the products of their genius after the limited period of exclusive control has expired.[8]

The 1976 Copyright Act uncovered a solution to disentangle copyright law from a difficult problem. Prior to the 1976 Act, copyright relied upon a categorical approach to subject matter. The Copyright Act of 1790 limited copyright to "books, maps, and charts." Later copyright acts added photography, movies, phonograph records, and cable television to the list of protected works. The categorical approach meant that the courts were compelled to examine each new communication format or technology to determine whether it could be interpreted as a "writing" within the constitutional scope of the copyright clause. Understandably, there was much judicial diffidence in approaching this difficult task. The courts believed it was the express responsibility of Congress to legislate whether a new technology should be covered under copyright protection. In the 1976 Act, Congress defined a copyright as an "original work of authorship fixed in a tangible medium of expression." The "fixation standard" was designed to cover existing and yet to be discovered technologies.[9]

In theory, the fixation standard was a choice based upon sound policy decisions. Congress could have selected various other points along a continuum as places to begin the copyright protection for a work. For instance, Congress could have offered copyright protection at the point of creation; at the point of publication; at the point of registration; at the point of placing notice upon a work; or at the point of depositing a work at the Library of Congress. The point of creation was problematic because it presented evidentiary problems and left no record for the innovator whose creation was still in his or her head. The points of registration, notice, and deposit were steps that our European counterparts had already rejected. Because the United States was attempting to move closer in philosophy and copyright formalities to the countries that were signatories of the Berne Agreement, Congress decided not to make copyright dependent on fulfilling any one of these mechanical steps. Thus, the fixation standard which goes into effect when a work is "fixed in a tangible medium of expression" became the new definition of copyright.

However, there were two unanticipated problems with this definition. First, the fixation standard, which initially seemed far superior to the older categorical approach, encountered difficulties in the electronic age. Imagine a Web browser that picks up an image and places it on a computer screen. When the image is placed on the screen, is it actually fixated? Can an individual use information that appears on the screen on the grounds that it is not fixated and therefore not copyrightable information? There were no clear-cut answers available to resolve this issue. There is reason to believe that fixation—but only at the margins—will be a problem in an electronic environment.

Second, the problem of judicial diffidence persisted. In the widely celebrated 1984 *Sony v. Universal Studios* case, Justice Stevens's majority opinion upheld home videotaping, but it also contained a strong protest that this was not the type of decision that the courts should be making. This complaint was more than a feigned sigh of anguish on the part of the Court in making a difficult decision. The Court felt ill-equipped to make such a decision where Congress had been silent on its intentions. Moreover, since Congress has the ability to conduct hearings, investigate industry policies, and legislate new initiatives, the Court understandably wanted to defer the decision making to an institutional setting that had more expertise. But the Court was forced to act when Congress defaulted on making a decision. In the *Sony* decision, the Court ruled that commercial copying was presumptively unfair, but that copying in the privacy of one's home was permissible. For the digital age, this holding opened the door for massive copying so long as it occurred in one's domicile. In *Campbell v. Acuff Rose* (1994), the Court sought to narrow this holding, retreating from the expansive nature of allowing home reproduction.[10] Home reproduction that looked benign in the eyes of the *Sony* Court was highly troublesome for the *Acuff-Rose* Court. Among the changes that had occurred in the decade between the two decisions were the increasing reliance on a home office, the widespread use of personal computers, and the growth of the Internet, which gave a vastly different coloration to "working at home."

FAIR USE DOCTRINE

Copyright law has long relied upon the fair use doctrine to minimize the clash between monopoly over proprietary information and access to information, and it serves as a device to weigh the competing claims between owners and users of copyrighted materials. How this doctrine will work in a digitally networked environment is yet to be determined.

In its application, the fair use doctrine involved the weighing of competing interests against the backdrop of promoting the public welfare. On the one hand, judges continue to emphasize the importance of providing incentives to authors and creators so that new knowledge and expression will be created. On the other hand, the law began to protect the limited appropriations by journalists, teachers, researchers, and other users of copyrighted materials if some overriding social purpose could be demonstrated. In effect, the fair use doctrine became a mechanism to balance the divergent interests of owners and users of copyrighted materials. Predictably, the balancing calculations were never precise or clearcut. As early as 1939, the fair use doctrine was labeled "the most troublesome in . . . [the] whole law of copyright."[11]

The fair use doctrine defies easy definition. For one thing, it does not mean "free" use or unlimited access to materials.[12] For another, it is regarded as a "rule of reason" that was developed by judges at common law and subsequently incorporated into Section 107 of the 1976 Copyright Act after its utility was demonstrated under the 1909 Act. The doctrine comprises four factors:

1. *Purpose of the use.* Courts are willing to grant wider latitude for some purposes. Section 106 mentions six purposes that receive special attention: criticism, comment, newsreporting, teaching–classroom, scholarship, and research. In addition, courts have been willing to grant breathing room to non-profit activities. In the *Sony* case, the Court stated a "for-profit" enterprise should be treated as "presumptively unfair."[13] The Court has been willing to read into the objectives of "purpose category" activities that recast, transform, or constitute a creative use of the original work toward desirable social objectives. In the *Sony* case, the dissent argued vigorously that a distinction should be drawn between productive and nonproductive use. A productive use involved something that was creative and required the user to add an element to what previously existed. A nonproductive use merely took the item and used it passively for entertainment. The dissent viewed off-the-air videotaping as a nonproductive use and contended it should never be treated as fair use.[14] This distinction between productive and non-productive uses has appeared elsewhere in recent court decisions, making it a key ingredient in interpreting the purpose of the work.

2. *Nature of the Work.* Some works are treated differently than others in the eye of the courts. News is treated with more leeway for the copier than a work of entertainment. A factual and nonfiction work receives less weight than a creative work. Items such as music sheets and work books are regarded as consumable items, and there is a presumption against using materials from them, while nonconsumable work may be treated with greater leeway. It is likely that items such as electronic mail, bulletin board postings, electronic journals, and online, fact-based databases will warrant different treatment, despite being common elements of the digital revolution.

3. *Amount Taken.* The courts examine the amount of material taken and weigh it against the work as a whole. Different ratios have been applied to different types of work. It is possible, for example, for a classroom teacher to take a chapter in a prose book if only one copy is handed out to each student, and the copying is regarded as spontaneous. At the same time, even taking a

limited number of words of poetry or music may trigger the claim of an unfair appropriation of another's work.

4. *Market Effect.* When the economic injury to the copyright holder can be demonstrated, making even a single copy or taking a limited appropriation, no matter how small the money involved in the case, may result in an infringement action. If the unauthorized use damages the market for the original work, then the courts have been reluctant to extend any latitude to the copyright users. Among the four criteria, the market variable has usually been given the greatest weight by the courts.[15]

Recently, Pamela Samuelson has written that there are two conflicting interpretations of how the fair use doctrine will be viewed in a digital environment. On the one hand, there are the accommodationists who see the fair use doctrine adapting to the new technologies. "Those who believe that copyright law will evolve without serious difficulty in the new digital environment," writes Samuelson, "look to this historical experience as a source of reassurance about copyright's potential to evolve to deal with digital networked environments."[16] Samuelson argues that accommodationists believe that because previous new technologies "have not threatened the viability of the core concepts of copyright law," that copyright law will adapt to cyberspace. On the other hand, there are the radicals who see the digital environment as being *sui generis* because the digital revolution may be interpreted as constituting a medium in itself–separate and distinct from analog communication. Samuelson maintains "copyright classifications have been quite medium specific," offering "thin or thick" copyright depending on the special characteristics of that medium.[17] As Samuelson observes, "Sound recordings, for example, have such thin copyrights that infringement can only occur by exact reproductions, whereas copyrights in other works can be infringed by less literal copying."[18] In a digital world, "[A]ll copyrighted works—pictures, sound, texts, music, or movies—consist of strings of bits."[19] It will therefore be more difficult, if not impossible, to apply the traditional fair use doctrine or to determine whether an infringing use has occurred, or to assess whether a derivative work has been made. In the radicals' outlook, a chart that sings, illustrates changes in time, and presents factual data in one single "work," challenges and uproots the traditional interpretation of fair use.

The viewpoint of the radicals, though acknowledging the novelty of a digital environment, seems flawed. It is very possible to imagine a creative work used for research or journalistic purposes that draws on a factual database and that would be covered under an "extended" fair use doctrine. Fair use may be more problematic in this digitally networked environment, but it will not necessarily be supplanted in cyberspace.

PROPOSITIONS IN SEARCH OF HARMONY

The following six propositions are set forth to indicate how copyright can survive in cyberspace. These propositions do not cover all of the major issues confronting copyright in a digital world, but they do offer an interpretation of several pivotal issues and even suggest where future controversies may occur.

1. *Electronic mail fits easily into the copyright model.* Currently, regular letters that are mailed physically belong to the receiver, but the copyright remains in the possession of the sender. The receiver may let the letters sit in an attic for twenty years, may destroy them immediately, or save them in a hope chest. The sender of the materials owns the copyright along with the five specific rights granted to owners in Section 106 of the 1976 Copyright Act: the right to reproduce, the right to make derivative works, the right to distribute, the right to perform publicly, and the right to display publicly. Letters are generally considered to be private, and there is no implied consent permitting the letters to be shown to others. Similarly, e-mail messages may be downloaded and saved on a hard disk, but there is no right to distribute the message further. The message may be stored on a hard disk for as long as a person would have stored a letter in a box in the attic. How should copyright law handle interspersing comments in a reply to the letter? Is this making a derivative work? O'Rourke observes that the noncommercial nature of such correspondence should qualify it under fair use, but that forwarding the letter to other receivers would be a copyright infringement that today is merely regarded as a "breach of manners on the Internet."[20]

2. *Bulletin board postings should be viewed as implied consent in the copyright model.* When an author sends a message to a bulletin board, it is assumed that there is a desire to disclose publicly the material, and that others may download the information. There is an implied consent to reproduce the material for private or research use. Whether anyone else may distribute that posting to other bulletin boards seems unlikely and presumably would serve as an instance of infringing use. For example, downloading pictures from *People* magazine and distributing them on a celebrity subscription service seems to violate the copyright owner's right to distribute publicly. But the subscription service may want to negotiate a licensing fee with *People*, creating a win-win situation for the magazine and the service. Bulletin board operators should be willing to negotiate a fee structure so that fair use is not simply regarded as free use. We may see several cases emerge in this area.

3. *Electronic journals should be treated as analogous to print journals.* Pool was particularly fearful about the implications of electronic publishing, because of his belief that "networked-computers will be the printing presses of the twenty-first century."[21] O'Rourke maintains that placing a journal on the Internet should be viewed as an implied consent to copy,[22] although it should not give a user the right to distribute the information publicly or to make derivative works without permission. On commercial services, users, like journal subscri-

bers, will pay for the journal at a price negotiated by the two parties. Hypertext may allow users to take portions of a work and use them in a new and transformed way. It may be difficult to determine such use by the fair use doctrine, and we may have to move to a fixed-fee license to cover any and all possible uses.[23] Unfortunately, this one-fee-fits-all may raise the price of the license fee.

4. *Transaction costs in cyberspace may be easier to monitor than traditional materials allow*. Computer technology will aid users of copyrighted materials to obtain works quickly and easily, but owners also will benefit from the technology. Goldstein maintains that transaction costs in cyberspace can be more easily monitored and billed, thus setting up a system that will continue to provide an incentive for individuals to produce works.[24] Copyrighted works downloaded in the home or in a place of business will be subjected to fees. The very technology that poses challenges to a system of copyright may be used to sustain and simplify the difficult tasks of billing and fee collection. The use of passwords, pin numbers, and other identifying mechanisms will minimize the transaction costs so that the copyright system is not spending dollars to collect nickels and dimes.

5. *Digital data will not displace all existing markets*. It is likely that books, magazines, newspapers, television, and films will continue to exist. Over time, all communication may become electronic, but users may still prefer to own hard copy newspapers, traditional books, and conventional formats for journals. Owners of copyrighted materials will continue to collect royalties and fees in these traditional markets. Cyberspace will serve as an option—an additional venue for owners to seek profits. Hypertext will provide special interactive qualities and provide a nonlinear learning experience which in time may become more attractive to users. But publishers who find that they are not making a profit in cyberspace will have an option to withdraw their works. In addition, a competitive market model should lower the cost of each item as the number of subscribers increases and should encourage other owners of materials to enter the market if profits are high. Cyberspace presumably will be governed by the economic laws of supply and demand and a market economy.

6. *Electronic fact-based databases are likely to be problematic for copyright owners*. Fact-based databases have a very "thin" copyright. The originator of such works can protect the selection and arrangement of materials but not the underlying facts themselves. These facts are open for anyone to use. As Goldstein points out, "For a database producer, the problem is that, by protecting only the selection and arrangement but not the data themselves, copyright has protection begin at the very point where his investment—the cost of collecting the data in the first place—ends."[25] In *Feist Publications v. Rural Telephone Service*, the Supreme Court rejected the "sweat of the brow theory" and its accompanying protection for facts.[26] This decision represented a major setback for companies who create and sell information from databases. The decision does not completely resolve the underlying controversy. The work

to create a data base is long and difficult, but the Court failed to view the work as creative or original enough to qualify for copyright protection. O'Rourke suggests that, absent the availability of copyright protection, publishers seek to use contract law to establish relationships with users of information.[27] If they failed to make money in these contractual arrangements, publishers could withdraw the information from the market. This option also presents a problem, and it may be in the best interest of all who want the information super highway to prosper for Congress to reexamine the status of fact-based databases. A solution to the problem, however, would be a noncopyright remedy.

CONCLUSION

The new digital technologies promise to alter the transmission and storage of information. These new possibilities will compel us to reconceptualize our notion of proprietary rights in information and the relationship between copyright owners and users in cyberspace. The shift to a digital environment, while providing users access to unprecedented information, will exert pressure on the medium-specific distinctions that currently govern copyright. Whether it is a digital sampling of music, computerized colorization of black-and-white films, recombined pictures, or wide-ranging and virtually indeterminate databases, users of information will have more choices than ever before. Happily, most of these choices will be available without leaving the house or the office.

Copyright pessimists fear that technology will undermine the system of intellectual property that has provided incentives to producers and creators to encourage them to bring forth new works. Meanwhile, copyright optimists, drawing on the long history of copyright and its successes in overcoming past challenges, see adaptations being made that allow owners of copyrighted works to continue to control the fruits of their own labor. As Paul Goldstein has observed, cyberspace "has the ability to separate paying from nonpaying audiences."[28] This should bolster the viewpoint of copyright accommodationists and optimists that the system is sufficiently elastic so that owners of copyrighted materials will continue to receive a reasonable compensation for their labors.

But Goldstein offers a perspective that should frighten copyright users: "The public today gets most of its daily information and entertainment 'free,' or at least for far less than it costs, over commercial television and radio and in newspapers and magazines, because these media get revenue from commercial advertising."[29] But with the expansion of cyberspace, "while the quantity of entertainment and information will doubtless increase for those who are able and willing to pay for it, it will probably shrink for those who are not. Will advertisers want to go on paying for air time, or for newspaper and magazine space, that will reach only poorer—and shrinking—audiences?"[30] The implication is that cyberspace and its many possibilities will reinforce the tendency toward a two-class society of "haves" and "have-nots." That would become a copyright nightmare, exerting pressure of a different kind on information users and forcing us to see anew the traditional question of whether copyright's cup is half-empty or half-full.

NOTES

1. M. ETHAN KATSH, LAW IN A DIGITAL WORLD 14-15 (1995).

2. *Id*. at 218.

3. CRAIG JOYCE, WILLIAM PATRY, MARSHALL LEAFFER & PETER JASZI, COPYRIGHT LAW 1 (1994).

4. ITHIEL DE SOLA POOL, TECHNOLOGIES OF FREEDOM 214 (1983).

5. *Id*. at 215.

6. U.S. CONSTITUTION, art. I, § 8, cl. 8.

7. Mazer v. Stein, 347 U.S. 201 (1954).

8. Sony Corporation of America v. Universal City Studios, Inc., 104 S. Ct. 774 (1984).

9. Ira L. Brandiss, *Writings in Frost on a Window Pane: E-Mail and Chatting on Ram and Copyright Fixation*, 43 JOURNAL OF THE COPYRIGHT SOCIETY OF THE USA 237-38 (1996).

10. Campbell v. Acuff Rose Music, Inc., 114 S.Ct. 1170.

11. Dellar v. Samuel Goldwyn, Inc., 104F.2d 661, 662 (2d cir. 1939).

12. Donald Fishman, *Instructional Materials and Copyright Dilemmas*, 25 COMMUNICATION EDUCATION 154-55 (1976). *See also* J. Jeffrey Auer, *The Rules of Copyright for Students, Writers and Teachers*, COMMUNICATION EDUCATION 245-55 (1981); Allen Lichtenstein and E. Phil Eftychiadis, *Student Video Productions: Who Owns the Copyright?* 42 COMMUNICATION EDUCATION 37-50 (1993). Some historical aspects of the economics of copyright are discussed in Ronald V. Bettig, *Critical Perspectives on the History and Philosophy of Copyright*, 9 CRITICAL STUDIES IN MASS COMMUNICATION 131-55 (1992).

13. Sony Corporation of America v. Universal City Studios, Inc. 104 S. Ct. 774 (1984).

14. *Id*.

15. Nicholas H. Henry, *Copyright, Public Policy and Information Technology*, 183 SCIENCE 384 (1974).

16. Pamela Samuelson, *Copyright, Digital Data, and Fair Use in Digital Networked Environments, in* THE ELECTRONIC SUPERHIGHWAY 119 (Ejan Mackaay, Daniel Poulin and Pierre Trudel, eds. 1995).

17. *Id*.

18. *Id*.

19. *Id*.

20. Maureen A. O'Rourke, *Proprietary Rights in Digital Data*, 41 FEDERAL BAR NEWS AND JOURNAL 514 (1994).

21. Pool, *supra* note 4, at 224.

22. O'Rourke, *supra* note 20, at 515.

23. *Id*. at 516.

24. PAUL GOLDSTEIN, COPYRIGHT'S HIGHWAY 197-236 (1994).

25. *Id*. at 212.

26. Feist Publications, Inc. v. Rural Telephone Service Company, Inc., 499 U.S. 340 (1991).

27. Maureen A. O'Rourke, *Drawing the Boundary between Copyright and Contract: Copyright Preemption of Software License Terms*, 45 DUKE L.J. 479–58 (1995).

28. Goldstein, *supra* note 24, at 32.

29. *Id.*

30. *Id.*

Part III

Law and Literature

7

Vichy Law and the Holocaust in France: Précis of a Talk to the Hofstra Conference

Richard H. Weisberg

BRIEF HISTORY OF THE PROJECT

In 1982, I began research in French documentary centers to find out the way in which lawyers behaved, spoke, and read during the dark Vichy years of 1940 to 1944. My project originated in a curiosity derived from both literary and legal texts dealing with Vichy. Camus' 1942 novella, *The Stranger*, and his 1956 final story, *The Fall*, both seemed to me to raise the question of the legal system's treatment of outsiders. In *The Fall*, Vichy explicitly colors the case history of the eloquent but self-deceptive legal protagonist, Jean-Baptiste Clamence. I had been teaching these stories since my comparative literature faculty years at the University of Chicago; when (as a law professor some years later) I perused the French legal reports of the Vichy years, I discovered that Camus' connection of legal language to the formalized ostracism of unwanted others was no mere fiction. Developing my intuition, I read with fascination the rationalized obfuscation of French lawyer Joseph Haennig who, in 1943, advised his colleagues in the pages of the official French reporter to adopt the "liberal model" of the Third Reich in determining who on French soil would be considered a Jew under what had become the *more* inclusive reasoning of Vichy law.[1]

By the time the empirical side of my project was completed in 1993, I had looked at some 2,500 primary documents—many of them previously untouched by any researcher—and interviewed some thirty lawyers, judges, and bureaucrats from the Vichy period. My work covered the full spectrum of French legal personnel: magistrates, administrators and judges, government ministers, functionaries, private practitioners, and law professors. My major findings were first published piecemeal, in English and in French, or have been offered at lectures and conferences in North America, France, Israel, Australia, and

Germany. They are fully elaborated upon finally in *Vichy Law and the Holocaust in France*.[2]

GENERAL CONCLUSIONS

The French legal system, following a brief period of aftershock with the Nazi victory in 1940, rapidly regained its prewar vigor. Not only in the negotiated "free" zone called Vichy, the spa town in which the autonomous French regime set up the wartime government, but also in occupied Paris, French law resumed its traditional patterns of discourse and reasoning. Only race stood out as an innovative legal matter. For Vichy made it one of its first goals to promulgate—long before any German pressure was placed on the regime—laws of 3 and 4 October 1940, calling for the identification of Jews and permitting the roundup and placement in "special camps" on French soil of stateless individuals defined under these laws as Jewish. Later, still with virtually no German influence, the definitive law of 2 June 1941 and then some 200 additional laws, ordinances, and regulations promulgated by the French, plunged the system into a detailed and legalistic debate about racial matters hitherto foreign to French law for the previous 150 years.

Surprising was not so much the "Franco-French" nature of the four-year-long development of anti-Semitic laws during Vichy—scholars had agreed on this since Marrus and Paxton's authoritative *Vichy France and the Jews*.[3] The Vichy approach was so rigorous and politically so helpful to the Germans that they imported it to the occupied zone, permitting it to trump their own less encompassing definitions and penalties. What my research perhaps indicates for the first time is the *pervasiveness* of the legal participation in the development, rationalization, and implementation of racial law. Thousands of legal actors, running the full spectrum of prewar political beliefs, willingly (if not usually gleefully) participated. And without the gradual consent of the French legal community, these laws—so estranged from its egalitarian tradition—could not have been enforced. Surely the Germans would then have brought about considerable suffering on their own; but there is little doubt that French legalistic reasoning spared the Nazis manpower and treasure and further implicated more groups and individuals than the German laws themselves had persecuted (hence the need Joseph Haennig felt to admonish his colleagues to be more like the Germans).

From the Justice Ministry to the private bar, Vichy racial law became a rich and nuanced source of legalistic conflict. Liberals and prewar antifascists were among the leaders in interpreting and giving life to these laws. The four-year-long discourse was rich and complex. The only issues that were never publicly raised (with one noteworthy exception) were the legitimacy and the enforceability of this discriminatory legislation, promulgated while French constitutional values still permeated the general discourse.

The sole protest aimed at the jugular of the Vichy racial laws was a piece written immediately after promulgation of the statutes of 3 and 4 October 1940. Professor Jacques Maury, who taught constitutional law in Toulouse, stated openly and on a high level of legal generality that these laws violated basic premises of French egalitarianism, and that they were thus no part of French law. Maury's confident style, projected to the mainstream legal world in a Parisian journal, seemed to assume that other leading voices would protest as vigorously against the new regime's bizarre statutes. He also demonstrated the courage of what he thought were his mainstream convictions, for his words were read by Germans and Vichyists alike. Maury was never punished in any way—indeed my research shows his own discourse developing away from this first jugular protest towards the more acceptable and compromising rhetoric that eventually brought him promotion and career success. People were willing to tolerate isolated voices of dissent. But no one else joined the chorus, and his lone appeal to constitutional tradition was simply buried by the quite different reaction to the racial laws of most of his colleagues at the bar and in the law schools.[4]

Hundreds of other lawyers instead found the central question in a lower-level, richly provocative loophole in the laws of 3 October and 2 June: Does an individual with two Jewish and two non-Jewish grandparents count as a Jew? Who, then, has the burden of proof in such cases—and there were thousands of them? What kind of proof would be admitted on the question?

Over the next four years—irrespective of military and political developments increasingly favorable to Germany's enemies—French magistrates, lawyers, ministers, and law professors argued the minutiae of religious definition, while their brothers and sisters at the bar represented many hundreds of clients whose interests required pro- or anti-Jewish legal strategies. My exploration of the wartime dossiers of one of twentieth-century France's most distinguished lawyers, Maurice Garçon, revealed that approximately 20 percent of his general practice during the war years touched upon French racial law. A pillar of the Parisian bar and a courageous defender of one of Vichy's (and the Germans') foremost political enemies—Georges Mandel—Garçon surely did not like these new laws, so foreign to his training and prior practice. But his willingness to work with them on low levels of generality and to integrate them into almost every area of his practice (landlord/tenant, estates, corporate, defamation, contracts and gifts) contributed to his profession's ratification of race as a valid feature of French law.

So, too, Garçon's bar association, under the leadership of Jacques Charpentier, found a way to accept the legislation, which brought with it a *numerus clausus* for Jewish lawyers and law students. Fiercely independent from the Vichy regime, the Paris Bar often managed to protest loudly and effectively against other strange incursions on French constitutional traditions (lawyer/ client, separation of powers, due process); but, with the help of the first official memorandum regarding its Vichy years ever issued by the Paris Bar, I learned that Charpentier and his colleagues actively implemented the quotas against their

Jewish brothers and sisters while quietly and privately lamenting the deportations of some of their most esteemed friends.[5]

Vichy racial law was big business at the bar. The complexities of racial definition joined with the aryanization of property to implicate billions of francs of Jewish holdings. Even before the first major roundups of Jews in July 1942 (although dozens of lawyers and others had been swept into French-run camps from the beginning) the careful nitpicking of legal lacunae produced the transfer of personalty, corporations, buildings, small businesses, entire careers. Many lawyers advised, or actually undertook the role of, the "administrateur provisoire" ("aryan trustee") over property and practices previously held by Jews.

The question of property extends through to today, of course, as countries such as France, Germany, and even neutral Switzerland grapple, at long last, with the looting of European Jewish wealth. In fact, the move to legalize the aryanization of Jewish property brought on one of the few moments of *public* hesitation before these laws by prominent French lawyers. Vichy's second justice minister was a prewar law professor of impeccable liberal and anti-fascist credentials, Joseph Barthélemy. Despite his sterling background, he had already managed, by mid-1941, to sign into law the comprehensive and punitive racial statute of 2 June. In July, he cooperated with the establishment of quotas upon Jewish lawyers and other liberal professionals. He had conducted, throughout 1941, the political trials in Riom against Third Republic leaders such as Léon Blum, accused by Vichy of demoralizing the country in the prewar years through socialist policies that Barthélemy and the prosecution subtly linked to "Jewish" ways of thinking.[6] But Barthélemy claims to have balked when his colleagues drafted a provision into the aryanization statute of July 1941 that would have placed the Jew's actual lodgings or principal domicile at risk for pillage.

Barthélemy managed to safeguard for French Jews at least their apartment or their house. (Typically detailed case law, however, made doubtful the preservation of a Jewish household where, for example, part of the lodgings had been rented out to tenants. There, given the commercial use of part of the premises, courts were less willing to read the statute as immunizing the resident from aryanization of the whole property). But in every other respect, his behavior confirmed the inclination of the profession as a whole to work with the racial scheme.

If men such as Barthélemy (whose grandson, a Parisian lawyer, generously opened to me many nonarchival documents from the period), Garçon and Charpentier acquiesced and even actively developed the laws, how or why would lesser lights manage to raise the kind of jugular protest first penned by Professor Maury? Yet, in Italy—an ally of Hitler whose racial laws were at least as harsh as Vichy's—persecution of Jews remained considerably more muted because, in part, the legal community simply ignored them. In Belgium, which had been granted no autonomous zone, leaders of the bench and bar immediately and publicly protested to the German occupiers about decrees persecuting their

Jewish colleagues. And in Denmark, communal refusal to ostracize Jews led to the survival of 7,300 of 7,700 Jews. For the French, on the other hand, all the archival and personal data paints the opposite picture. The leading figures—no mere martinets or Quislings but active and autonomous practitioners of French law—indulged a statutory scheme that, only months before, they would have found odious and heterodox. Interweaving race into the still otherwise fully operative rhetoric of French law, the legal community took upon itself a pervasive, systematic and even logically compelling discourse of anti-egalitarian and anti-French persecution.

Camus had it right. Writing in 1942, in the midst of the rationalized legalistic violence, he had shown in *L'Étranger* (without mention of Vichy) that an eloquent system of laws can lose sight of basic premises and even realities in its urge to destroy unwanted others. And then, in 1956, through the words of his self-deluding, Dostoevskian lawyer, Jean-Baptiste Clamence, Camus placed the "fall" of France explicitly under the sign of Vichy legalism.

AN ATTEMPT TO COMPREHEND

Several years of pondering dovetailed with the conclusion of the empirical work and the beginning of the writing of the book. The first premise had to be that I, as one trained in America, might well have acted the way the French did. I had learned that unexceptionable, and even a few otherwise sterling individuals, brought about a good deal of the suffering of Jews on French soil. And I had learned that they did this willingly and without any substantial German intervention. In other words, I surmised that a lawyer like myself, working within a still explicitly egalitarian legal structure,[7] could join with my colleagues to accept, tolerate and in fact develop and sustain a rhetoric of ostracism against a small part of an otherwise protected national community. No matter how stable the tradition of equality, no matter how superb the professional reasoning and practice, nothing and no one slowed, much less stopped, the weird new growth that invaded a constitutional organism similar to our own in this country.

A Desiccated Cartesianism: Logic at Any Price

Part of the explanation, I felt, lay of course in special aspects of French practice. (Yet, even these resonated finally with my sense that the Vichy experience has particular meaning for American lawyers). Piling one judicial decision or administrative decree on another, one internal office memorandum or legal argument on another, one law review article or full-length book treatment on another,[8] French lawyers played out their own approach to race with a logical fierceness that defied global events, D day, or even the dropping of allied bombs on French courthouses, which rigorously pursued French racism until each town was finally liberated.

Although, during Vichy, my research indicated that there was a kind of "common law" reasoning about the new statutes that at first might have permitted their total rejection if legal genius, creativity and leadership had so desired, eventually we find a four-year discourse of immaculate logic, a kind of desiccated or degraded Cartesianism. Just as the words of Jacques Maury, the courageous protester of late 1940, developed into the compendious and scholarly Maury of March, 1944, who had fully accepted by then the "Frenchness" of racial ostracism, so the system as a whole built an elegant structure of piece upon legalistic piece, rendered grotesque only because none of its architects managed to step back for a moment and publicly declare the bizarre nature of the whole.

I could not, however, dissociate even this peculiarly Cartesian risk from American practice. The antebellum laws already indicate how legalistic discourse and logic blinded many good men and women to the antifoundational and anti-religious core of their words and deeds. At any moment, the legal practitioner risks devolving into the low-level thinker, delighting in the technical games that tiny issues and loopholes give rise to; Vichy and America are here virtually indistinguishable.

Embedded Cultural Prejudice

1. Dreyfus and Vichy

Secular, "polite" anti-Semitism has existed in France for centuries. Only a few decades before Vichy, the Dreyfus affair brought this to the surface. As was true then, so in Vichy itself, there was far more the sense that Jews simply could never become truly French than that they were racially "inferior." But Vichy differed dramatically from Dreyfus, or any other development for the prior 150 years, because Vichy made anti-Semitism *lawful*, and instantiated the polite "otherness" theory into a still durable constitutional structure of laws and practices.

Yet, anti-Semitism may be less complete as an explanation of Vichy than it was to understand the Dreyfus affair. There were vicious anti-Semites at work upon Vichy law, of course. Raphaël Alibert, the brilliant legal technician who crafted the laws of 3 and 4 October 1940, was an anti-Semite of the worst order and also Vichy's first justice minister. But his equally fierce anti-Germanism led to Alibert's replacement by the prewar liberal, Barthélemy, a man whose egalitarian impulses were previously marred only by a polite sense of the Jew's "otherness" that became overt finally in his Riom courtroom anti-Semitic jottings against Léon Blum. Alibert's statutes meant nothing until Maury's protests were ignored, until Charpentier and Garçon and other leaders at the bar ingested the laws, and until Barthélemy—previously revered somewhat like our George Ball or Floyd Abrams—ratified Vichy anti-Semitism by his everyday practice in the ministry of justice.

Strikingly, too, my research indicated that the rigorous logic of Vichy law permitted *philo-Semitic outcomes* in some doctrinal areas, with courts, for example, usually but not always placing the burden of proof on the state in mixed-heritage cases or finding for Jewish tenants in landlord-tenant disputes in many of Paris's arrondissements or protecting Jewish out-of-wedlock children from examination of their "racial" heritage, because of prewar French code provisions favoring illegitimates.[9]

Anti-Semitism may have been a factor in the promulgation of the first Vichy racial statutes and in the failure of some leaders to muster effective protests against them; but nothing in what followed can be explained except by the behavior of the community of French lawyers, few of them rabidly anti-Semitic, some of them pro-Jewish, most of them increasingly secure, despite the German presence in their midst, that traditional patterns of French legal reasoning remained in place and could manage to assimilate fruitfully these strange new laws.

So here, too, Vichy and America were difficult to distinguish. How, usually quite subtly, does *our* system persecute those against whom there is a culturally embedded prejudice? Does the Fourteenth Amendment alone—any more than the extant "rights of man" language during Vichy—provide protection when judges and politicians and citizens feel threatened from without (the Japanese internment cases; the World War I speech cases devolving upon state as well as federal law) or within (*Bowers v. Hardwick*; recent incursions on *Roe v. Wade*; the chipping away of affirmative action)?

2. French Catholic Ways of Reading: The Vichy Hermeneutic

Research into Vichy law quickly interweaves with what at first seems finally to be a unique feature of French legal culture. From the very onset of legalistic analysis and rationalization of the laws, a religious imagery of the "Talmudic outsider" explicitly colors and infects the ostensibly "neutral" assessment of positivistic writers. Unlike the culturally embedded anti-Semitism that I found to be relevant but not overly significant, the conclusion by many writers that the Jews deserved special legal treatment because they had always thought of themselves as legally distinct[10] strongly contributes to the acceptance of the racial scheme and integrates into the fabric of constitutional egalitarianism a "reasonable" counterdesign influenced by centuries of religious dogma about the Jews.

Hence into scientific positive law there crept a key rationalizing principle that both exemplified and permitted thereafter what I have called the "twinned Vichy hermeneutic": the Janus-like face of Vichy law reflected a flexible (deconstructive) assimilation into the foundational equality of French law of an exception for the Talmudic outsiders and, on the other side of the face, a niggardly, low-level positivism when dealing with the interpretation of the actual racial legislation.[11] This is a way of *reading*, not traditional prejudice.

That adoption of the Talmudic interloper into French law books exemplified the malleability of positive law within a still dominant foundational story premised on equal protection. Lawyers mimicked Catholic theology in a manner demonstrated by an incident in 1941, when Vichy's leader (the octogenarian hero of Verdun, Marshal Pétain)—perhaps concerned that his racial laws might imperil his immortal soul—asked his emissary to the Vatican to find out if Vichy's anti-Semitic laws bothered anybody there. In a single-spaced twelve-page reply, ambassador Léon Bérard, himself a lawyer, comforted his head of state by reporting that Rome essentially approved the racist laws. Of course, the Church theoretically detested racism. A Jew converted to the faith would be as welcome as one born and baptized into it. So the idea that an individual might be deemed Jewish—even though baptized—because he had two Jewish grand-parents and was either married to a Jew or unable to disprove his Jewishness (the then state of Vichy law on the subject) was not in conformity with Catholic doctrine. *However,* on the time-honored Catholic hermeneutic distinction between "thesis" and "hypothesis," Church doctrine could yield to the pragmatic needs of the state. Pétain, with such theological flexibility conferred upon his laws, had nothing to fear.

French law had within it, quite apart from the prejudices of its practitioners of servants, a hermeneutic—a system of reading—that sanctioned from the outset flexible variations from the foundational 150-year-old egalitarian story. The exception for the Talmudic interloper once admitted, the positivist, literal reading of the statutes could be pursued to its logical extremes.[12]

Important though this move was—and, in my opinion, even today it is a factor in French legal reasoning[13]—the twinned hermeneutic unique (I argue) to Catholic France (considerable flexibility in retaining foundational stories while altering them in one or two respects, coupled with the desiccated Cartesian literalness dealing with the positive law) also implicates the quite different way of reading law practiced by contemporary American academicians, influenced significantly by two "postmodern" approaches in the literary disciplines: deconstructionism and reader response, situationally constructed meanings.

There are provocative similarities to Vichy contained in these post-modern approaches to reading and understanding. Because this understanding had its origins at Cornell, where some thirty years ago I was being trained in literature by two soon-to-be leading deconstructionists,[14] I will conclude with the perhaps surprising and admittedly not fully developed thesis that Vichy lawyers were the major deconstructionists of the twentieth century and that their flexible hermeneutic constituted a violent and persecutory negative model for late-twentieth-century thought.

THE POST MODERN CONDITION FOR LAW AFTER VICHY

Deconstructionism

Let us start with what I consider to be a foundational (forgive the paradox) premise of deconstructive writing at its best and a corollary of that premise. In a recent exchange over a month's mutual residence at Bellagio, Geoffrey Hartman consented to my description of this: that postmodernists have insisted on avoiding what he has called the "slavishly immature use of language" or (variously) "the residue of a sublime and vulgar rhetoric" associated with the Third Reich (its leaders, including its philosophers); that the complexity of recent discourse at least in part reflects a programmatic turn from the obscene and knee-jerk referentiality of Hitlerian language; that, although Jacques Derrida, for example, has not yet explicitly connected his "écriture" with what Hartman calls "pressures on language after the Holocaust,"[15] poets and thinkers like Celan (and I would add Günther Grass) have done so. The corollary, otherwise also furthered generally by such thinkers as Lyotard, is a rejection of all "metanarratives," a distrust of unifying stories and of the colonialization of history and culture by those powerful enough to achieve power over the production of our shared memory and language. All structures are suspect. What Hartman is calling "the question of our language" is pervasive, too, but although we can try to destructure domination stories, we cannot entirely remain silent, even in the face of the Holocaust.

However, as I have been discussing recently with Hartman, Vichy tends to reverse the premise and to see the Holocaust as the result of subtle rhetoric in the service of what I have called the flexible hermeneutic. Whatever may be said of the German example, scrutiny of French discourse reveals perhaps a more pan-European (or "western") model of reading and speaking. Simply put, pending more sustained inquiries particularly in the domain of theology, Vichy identifies a kind of Catholic manipulation of foundational texts to *be* the deconstructive paradigm—against metanarrative, in favor of destabilizing readings.

It may follow[16] that the commendable post-Holocaust rejection of simple speech and even of a comprehensive narrative becomes methodologically suspect. If, as I contend, subtlety and the rejection of basic stories more define the Holocaust than the "slavishly immature" language of the Third Reich, our thoughts may have to turn to the *construction* of a metanarrative capable, in its simplicity of language, of moving our legal culture always away from ostracism and towards justice.

It may further follow that we will need to explore the differences between French Catholic ways of reading texts and other models, for example, the very Talmudic model suppressed by Vichy law and theory. For a mode of reading that carries with it a dominant tendency to undermine the established sense of a text may—even in a just culture environment—at any moment yield (usually under pressure) to antithetical and unjust meanings.

Reader Response

Nonetheless, under any model of reading, interpretive communities control the meanings of important texts. To say this is not, however, to assume that "anything goes," or that communities easily change their readings.[17] But Vichy teaches that communities discharged from any allegiance to a "metanarrative" (by which I mean here a commitment to long-established ways of understanding foundational texts) can alter meanings overnight.

I speak to Stanley Fish's view of situational control over meanings in the final chapter of my Vichy book. Unlike, for example, Richard Posner—who has openly accepted the manner in which Vichy discourse developed as being some-how inevitable[18]—Fish may be read as *empowering* the practitioner to reject any "given" of meaning; for the Vichy lawyer, in other words, there could never be the excuse of accepting racism because the statute required it or even because the dominating discourse among authoritative lawyers (like Garçon, Barthélemy, Charpentier and Maury) was moving towards acceptance. The individual practitioner is always situated to argue the other way and can never yield his or her own individual responsibility of the community as a whole.

But even on this reading—and other intelligent readers do not see Fish as encouraging individual responsibility at all[19]—something more is needed. Whether we speak in terms of Owen Fiss' "disciplining rules" (i.e., interpretive practices that yield less easily to change than the readings of individual texts) or what I would prefer to place on the level of "Talmudic allegiance to the meta-narrative," the practitioner in a just system requires *both* an already-embedded foundational narrative of equality and a method of practical response to that narrative that discourages alterations in its received pattern of understanding. The practitioner must be ready (taught?) to take a half-step backward from the immediacy of the professional moment (Fish wrongly considers this to be impossible) whenever his or her trained intuition senses that the dominant narrative is being violated by the contextual, situational flow.

If, as I continue to try to develop so that the issue will be joined on this level, Catholic (or some subcommunity of Catholic or Christian) hermeneutics encourages deviation at times of stress or change (the "hypothesis" mentioned by Léon Bérard or the misappropriation of the Old Testament stressed by Nietzsche), the "nature of our moral condition" after Vichy may lead us to inquiries linking law and religion quite different from the connection made by wartime French lawyers.

NOTES

1. For the ensuing debate on Haennig, *see e.g.*, Richard Posner, *responding to my* THE FAILURE OF THE WORD (1984) in his LAW AND LITERATURE: A MISUNDERSTOOD RELATION 170–74 (1988).

2. RICHARD H. WEISBERG, VICHY LAW AND THE HOLOCAUST IN FRANCE (1996).

3. MICHAEL R. MARRUS & ROBERT O. PAXTON, VICHY FRANCE AND THE JEWS (1981). Until two years ago, most of the work has been by North Americans.

4. For the degradation in Maury's own rhetoric between October 1940 and June 1944, *see* my *"Three Lessons on Law and Literature,"* 27 LOYOLA (L.A.) L. REV. 285-303 (1993).

5. *See* ROBERT BADINTER, UN ANTISÉMITISME ORDINAIRE (1997).

6. In the book, I further discuss the *political* context of the early Vichy years, which made statist anti-Semitism more acceptable to the masses than it could have been hitherto.

7. The great principles of the 1780s still survived through never-repealed constitutional texts of 1875 and 1884, which were often still cited by Vichy lawyers.

8. Professor François Dominique-Gros has recently studied some forty legal manuals on race published during Vichy. There were also at least six books, one of them a prize-winning dissertation written in 1944.

9. The jurisprudence in each of these philo-Semitic areas is complex, elegant, fascinating. *See* my book at chapters 5, 7, and 10.

10. *See* the arguments of legal writers Broc, Baudry, and Ambre, my chapters 2 and 10.

11. I have debated with Danièle Lochak, a French law professor, her contention that Vichy constitutes positivism gone haywire; rather, I believe that it proves the constant susceptibility to Catholic structures of theology implicit in the seeming neutrality of French law. *See* my chapters 4 and 10.

12. Even the philo-Semitic exceptions for tenants and out-of-wedlock children can be explained according to Catholic principles of mercy and forgiveness for those who have suffered and are "innocent."

13. In a recent address at the Cardozo Law School by an esteemed judge of the French high administrative court (the Conseil Constitutionnel), the continuing influence of Catholicism upon French law (here, of bioethics) was stipulated, but an exception to permit abortions was flexibly integrated into it.

14. Geoffrey Hartman and Paul De Man, then in Cornell's Comparative Literature department and its program in Zürich.

15. Quotes from Hartman's draft of a forthcoming essay.

16. Hartman has accepted so far only that we need to be considering closely the question of the nature of our moral condition after the Holocaust which has been further understood (empirically and through reflection on what we know of it) and also the question of the relation of that moral condition to language. Others have argued that my approach conflates Vichy's "program" and lack of irony with deconstructionism's always self-critical lack of a program. But when pressed to further thought, these respondents see that all the distinctions and assumptions break down. This is for further debate and inquiry.

17. *See, e.g.,* STANLEY FISH, IS THERE A TEXT IN THIS CLASS? (1980).

18. In answer to my "Haennig" question, *op. cit.*; book, chapter 2, n.80.

19. Robin West feels strongly that Fish's approach cannot yield, or at least predominantly discourages, this outcome.

8

A Comment on Richard H. Weisberg's Work on the Vichy Lawyers

Robin West

Richard H. Weisberg has done an admirable job[1] of using his work on the race laws of Vichy France, and their interpretation, legitimation and implementation by the bar and bench,[2] toward three different arguments, all of which should be of interest to law and literature scholars: First, he suggests, albeit in passing, that both the race laws of Vichy France and the French legal mindset that failed to mount a resistance to them were the historical model for and instantiation of the legal world depicted in Camus' acclaimed legalistic novels, *The Stranger* and *The Fall*.[3] Second, he has asserted here, and he argues at great length in his book, that the reason for the Vichy lawyers' acquiescence in this evil was not only, or even primarily, their own overt or covert anti-Semitism, but more importantly, a "hermeneutic of reading" that combined a willingness to ostracize and exclude the Talmudic, Jewish outsider, with a willingness to "insinuate" into the French constitutional texts a condemnation of him, and hence limits to the otherwise universal promises of fraternity and equality which those texts seemingly guaranteed.[4] Third, he suggests that this history should be read as a cautionary tale about the morality or immorality of deconstructive readings of comparably embracing and seemingly universal constitutional phrases in contemporary American life.[5]

All of these are tremendously important claims. It matters what it was, precisely, that Camus was criticizing in his opaque novellas. And of greater import, it matters why the Vichy lawyers, judges, and legal academics failed to act in the face of the massive and historical injustice with which they were faced. It matters, of course, in part, simply as a matter of historical integrity. But it also matters because it may indeed, as Weisberg suggests, carry lessons of broader applicability. Not only in Vichy France, but in America as well, seemingly upstanding and otherwise moral legal actors have accumulated a less than stellar record when faced with state-sponsored evil. In fact, the record of lawyerly complicity in legalistic injustice is so appalling—falls so short of decency—that it virtually demands scholarly attention, inquiry, investigation, or cross-examination. If there are any connecting threads—of psychological mindset, of styles of reading, of strategies of interpretation, or of public morality—between these legal actors—if there is anything at all that the study of one can tell us concerning the occurrence of the others—it well behooves us to know what those threads might be.

As important as these historical and psychological questions are, however, we might also pose the general question that Weisberg's history engages in a somewhat different, and more explicitly jurisprudential way. In addition to asking why it is that lawyers acquiesce in, rather than resist, state-sponsored evil, or legal wrong-doing, we also need to know how we should best character-ize, so that we might best understand, this phenomenon. Although he has rarely characterized his own work as having distinctively jurisprudential rather than literary, psychological or historical implications, in my view Weisberg's great-est and most original contribution to legal thought may be the jurisprudential one. In my comments, therefore, I want to focus attention on that contribution.

Again, my general claim is that Weisberg's recent historical work on Vichy France profoundly deepens some of the jurisprudential suggestions—made more often indirectly than directly—in his earlier work in law and literature.[6] Because I think those indirect suggestions are both novel and largely right, I want to try to spell out what they are. I will then spend a little bit of time putting forward a criticism and a friendly amendment.

THE LEGAL ACTOR AND STATE WRONGS

The questions to which I want to direct Richard's work, again, are these: How should we best understand the dilemma of the state actor—a judge or lawyer—faced with apparently lawful, state promulgated evil? How should we understand, and how should we characterize, the dilemma of the Vichy lawyer faced with the Jewish race laws, or the antebellum North American judge faced with the fugitive slave act, or the fictional Captain Vere, for that matter, on the ship of war, the *Bellipotent*, faced with a risk of mutiny, a morally innocent defendant, and a legal text that seemingly imposed the ultimate penalty with no process for an unintentional crime? The first sort of answer that might be given to this question might be characterized as the "traditional" or jurisprudential answer. The Vichy lawyer, the antebellum judge, and Captain Vere were all faced with a conflict between law and morality, or between positive and natural law, or between law and justice. They are faced with the demands of an unjust law, and they must decide whether their first loyalty should be to the law or to justice. They can only follow the law—the positive law—at some cost to justice, morality, or natural law. If they do the lawful thing, or the legally required thing, they will not do the right thing. When faced with a conflict between the law and justice, under this conception, the legal actor must choose. He must either comply with his very concrete lawyerly obligations to the king, to the state, to the law, to the profession, to the Constitution, or to the people, or his far more opaque obligations to God, or to justice, or to the right, or the good.

Should he choose to follow the law, at the expense of justice, he may, of course, have done the "right" thing in the long run, or in some larger sense, even if he has concededly done the wrong thing in the short run, or in some narrower sense, again, at least according to the traditional conception of the problem. Whether or not the long run requires compliance with a bad law in the short run—whether or not justice overall requires complicity in injustice in the particular instance (which turns out to be the question at the heart of tremendous amounts of traditional jurisprudence) obviously depends on the value of the idea of law or the rule of law or the order and security and peace of mind that kings impose. If one holds the idea of law itself in high regard one will obviously be more willing to tolerate or forgive or even applaud the tough minded judge who can resist the weak-kneed impulse to side with the moral innocent. The more that one esteems the king's peace or the captain's order on ship or the value produced by peaceful living, or, correlatively, the more one fears mutiny or the state of nature or outbreaks of violence, the more one will be inclined to grant Vere the necessity to hang the innocent Billy or the antebellum judge the moral logic of the need to return the escaped slave to his owner or the Vichy lawyer the need to persecute the outsider Jew. On the other hand, the greater the skepticism one has regarding the internal morality of law, the more likely one will be to regard Vere, the judge, or the Vichy lawyer as a scoundrel, a coward, an opportunist, or—at best—as a tragic figure forced to do wrong no matter how he chose.

Robert Cover may have been the first important legal theorist to notice that at least many times this traditional way of looking at the problem of legal injustice depends upon a degree of legal determinacy that is simply belied by the positive law.[7] Rather, Cover argued, what the legal actor faces in some of these cases is not a choice between law and justice, or law and morality, but an interpretive choice about what the law *is*.[8] The Articles of War Vere had to read and implement in fact did not put him in the straightjacket of strict liability and mandatory sentencing that he disingenuously claimed: the positive law provided considerably more flexibility and free play, for the astute judge willing and able to fashion the argument. Vere in effect *chose* the harsh reading—and hence the harsh sentence—imposed on the innocent Billy.[9] Similarly, Cover went on to argue, the antebellum judge was not faced with a stark and unjust Fugitive Slave Act, underscored and supported by a starkly unjust Constitution. Rather, the judge had at his disposal legitimate constitutional arguments that could have been made so as to strike the law, had he so chosen, and that he did not so choose, in effect, means that he too, like Vere, chose to return the slave to his owner. He, like Vere, was faced with a choice of meanings, a choice of legal interpretations, and not a choice between law and justice or law and morality.[10] He, like Vere, should accordingly be held responsible for the interpretive choice made.[11] Similarly, Cover might conceivably have said, the Vichy lawyer was faced not with a choice between moral right and legal wrong, but with an interpretive choice between possible readings of the French Constitution.

I would like to refer to this second and dramatically different understanding of the dilemma the "interpretive approach." According to the interpretive understanding of the problem, the lawyer or judge is only rarely, if at all, faced with the problematic choice between following a bad law or doing the right but unlawful thing. Rather, the choice between doing justice and injustice—between the right and wrong thing—is much more often than might initially appear entirely internal to the law itself. The morally responsible legal actor finds within the legal materials the necessary grounds for the just decision. The legal materials, far more often than one might think, and perhaps always, are sufficiently malleable to permit or facilitate moral action. The lawyer's or judge's ability to do the right thing without disavowing his obligation to obey the law is fragile: it is dependent upon his own legal creativity and intelligence and the law's malleability. Without either ingredient, the interpretive freedom disappears. But the possibility for it is nevertheless usually present.

It would be impossible to understate how dramatic a reversal, and how significant a change, this turn away from the traditional approach, and toward the interpretive, occasions. The latter was clearly intended to be, and indeed is, a serious challenge, or rebuff, to the former. The conscientious judge, according to the advocates of interpretation, is almost never faced with the moral dilemma that has captured the attention of traditional legal philosophers: the conflict of legal wrong and moral right. It is a false dilemma. The moral judge never need choose between conscientious judicial disobedience and complicity in lawful injustice. The choice facing such a judge is not between the king's law and God's law, between allegiance to law versus allegiance to right. Rather, the conscientious judge can find, *within* the law, the grounds for moral action. The traditional understanding of the deep and historical conflict between positive and natural law, and the particular choices and pitfalls that conflict presents the legal actor, is simply misguided. The conscientious judge who insists on doing justice need not commit an unlawful act in order to do so, or resign his seat. The judge who sides with the law, on the other hand, can take no refuge in the disingenuous disclaimer that the law dictated a bad outcome, and that obedience to law is a higher obligation than allegiance to justice. Both horns of this dilemma are false. The good judge can and should read and then restate the law so as to accomplish the end of justice.

The *reason*, again, that the judge has this option—the reason the traditional moral problem is illusory—lies in the nature of judging: judging is at heart interpretive, and interpretation, properly understood, implies choice of meanings. Because judges interpret, they can and, therefore, should read the law so as to do justice. And, with interpretive freedom and power comes responsibility, and accountability: because they can, and should, do so, they can *also* be faulted for their failure to do so. The judge who upholds the Fugitive Slave Act should indeed be faulted—but not for failing to engage in judicial disobedience or failing to resign—for failing to sacrifice positive to natural law. Rather, the antebellum judge who so acts should be faulted for having failed to strike the law as unconstitutional—a reading of the law and of the Constitution clearly within the boundaries of interpretive permissibility. The Vichy lawyer should be criticized, not for failing to disavow law, but for failing to choose an interpretation of the Constitution and of the race laws themselves that would have nullified or minimized their force. Vere should be faulted, not for his allegiance to the king over morality, or nature, or the right, or justice, but rather, for his interpretive failure to read the Articles of War in a way that would permit the just outcome. And in all three cases, none of them should be heard to defend their decisions with the claim that the law constrained their judgment, forcing an unjust decision in compliance with its dictates. Such denials of choice, freedom, and responsibility are paradigmatic acts of bad faith.

This brings me finally to Weisberg. Richard Weisberg's jurisprudential contribution is that he has carved out a position on this issue that is strikingly different from both the traditional jurisprudential one and the Coverian, postmodern or interpretive one. I would be inclined to call that position "naturalist." Let me illustrate the difference first by drawing on Weisberg's work on Captain Vere. In Weisberg's view, in essence, Cover's insight into Vere's predicament did not go far enough. Like Cover, Weisberg agrees that the positive law—the Articles of War—did not in fact force Vere to do the unjust thing, and he agrees that we should be for that reason deeply skeptical of Vere's protestations that his allegiance to the king, law, and order forced him to do an injustice.[12] Vere was not a man forced to make the unpalatable choice between upholding the king's law by executing a moral innocent, or disavowing law (and thereby threatening mutiny) to uphold justice.[13] But *unlike* Cover, Weisberg argues that Vere's action, far from being one of several permissible choices, was in fact illegal. The choice Vere made—to read the law as imposing the ultimate penalty for an unintentional strike without legal process—was *not* in fact a lawful one: It *violated* the Articles of War. The law did not permit two options, one just, the other unjust; it mandated the just and forbade the unjust. Vere is not a tragic hero, as under the first, traditional, jurisprudential account of the problem. Nor is he someone who failed to see an interpretive choice by virtue of a knee-jerk, Hitlerian positivism. He is an outlaw—but an outlaw clothed with legal authority. His act was not only unjust it was criminal, and the crime was not that he acted in bad faith. His crime was murder.

Let me turn to the Vichy lawyer. The traditional, jurisprudential description of his dilemma is that the lawyer was posed with a conflict between positive and natural law, or between law and justice. If he accepts the law, and does the injustice, he may or may not be able to claim that the long run benefits of order and law justified the act, depending on the size of the evil, and the benefits to be had from upholding law; clearly, in this case, the evil is not so outweighed. The interpretive description of his dilemma is quite different: The lawyer is faced with an interpretive choice *within* the law between just and unjust meanings. If he chooses the latter, he cannot escape or evade responsibility by claiming that the law constrained his judgment: it did not. Weisberg's account, again, differs from both: The Vichy lawyer, Weisberg argues, accepted an *unconstitutional*—and therefore unlawful—as well as unjust regime. The lawyers' actions, in so doing, were themselves unlawful as well as unjust. Like Vere, the lawyers were outlaws. The evil did not lie in the constitutional law itself. The evil laid in the lawyers who ignored it.

Let me sharpen the distinction between these three conceptions of the problem by highlighting the evil each intends to address. The traditional jurisprudential conception casts the evil of legal injustice as the immoral law itself, and the dilemma is for the man or woman of conscience asked, in the name of law, to uphold, implement, or apply it. Whether one thinks that such a person can ever in good conscience do so depends largely—perhaps entirely—on the abstract or concrete value one attaches to the idea of law itself. Thus, and as Weisberg insightfully pointed out some time ago, whether one views Vere as a tragic hero or a scoundrel on this traditional approach, depends largely on the value attached to legalist virtues. The interpretive turn in jurisprudence had many effects, but one of the most salient was to redirect attention away from the unjust *law* and instead to the unjust *interpretation*. No law, standing alone, is evil; only interpreted laws, only particular interpretations can have such a quality, and particular interpretations are, on some level, chosen by the interpreter or perhaps the interpreter's community, not mandated by the text itself. The cause of legalistic evil, then, is the judge who chooses the unjust interpretation, and more specifically, the judge who does so in bad faith: because of an allegiance to a Hitlerian, superficial style of reading that denies choice and responsibility where both are clearly present. The evil is the judge (or interpreter) who denies the freedom of interpretation, and the responsibility it entails. There are not irretrievably bad laws on such a view—only bad interpretations and bad faith: the counterfactual denial of freedom.

Although the interpretive turn unquestionably underscores the freedom—and hence the responsibility of the interpreter, it *also* provides cover for the dissembling, rationalizing, deceiving outlaw who is clothed in the forms of legal authority. This is the jurisprudential insight that ties together Weisberg's work in legal history and in legal literature both. For, if no choice is *compelled*, it is also clearly the case that no choice is forbidden. If Vere cannot in good faith claim that the law forced his hand—because no adjudicated outcome is so compelled—then no critic can be heard to complain that he lied about or misstated or ignored or refused to follow the law. Although the interpretive turn, then, focuses our attention on the judge (or lawyer) acting in bad faith—the judge who escapes responsibility for injustice by claiming, in effect, legal compulsion—it diverts our attention from an arguably greater evil: the dissembling, articulating, resentful, bookish, wordy lawyer or judge who clothes his perverse, illegal, and utterly personal motives and ends in the forms of law.

To put it another way, while the interpretive turn unmasks the judge who in bad faith denies the existence of interpretive freedom, the naturalist turn, for which Weisberg argues, unmasks the judge or lawyer who deceitfully claims under the forms of law the legal authority to accomplish some unlawful and often quite violent end. Let me try it one other way: The problem of evil that has absorbed Weisberg's attention is *not* the problem that has captured his postmodern colleagues in law and literature both, and that is the problem of the "Hitlerian" judge who out of misguided commitment to positivism and positive law both fails to acknowledge the interpretive freedom he, in fact, possesses, and the responsibility for judgment such freedom entails. It is, rather, the problem of the dissembling, verbose and perverse legal actor who *wrongly* and *falsely* and *dishonestly* and, therefore, illegally assumes and asserts the availability and hence the legality of a law's meaning. It is the problem of unlawful injustice clothed in the forms of law. It is the judge who truly acts outside the bounds of law, and who does so in furtherance of personal and perverse ends, not the judge who in bad faith fails to acknowledge his options within it.

Now, let me quickly describe the scope of my agreement with Weisberg and then pose one criticism. I think that Weisberg is entirely right to highlight the evil done by legal and judicial outlaws. He is right to claim, in other words, that whether or not there exist unjust laws, and whether or not there exist bad faith adjudicators who deny their freedom, there do indeed exist judges and lawyers who are outlaws: who misstate, twist, and lie about the law—and particularly the constitutional law—in such a way as to further injustice, and who do so to accomplish their own personal and perverse ends. I think Weisberg was right twenty years ago to argue that the operation of this dynamic on a very individual level is in some sense the subject of Melville's classic tale, and I am convinced from reading his book on Vichy France that the operation of a similar dynamic, albeit on a cultural scale, was at work in Vichy France as well. I also think he is right to claim that the logic of deconstruction—or, more broadly, the logic of indeterminacy—masks the evil of disingenuity, of dissemblance, of articulate but dishonest formalism. Deconstruction and indeterminacy permit all interpretive choices, including any number which are not only horrific, but unlawful as well.

What, though, is the cure, if Weisberg has correctly diagnosed the problem? Weisberg actually has two suggestions, and I want to endorse one and criticize the second. First, the false hope. I don't think that the solution to the problem of the outlaw dissembling adjudicator or lawyer lies in reader-response modes of interpretation, or for that matter in any sort of interpretive theory.[14] Although interpretive theory may indeed be part of the problem—deconstruction and indeterminacy may well hide duplicity—it doesn't follow that any alternative *way of reading* provides an answer. Deconstruction or indeterminacy might well *mask* evil. But they are not themselves evil, or even the cause of it.

The second sort of corrective Weisberg urges upon us—with which I am in full agreement—is the recognition, or acknowledgment, or reowning, of the very particular metanarrative ethical ideals that are a part of positive constitutional law—ideals of equality and fraternity in the case of France. It is, after all, abandonment of that law that constitutes the evil with which we are here concerned—the illegal and unjust act of the legal culprit. That is the evil—the decision, by powerful people within law, to jettison the ideals of inclusion, fraternity, equality, and due regard for the humanity of others—which, when it occurs, is obscured by the deconstructionist's zealous insistence on the "free abandon" of the liberated interpreter. It is because these ideals are a part of our positive law, that the legal actor becomes a lawbreaker when he abandons them, and it is because this part of law is indeed morally demanding, that he by so doing acts unjustly. And again, it is true, as Weisberg argues, that the interpretive turn in jurisprudence has obscured the harm done by the legal outlaw who for no reason or worse whimsically disregards their dictates. But to obscure an evil is not the same thing as to cause it. The claim that the law has no determinable and determinant content, moral or otherwise, that binds, may well obscure the outlaw's refusal to comply with the constitutional dictates of fraternity and equal regard, no less than the same claim may obscure the illegality of Vere's refusal to comply with the demands of the Articles of War. And it also may, as I have argued elsewhere, wildly confuse and in some cases blunt and even blind our critical capacities. But neither the indeterminacy claim nor a penchant for deconstructive readings causes the legal outlaw to abandon the constitutional demands of inclusion.

Again, the evil that Weisberg so powerfully explored in his early essays on Billy Budd was the abandonment, by Vere the adjudicator, of relevant portions of the Articles of War—the articles that required mitigation and process, and forbade executions without review. It was by virtue of his perverse abandonment of law—his refusal to apply it—that Vere is a murderous outlaw, rather than, as traditionally conceived, a tragic hero caught in a moral conflict between his duties to the state and to God. The evil Weisberg has so convincingly and so painfully recounted in his current book, is the abandonment, or jettisoning, of a part of French positive law—the part that demands fraternity and equality; the part that forbade ostracism, and persecutorial exclusions—the part that forbids the slaughter of innocents. It is by virtue of their perverse abandonment of those demands that the Vichy lawyers and judges and academics became complicit in the evil they failed to challenge. But if I am correct to argue that is the evil Weisberg has exposed, then it is surely the case that disingenuous claims of interpretive freedom at worst obscure it, and it is also the case that there is no method of reading that will cure it. If the evil is the unlawful neglect of constitutional mandates—here, mandates of inclusion and fraternity and equality—then the only appropriate counter force is to reembolden the Constitution that requires them. We have to endow our metanarratives not only with their lost moral sense but also with their lost legal force.

Let me close by looking at a more local example. Were a legal actor—say, the Supreme Court—to act in accord with legal forms but in such a way as to knowingly uphold the execution of an innocent man, that Court, by virtue of its abandonment of constitutional mandates precluding precisely such an outcome, would become, no less than Captain Vere, a lawbreaker. To take such an action, in violation of constitutional principle, is, as Justice Blackman said in dissent, perilously close to murder.[15] It is not simply sad or tragic or unavoidable or avoidable. Rather, he said, it is perilously close to *murder*. If one worries that this evil—to which Richard Weisberg has devoted his career—might on occasion occur here, or might recur in waves here, one might appropriately set oneself the work of dispelling the aura of permissibility around such decisions imbued by disingenuous claims of interpretive freedom. But that is clearly not sufficient. To address the evil, as well as simply unmask it, requires a recommitment to the relevant but abandoned constitutional law: those principles of law, with imperative force, grounded in narratives of our past, that unequivocally forbid the prosecution and murder of the innocent, whether the innocent be found in shelters for the homeless, in private homes, or on death rows, and whether the state-sponsored murder be by act or inaction, execution, or willful neglect. It is toward that recommitment, I believe, that Richard Weisberg's work compels us.

NOTES

1. Richard Weisberg, *Vichy Law and the Holocaust in France: Précis of a Talk to the Hofstra Conference in* LAW AND THE ARTS (Susan Tiefenbrun, ed., this volume) [hereinafter Précis Of A Talk To The Hofstra Conference].
2. RICHARD WEISBERG, VICHY LAWYERS AND THE HOLOCAUST (1996).
3. Précis of a Talk to the Hofstra Conference, *supra* note 1, at 81.
4. Précis of a Talk to the Hofstra Conference, *supra* note 1, at 86-88.
5. Précis of a Talk to the Hofstra Conference, *supra* note 1, at 88-90.
6. RICHARD WEISBERG, THE FAILURE OF THE WORD (1984) [hereinafter THE FAILURE OF THE WORD].
7. ROBERT COVER, JUSTICE ACCUSED (1975).
8. *Id*. at 62.
9. *Id*. at 3.
10. *Id*. at 253.
11. *Id*. at 258.
12. THE FAILURE OF THE WORD, *supra* note 6 at 131-76.
13. *Id*.
14. Précis of a Talk to the Hofstra Conference, *supra* note 1, at 89-90.
15. Herrara v. Collins, 506 U.S. 390, 446 (1993).

9

Legal Fiction and Literary Fiction in Seventeenth- and Eighteenth-Century France

Christian Biet

I would like to introduce myself as a scholar who has spent several years researching the connections between law and literature during the second half of the seventeenth and the beginning of the eighteenth century.[1]

While looking specifically at several aspects of civil law and its relationship to the novel and to comedy (for example matrimony, paternal power, inheritance, the role of the youngest son (*cadets de famille*), of illegitimate children (*bâtards*), and of free women, (i.e., widows and unmarried women under the age of twenty-five), my research has revealed that the aesthetic of this period made use of a new set of heroic figures. Although these heroes were somewhat marginal and in breach of the common law (*en défaut de loi commune*) with respect to both the law and to lineage, they were able to represent new, more relative values. Writers were faced with the challenge of inventing a different kind of fiction, an autonomous fiction, which did not constitute an exact replica of the lives of their elders and fathers.

Writers were in search of new, more autonomous characters, closer to the modern status of the individual. They were also in search of new relationships between the different players in novels and in the theater (author/reader, narrator/narratee, author/characters/spectator). Such new relationships allow greater freedom within these roles by granting each player a more individual sense of judgment.

During the same period, the notion on which the classical aesthetic doctrine is based (i.e., verisimilitude) seems to step aside, making room for the probable, the uncertain, and the possible, which can be negotiated by various members of the literary system. In this way, the author becomes a sort of lawyer, using, like real lawyers do, literary means to present the case; the story is based on the life of new individuals, and the narratee, or the reader, is an individual and arbitrary judge who can hear the represented story and the moral conclusions of the author-lawyer and who can then make his own judgment.

I will begin by examining a legal case, a "factum," from the end of the seventeenth century, in order to demonstrate the constant relationship between legal and literary writing. Both make use of the same themes, the same narrative mechanisms, and the same aesthetic systems.

THE CASE

On the night of September 23, 1687, François Count of Montgomery was robbed of the fat sum of 30,000 livres (about $800,000 U.S. dollars today). The robbery was achieved by the use of copied keys. Montgomery shared a building building with his two neighbors, Sir and Lady de Langlade, who had declined the count's invitation to come to the countryside on the very evening of the robbery. They declined the invitation on a pretext that was later judged to be trivial. Sir Langlade not only knew that Montgomery had some cash, but he also knew the count's property well and had keys to his property. During a search led by Montgomery, a roll of seventy gold louis, *louis au cordon* (rare coins that were brand new and minted in 1686 and 1687) were found in Langlade's wardrobe. According to witnesses, Sir Langlade trembled and Lady Langlade fainted during the search. Furthermore, their arrogance, embarrassment, and uncertainty seemed to confirm the general suspicion that they were guilty of the robbery. Following this search, Montgomery filed charges against the couple who were convicted of a domestic and abominable crime. The aggravating circumstances of the case were that the perpetrators were well acquainted with, and friends of, the victim. Sir Langlade was immediately convicted and sent to the galleys, and his wife and daughter were sent to prison. Montgomery, then, took possession of everything belonging to the Langlades, who were merely of the ennobled bourgeoisie but who, nevertheless, lived quite well. Sir Langlade was a usurer. The case was considered to be settled. Some time later, a man about to be executed swore that he had not committed the crime for which he had been condemned to death, but he had confessed to another less serious crime, the theft of the Count of Montgomery, in order to prove his good faith or to escape divine punishment. This man named Gagnard, who was not spared by his execu-tioner, was the count's valet. Gagnard named Montgomery's previous chaplain as his accomplice, a man named Bellestre, who had died in his home in Mans soon after the robbery. This confession appeared particularly plausible because it was made by a man about to die. The Langlade's case was then reviewed and the couple absolved of guilt. Lady Langlade was released in 1691, but her husband did not survive the galleys. He had already died in a hospital in chains. As a widow, Lady Langlade was now free to follow her own desires. When released, she filed a petition not only to recover her confiscated fortune, which Montgomery seemed reluctant to relinquish, but also to press charges against Montgomery for her pain and suffering. She felt that the count, overly anxious to accuse both her and her husband, had pressed charges in a hasty and partisan manner without following up on other leads. The Langlades committing slander, bribing witnesses, and murder.

Thus, the widow Langlade's case is civil in nature (a claim for damages), but it has at its origin a criminal component (larceny of a large sum of her money with breaking and entering her property to obtain the money).

FACTUMS: A NEW LITERARY GENRE

My summary of this sample case is based on three texts included in what was in 1710 apparently the first published collection of factums and case statements available in bookstores in Lyons and Paris.[2] Taking these three factums as a starting point is, in my opinion, quite productive, for factums constitute an ideal lookout for the researcher. They are somewhere in between the reality of facts and behavior, and the symbolic (literary and fictional) image that we have of such a reality.

Factums are case statements that contain "a summary of the facts, with the interventions and objections of both parties, each of whom states the basis of his case, and his response to the opposing party's case and claims." Factums constitute legal evidence (petitions, summaries of the facts, etc.) that are admissible at trial, and that judges use in making their decisions. They constitute the lawyer's written conclusions and are presented to the court before the hearing.

Before the 1710 publication, factums appeared in small books generally sold by lawyers or available in the bookstores found in law courts. These publications were naturally of interest to an exclusively legal clientele such as the people involved in the case and to specialists interested in legal cases and their treatment. Because lawyers have the right to express themselves freely in these texts, which constitute admissible legal evidence and are considered to be "true," lawyers escape literary censure when publishing such texts. For this reason the texts eventually serve as a sort of outlet for the resentful lawyers who had not been allowed to express themselves freely in the courtroom (in particular with respect to criminal law).

However, a trend, still in its infancy in 1710, was developing whereby a new kind of reader would begin to read these texts. Although the theme of this conference does not lend itself to a general talk about factums and their significance, let me just say that at the end of the seventeenth century and well through the eighteenth century, these publications were beginning to have a profound effect not only on the evolution of the law but also on other disciplines, including literature. The preface to the collection of factums containing the sad story of Lady Langlade is quite enlightening in this respect. The author (probably a well-known Parisian lawyer named Cochin) claims to publish his first collection of factums in response to the wishes of a wide audience.

Moreover, while the collection will naturally serve as a stylistic handbook for lawyers, Cochin hopes that it will also help them to obtain a "fame that they so legitimately deserve," one that much resembles a literary or worldly fame. And for other readers, those hoping to find a mix of the "useful and [the] pleasing" (i.e., those hoping to find cases able to "form [their] style"), the collection of factums offers an idea of the "organization that is so important in the development of the circumstances surrounding the facts, which always determine the final decision in trials up for judgement." Within Cochin's preface, we are witnessing the creation of a genre at the outermost boundaries of law and literature. In choosing certain pleas taken from famous cases that are able to serve as models to lawyers and prosecutors, and also able to please the vast "public," the author does not intend merely to instruct professionals. He claims another status for these texts: "It is through such readings that within the thorns of jurisprudence can be found some roses to be picked, roses which soften the tedium of such dry and off-putting study". The lawyer wants to instruct while pleasing; at the same time he wants to expose judicial texts to a wider public in order to grant lawyers the fame that they deserve.

In so doing, he provides "cases" or anecdotes for all concerned that may interest or entice his audience. Such collections, which will subsequently multiply, are, first, veritable law manuals (the role of indexes classed by case is important, even if the sentence doesn't appear with the factums); second, stylistic models for lawyers (and incidentally for all those who would like to narrate a story in defending or in accusing a character); and third, "stories" for honest people.

Indeed these collections will appear soon thereafter in the library of the noble gentleman, who is not only more keen on law than today's gentleman but also more capable of understanding and appreciating a complicated story. A genre more elevated than the rumor rag, but less "literary" than the tragic story (*l'histoire tragique*), the factum will play in the eighteenth century a determining role in the expansion of the novel and in the public's interest for what will later be called in French *faits divers* (the trivial news item, the journalistic anecdote). Beyond the bounds of literary censure, these texts have both the appeal of the true and the interest of the exceptional.

What interests us here is that factums are at the juncture of the real and the fictional. Factums mix the real and the fictional in order to persuade the audience. As they argue their cases, lawyers guide the judge in his decision. In so doing, lawyers must entice the judge by putting him in the position of a reader.

Therefore, the lawyer presents his client's story in a certain light in order to convince the judge, the text's first addressee. The lawyer must keep in mind both the images traditionally associated with various social categories and conditions and the rules and motifs common to legal argument and to literature. Such rules and motifs include, above all, verisimilitude and veracity, but also organization, repetition, and ellipsis within the statement of facts, a certain "staging" of the facts and circumstances *pro* and *contra*, and finally the insertion of portraits and clauses for persuasive sequencing.

HOW TO PLEAD AGAINST A WIDOW?

But what do we actually see if we consider the way in which the widow is attacked or defended in the case before us? In his two petitions, Montgomery's lawyer naturally insists on the elements that will lead to his client's discharge. First of all, he makes note that in telling her story in a preliminary petition not included in the collection, the widow Langlade seeks the judge's compassion, hoping to turn his emotion to her financial profit. However, faced with this emotionally manipulative woman, the appellant "supplicant" (Montgomery) creates a flawless solidarity among himself, the count, and the magistrate. He argues that the case was decided by the judge on the basis of compelling evidence. The couple was convicted by the judge. If the magistrate made a mistake, then Montgomery must have made the same mistake. After all, isn't to err only human? Since a judge is always beyond suspicion because he is "exact," the widow must have accused Montgomery unjustly.

Moreover, in going after Montgomery, she is also attacking the legal institution and its authorities. In the face of the common front, put up by the magistrature and the appellant, Montgomery, the widow becomes a canonical figure of widowhood: a woman who is "avid," tricky, hypocritical and self-interested, as all the widows are in literature during this period. The petition proceeds by reviewing the reasons behind the original decision. Hammering out the circumstances again and again in just the right order to persuade the judge, the appellant Montgomery is thus able to emphasize a network of presumptions and clues. And, in the absence of proof, a body of prejudices takes its place. This reiteration has the effect of proving not only that the magistrate and the appellant had good reasons to believe the couple guilty, but also that the presumptions and the clues still remain, even if Langlade's innocence has been established by the confession. The network resists and remains credible. Even if the couple's innocence is proven by Gagnard's confession, their innocence remains contentious. To explain why, it is necessary to go one step further by going back to the canonical image of the nasty widow.

The appellant insists on the fact that a wife is bound by her husband's faults and conditions which exist both during his life and after his death. Langlade was an unjustly ennobled commoner, a usurer, a quick-tempered man, a defendant in the first suit brought by Montgomery. Longlade's guilt was confirmed when he reacted badly upon being accused. All of this together spills over onto his wife, who naturally has augured the usurper's arrogance and his violent nature.

Furthermore, in taking it upon herself to press charges against Montgomery, the widow demonstrates a shameful obstinacy; instead of seeking to strip the count of his fortune by imposing compensatory damages, she should merely take back her belongings, restore herself to the position she was in before, and blame herself for her misery and misfortune. As a woman, she lets her passion rule and takes her husband's villainy to new depths. In taking the law into her own hands and using it toward her personal gain, this widow breaks the code of ethics inherent in the law itself. Thus, the good faith of the appellant Montgomery and of the magistrate corresponds to the bad faith of the widow, who takes advantage of her legal powers to make a windfall in a bad trial.

In reviewing the circumstances of the original trial, the appellant suggests that the initial body of evidence can still be used to prove the woman's guilt, and furthermore that the justice system was not entirely at fault in convicting the falsely accused couple. Because "natural conjecture" formed a "fair presumption," it is clear that the proof brought by Gagnard's declaration can only be unnatural, and that it is an offense to verisimilitude and even the very rules of law.

In other words, the genuinely guilty person exists only because of a fortuitous "miracle." The widow, who knows the law and wants it to be exercised in her favor, finds herself pushed aside into the realms of the fantastic and the implausible, in other words, the illusory.

Furthermore, she shows herself to be prone to excesses, exaggeration, and malice by directing invectives, insults, and rage toward the court. Such a being cannot be believed, especially when she pursues legal actions against honest, calm, noble gentlemen such as Montgomery and the magistrate. The link between social class and widowhood is patently obvious and condemns both the ennobled bourgeoisie and women to disappear from the judicial stage when they are opposed by nobles who claim that these women are greedy and their sense of honor cannot be trusted.

Consequently, it is verisimilitude that must guide judgments, rather than the "incoherent" truth. The plausibility and the probability of the evidence, the clues, and the psychological and social observations, along with the coherence and the decorum of the person attacked by the widow, all serve to discredit Gagnard's confession.

The argument is that one should be skeptical about this miraculous, incoherent, and implausible confession. Because she is a woman and, worse a widow (whose status constitutes an aggravating circumstance), Lady Langlade comes to represent all that is excessive, fantastic, hypocritical and, uncontrollably passionate. The law has no room for passion and allies itself rather with "prudence." Some argue that since the widow by definition is outside of the law, she should never have had access to the law. As the lawyer concludes his oral arguments, order is restored: Just as in novels and comedies, the widow is at best a being who, is "competent" in law and who does not know how to exercise this power. At worst the widow is a dangerous character who robs honest people.

Lady Langlade, a permanent feature of the social canon, has become both a literary and a real image. Her violent and excessive expressions prove that the most reasonable actions often contain passions and unjust motives, and that anger and self-interest play as much of a part in Lady Langlade's conduct as do her desire to justify herself and protect her husband's memory.

HOW TO EXCUSE A WIDOW?

When faced with this petition, written in the form of a closing statement which incorporates standard patterns from the social and literary consciousness of his time, Lady Langlade's lawyer must be tricky in order to turn the argument to his advantage. How can he defend a woman who demands not only that the law restore her lost belongings but also that it compensate her for the loss of her husband, the confiscation of her fortune, her own and her daughter's imprisonment, all of which constitute five years of misery?

The lawyer's first task is to legitimize the presence of this woman in the legal forum and to validate her courage in standing up and accusing a nobleman. Therefore, Langlade's lawyer must prove first that she and her husband have both honor and birth, despite allegations to the contrary. Next he must prove that it is not self-interest that brings her to court, and that she, unlike most widows, does not seek to rob others.

On the contrary, she seeks merely to recover her own fortune (and to gain a sum of money that will punish the slanderer). This belief would restore to both her and her husband their credibility, innocence and irreproachable virtue. To win the case her lawyer must contest the social and literary image painted of women and widows, of a recently ennobled wife of a usurer, a hypocritical and self-interested widow, a woman who has broken into the legal arena in an almost criminal sense. To turn this image on its head is to represent Langlade as a good husband and a man of quality, and his wife as an innocent victim, devoid of self-interest, passion, and rage.

The perfectly plausible fiction written by Montgomery in his petition is that of a woman who has pressed charges wrongfully, a *necessarily* self-interested widow. This fiction must be replaced by an equally aesthetic and plausible story based on the exceptional. According to this story, the Langlade widow is a woman of worth, falsely convicted on the basis of alleged facts and prejudicial opinions. Instead of challenging the social image of certain classes or of the widow in general, Lady Langlade's lawyer merely claims that they do not apply in this case. In response to the count's plausible fiction, the lawyer constructs a reality all the more real because it is difficult to believe. As in novels, this truth is too incredible not to be true.

Because all of this may be quite difficult to believe, even unreadable in the eyes of the collective consciousness, the lawyer must push his argument even further. He not only claims that public opinion is on his side, but, above all, he claims that divine Providence is behind him along with the most noble literary works.

First, Longlade's lawyer makes the claim of popular legitimacy by arguing that the widow, despite her status and condition, has the will of the people behind her in a case that has become well known in the public arena. Then, it is up to the magistrate to break the bond between the count and himself and to break down images of social class if he wants to be on the side of public opinion and innocence. But this argument is hardly sufficient in 1692; Longlade's lawyer will need an authority more absolute than that of public opinion to persuade the judge.

Because Montgomery's petition had described Gagnard's confession as a "miracle," the widow's lawyer takes the miracle even further: According to him, the truth had come to the surface thanks to a "blow from the Heavens," and "in a series of circumstances provoked from above, the truth was revealed!" If she wants to escape her social status, this particular widow cannot afford to count on social, legal, or logical arguments. She can save herself not by having recourse to knowledge and social standing, but by allying herself to God. For if the court considers that God or Providence saved her in order to protect innocence, human justice must bow under God's pressure and take the consequences. Thus, because Providence has intervened to prevent the sacrifice of an innocent victim, innocence will be "universally" recognized. The judge, who makes his judgment before "the whole world," will surely agree.

THE WIDOW AS A CHARACTER; THE FACTUM AS A FICTION

I don't know what the judge did, and I doubt that in this particular case he followed the divine argument. However, because we have been discussing women's knowledge and the law, I would like to add a thought to this anecdote. A woman, and furthermore a widow, can have legal knowledge and the law on her side when she comes before the court. Obviously her right to speak, to plead her case, and to defend herself cannot be contested, because she is clearly "competent." However, in the judicial arena the widow keeps her special social image, her suspicious status as a woman, especially when she stands up to a count, and even more when she is the wife of a usurer who was born into the minor nobility. Consequently, her knowledge and her personal status do not help her very much as long as she merely defends herself with the legal arms that are available to all citizens (i.e., to all men).

As her lawyer understood so well, in order to convince, or even to attempt to convince, it is not enough for the widow to prove that she is actually, as she claims, a noble and honest woman; she must also call upon another judgment, that of God. For wherever a woman may be, how can she conquer or convince without the help of Providence?

I would like to conclude at this time with a remark that is also a possible direction in research. The writing of factums, like that of novels at the end of the eighteenth century, reveals the advent of a new aesthetic. This new aesthetic is based on a new and distinctive conception of the individual that puts authors, narrators, characters, narratees, spectators, and readers in a position of autonomy. The author becomes a sort of lawyer, using, as real lawyers do, literary means to present the case. The story is about the life of new individuals. The narratee, or the reader, is like an individual and an arbitrary judge who, upon hearing the represented story and the moral conclusions of the author-lawyer, can make his own decision about the case.

As a matter of fact, each and every one of these factums assumes a complete and modern individual, capable of forming his own judgments according to a set of relative values, values which in fact criticize the very idea of an absolute value or an unshakable truth. Authors, lawyers, readers, spectators, and judges are now free to decide as to the legitimacy of a fiction and the lessons developed by its author (and illustrated by its characters). This new aesthetic introduces, in addition to relative values, a sense of contract and of play, while making room within the practice of writing and within ideological lessons for decisions, criticisms, and reflections Thus, for quite some time, and in a "modern" sense, the novel and the law have been intimately linked.

REFERENCES

Some references include:

Christian Biet, *Droit et Fiction, La Représentation du Mariage dans La Princesse de Clèves, in* LITTERATURES CLASSIQUES (1990);

Christian Biet, *Le Cadet, Point de Départ des Destins Romanesques et Révélateur des Mutations Familiales, in* LES CADETS (1993);

Christian Biet, *De la Veuve Joyeuse à l'Individu Autonome, in* 187 REVUE XVIIEME SIECLE (1995);

Christian Biet, *Droit Divin, Droit Naturel et Droit Humain dans l'Antigone de Jean Rotrou, in* LITTERATURES CLASSIQUES (1992);

Christian Biet, *La Justice dans les Fables, La Fontaine et Le Droit des Gens*, REVUE *LE FABLIER* (1992);

Christian Biet and Jean Bart, *Les Illustres Françaises*, Roman Moderne, "Exemple d'un Romanesque Juridique," REVUE *XVIIEME SIECLE* (1992);

CHRISTIAN BIET, *OEDIPE EN MONARCHIE, TRAGÉDIE ET THÉORIE JURIDIQUE À L'AGE CLASSIQUE* (1994);

RECUEIL DE FACTUMS ET MEMOIRES SUR PLUSIEURS QUESTIONS IMPORTANTES DE DROIT CIVIL, DE COUTUME ET DE DISCIPLINE ECCLESIASTIQUE, 2 vols. (Anisson and Posuel: Lyons, 1710).

Part IV

Law, Literary Theory, and Critical Legal Theory:
A Forum

10
Critical Legal Theory

Mitchel Lasser (Moderator),
Duncan Kennedy, David Kennedy,
Nathaniel Berman (Discussants), *Norman Silber and*
Lawrence Kessler (Commentators)

Mitchel Lasser:

First, I would just like to thank Susan Tiefenbrun for inviting us all to take part in this terrific conference. I would also like to take a couple of minutes to explain what, after lengthy negotiations, we've decided to do and, furthermore, how we're going to try do it.

This panel is called "Law, Literary Theory, and Critical Legal Theory: A Forum." What we've decided to do is simply to have a conversation among a few people who are engaged in some project that seeks to bring together the three elements of the triad: law, literary theory, and critical legal theory. The subject of the conversation really boils down to this: What should be the relation between the three elements of the triad, bearing in mind that the meaning of any of the three elements is quite up for grabs?

In order to highlight the similarities, nuances, and differences between us on these issues of so-called interdisciplinary practice, and in order to promote a conversational approach, we've decided to structure the debate in the following manner. The discussion will move forward in three phases, each of which will begin with a question that I'll throw out and to which we'll each have about five minutes to respond. We'll then move on to the next question. After the last question, we'll pass the buck to our two respondents who can respond in whatever way they'd like.

So what are the three questions? The first is a set-up question that is intentionally problematic: Insofar as each of us is engaged in some project that brings some "other" discipline to the table in the performance of our legal scholarship, what "non-legal" works—be they drawn from "lit theory," literature, or the visual arts—are, or have been, or should be the most important to you in the furtherance of that project?

Having hopefully gotten some field of references from the answers to this first question, the second question will be: What is or should be the relation between that "other" discipline (whether it's literary theory, literature or the visual arts) and "legal" scholarship?

The third question will then seek to refine the discussion. If, as I suspect, we will each tend to answer the second question by propounding some version of what might be called "counterdisciplinarity" or "antidisciplinarity" (as opposed to "interdisciplinarity"), what do these slogans really mean? The ensuing discussion will, I hope, refine our answers and flush out certain subsidiary issues. For example, what is meant by the terms *eclectic borrowing* or *ruthless appropriation*? Furthermore, do you, or should one, feel some sort of responsibility to the projects of the "other" discipline or to the projects or boundaries of our "legal" discipline?

That said, allow me to introduce quickly the three other members of the panel. They are David Kennedy and Duncan Kennedy of the Harvard Law School, and Nathaniel Berman of the Northeastern University School of Law. Our two respondents, both of whom teach here at the Hofstra University School of Law, are Norman Silber and Lawrence Kessler.

Let us begin then with the first question. To reiterate: Insofar as each of us is engaged in some project that brings some "other" discipline to the table in the performance of our legal scholarship, what "nonlegal" works—be they drawn from "lit theory," literature, or the visual arts—are, or have been, or should be the most important to you in the furtherance of that project?

Duncan Kennedy:

Hi! It's nice to be here. The morning session was just riveting.

I thought what I'd do is to talk for five minutes and try to answer the question by beginning with the distinction between policy work and theory work. I do both as a law professor. I teach low-income housing law and policy, and I do quite a bit of work which amounts to trying to figure out what left-wing proposals for changing the legal system ought to be, or how leftists can relate to the American legal system from a point of view of challenge, from a perspective that's to the left of American liberalism, that's more radical than that. For those of you who were at the luncheon, I, too, read *Citizen Tom Paine* in my fifteenth year, and it had a big effect on me.

So that's one kind of work. There's another kind of work which has been going on the left since the beginning of the left, which is the "theory" stuff. This theory stuff in the United States often has a bad name, and seems unbelievably abstruse and irrelevant, and who cares about it? It's all in hopelessly technical language which I'm now going to use absolutely shamelessly on the grounds that I'm going to talk at a conference at NYU on Friday about homelessness, and as far as I'm concerned, this is an occasion for being as "fancy" as you want to be. If you hate theory talk, you're probably just going to find this discussion intolerable. But in that case, I invite you to the REACH Program's event on homelessness and housing policy at NYU which starts at 11 o'clock in the morning in the NYU auditorium.

So: Theory. What's it got to do with anything? From the beginning, a left-wing project in the area of legal theory seemed to me to mean something not too far from what Robin West was describing this morning when talking about the contribution of Robert Cover. In the sixties and seventies, the left legal academics and leftists interested in legal theory were overwhelmingly preoccupied with demonstrating that the right legal answer to legal questions was on the side of the oppressed, so that the Constitution showed that the people whose struggles you endorsed had constitutional rights to all the things that you thought they ought to have. At the lower levels of legal theory, this meant adhering to the conviction that the common law embodied exactly our most cherished political ideals, and that when judges didn't go along with this vision, they were doing something that was in violation of the norms of the legal order.

As opposed to this approach, people like me, who thought of themselves as radical intellectuals in that period (and still today), thought that it was a good idea—and would be ultimately a politically correct and politically desirable left-wing thing to do—*not* to engage in that activity alone. I did my share and I still do my share of engaging in the activity of arguing that the correct meaning of the legal materials is that the left should win, and I believe it is often the case that the correct interpretation of the legal materials is that the left should win.

But we also wanted to do something else, which was to criticize the effect of necessity that people underwent or experienced when confronted with an argument that claimed that there was a correct legal outcome. In other words, as opposed to going on arguing just that the left was legally correct and that's why we should win every case, we wanted to attack legality itself, that is, to attack the idea of "right answers" by trying to open up a consciousness of the multiplicity of possible interpretations. The idea was partly to show how much of the actual law in force was the product of political projects either of the right or of the moderate left, so that we could then argue for more radical projects, not on the grounds that they were legally correct, but on the grounds that they were right and that if people wanted to do them, the fact that the law didn't do them was no criticism.

So the idea was actually to attack legal determinacy and the experience of being bound that classic American civil libertarian and civil rights rhetoric emphasize, and to push for the plurality of plausible interpretations of the law and for the presence of nonlegal or extralegal or prelegal political motivations in judicial lawmaking. Earl Warren was a liberal. He wasn't just a judge who was doing what the Equal Protection Clause required; he was putting a legal/ political ideology into effect as positive law.

So what seemed to be useful in order to engage in this project? I myself was just a complete pack rat, cannibalizing, you know, like an abandoned car pulled apart in no time flat. My view of literary theory, Marxist theory, or structuralist theory was that it was an abandoned car, and I was a kid in the neighborhood, and there was no reason why I shouldn't steal the hubcaps, use a hammer on them, and turn them into Art Moderne dinner plates if I wanted to.

The idea was just to pull pieces out of the theory of the people who seemed most useful to cannibalize and put them to work to support the proposition that law was more like a language in which you could say a lot of different things than it was like the Code of Hammurabi telling you what to do to a thief. Legal discourse is more like a language in which you could say a lot of things, but not just anything.

So what was useful? Well, I actually found useful a lot of things inside the left or progressive legal tradition in legal realism, but also quite a few things that are in some sense part of literary theory. For instance, I think that anyone interested in doing legal theory should begin by reading Saussure's *Course on General Linguistics*, the message of which is the distinction between a language and a speech or sentence uttered in that language. That's the first basic message, which insists that we think about legal talk as a language inside a language. In other words, saying it in English is restrictive because English is a particular language of a particular vocabulary. Saying it in legal English means that there is another language or another set of restrictions on speech when you are doing legal discourse.

So what does that mean? Here is an example of what it can mean, borrowing directly from Saussure. It's the idea that when lawyers and judges produce legal arguments, there are a very limited number of conventional arguments that they use over and over again.[1] For example, if you adopt this rule, no one will know where they stand; or this rule is much too rigid; or this rule makes people responsible without fault; or if between two people one has to pay, the person who caused the injury should pay even if she isn't at fault. These are typical, recurring legal arguments. There are maybe a thousand of them used over and over again. They're like the words of a language that can be combined with other arguments that are also words in the language of law to produce the equivalent of a sentence in English that is a complete and formally correct legal argument in law.

That emphasis on legal discourse as a language with words that are arguments defined partly in relationship to each other turned out, I think, to be incredibly useful in understanding how it could be the case that very right-wing and very left-wing positions can be taken in a way that's apparently fully consistent with interpreting the Constitution in good faith. That is, the question is how can good faith interpreters turn the Constitution into a right-wing document and also into a moderately progressive document? The theoretical borrowing had the purpose of demonstrating this kind of interpretive possibility and was, I think, useful to that extent.

David Kennedy:

I would like to respond to Mitch's question by talking about some dilemmas that arise in trying to carry out the interdisciplinary projects Duncan proposes. The first difficulty arises from the fact that the law is itself ravenously interdisciplinary. People who wish to enlist interdisciplinarity in the project of critical writing about law face the difficulty that there are a lot of texts out there, lots of books, ideas, disciplines that would or ought or should or might be relevant. To pick up on Duncan's metaphor, there are a lot of abandoned cars lying around. And most of them have already been picked pretty clean by interdisciplinary borrowers committed to restablizing rather than criticizing law. As a result, saying you favor interdisciplinarity is not enough—we need to speak about the strategy for specific borrowings in service of particular projects.

Perhaps one can simply revisit the old junkyards and reenlist sociology or literary theory or psychology in a critical rather than a reconstructive way. And it is nicely liberating to think that there are no classic texts one needs to read. One mustn't feel demobilized by not having (yet) read Hegel or Rousseau or Derrida or whomever. It's abandoned automobiles all the way down. But we might also think strategically about which abandoned car to approach, which hubcap to take, whether the fender might also be useful, and so on. Some texts—Wittgenstein, for example—have been cannibalized by a variety of both critical and reconstructive legal projects.

In my own field of international law or international economic policy it has seemed to work to take a bit of this and a bit of that. One could argue about what Adam Smith or Keynes really meant, but it may be better simply to juxtapose a few sociological hubcaps with some bumpers from postcolonialism. In general, I am skeptical that any one interdisciplinary key will unlock the field. But this creates a problem in interdisciplinary forums when you are asked what texts are most important—as if the work were being done by the texts you scavenge rather than by your own strategies of reading and intervening in your own discipline. Talking about interdisciplinarity can be a way of not talking about one's actual scholarly projects and objectives. For scavengers, there is also the anxiety of ignorance: "If I name a text, then I'll have to remember what was actually in it, and perhaps I don't remember; and I'm just a lawyer and not a philosopher, and so on."

And then there is the rat hole problem—if you say the name of your cross-disciplinary guru, you can easily disappear into the guru's own fifteen minutes of fame. If you don't pick a classic text but rather something lying around in today's academy, you might make the error of picking whatever you studied as an undergraduate. If you studied literary theory in the eighties, for example, and picked Derrida, by the time you write a law review article applying Derrida's fourth insight to your field's eighth dilemma, it's too late. You're the Derrida guy, and we all know what his problem was, and you've got it, too.

Moreover, the strategy of interdisciplinary text selection looks somewhat different in teaching than in writing. In the classroom, in my experience, you don't want Hegel, but you don't want Dale Carnegie either. You want a middle-level text, preferably short and entertaining. The more theoretical, the shorter, to add the powerful feeling that comes with saying "We've now read three paragraphs of Wittgenstein and will discuss how he would have us rethink all of constitutional law." Two short pieces of this sort that I've used are cuts from Clausewitz, describing war as a language, and an essay by Roland Barthes on the Eiffel Tower. Reading both texts can get students asking new questions—what if I saw the United Nations like Barthes sees the Eiffel Tower?

Mitchel Lasser:

I really like this hubcap image, so I think I'll run with it. The problem that I face is what to do if in some way, shape, or form you have a claim of some sort on the car that's being cannibalized. In my case, the issue is that I teach in a law school but that I have a degree in comparative literature. I'm therefore constantly faced with the question: How am I supposed to react to the kids on the block taking the hubcaps of an intellectual automobile that I'm in some way deeply implicated in? The answer is that I actually feel fine about it, primarily because I'm sitting on both sides of the disciplinary fence. I don't actually feel, or believe in, the disciplinary divide; it's not something that I take seriously, despite the fact there are people who seem to have a lot of stock in that divide's supposed existence.

Moving to the pedagogical issue: Since my place on the divide depends on the context that I'm in, I'm going to assume that this is a predominantly legal context, and that I'm faced with the questions, "What are you taking from the 'other' discipline, and how are you using it?" The answer would have to be one that might be expected from one of David's old students. There's no pantheon of "literary" or "theoretical" texts to which I would claim adherence, if only for defensive reasons, precisely in order to avoid the response, "Clearly this person is an adherent of so and so, and given so and so's problems, we can just relegate this person to the side."

I would claim adherence, however, to a certain pedagogical method, a certain mode of reading, a certain strategy toward approaching texts that I was first exposed to on the "lit" side. I actually have quite a bit of faith in this mode of reading which, as I understood it, worked on the basic premise that one should engage in what we used to call, quite simply, "close reading." I took this to mean that one should pay particular attention to the way in which a text talks about itself. The fundamental notion is that a text—whatever the text may be—is composed of a series of signs that tell you something not only about the nature of the relationship between the text's constitutive elements, but also about why the text is put together the way that it is. Those signs represent claims of one kind or another; and these claims need to be taken seriously, and therefore need to be evaluated, at the very least, on their own terms.

This approach to reading is one that I totally adhere to in both the "lit" and the "law" contexts. If I had to list the pantheon of canonical "lit theory" texts that were always introduced as those that called for such "close reading," engaged in it, and served as the pedagogical models that gave students the means to arrive at the vantage point of the "close read," the series of names would start with Saussure, go through such structuralist texts as Genette,[2] Jakobson[3] or Barthes,[4] and continue through De Manian deconstruction.[5]

If this discussion were occurring somewhere else, and if I were asked the same question in a predominantly "lit" context, I would tell the same story and give the same answer. The only difference would be that I would construct a different pantheon, this time a "legal" one, and produce a series of names that would begin this time with Hohfeld.[6] That said, I think that the form and substance of the answer would be identical.

Nathaniel Berman:

I want to pursue the notion of the "strategic" use of theory in order to contrast "counterdisciplinarity" with "interdisciplinarity." Many critical alleged writers have deployed theoretical techniques form other disciplines' "master thinkers" to crack the unitary facade of their own disciplines. The counterdisciplinary strategy is quite different from the interdisciplinary aspiration to establish some kind of "dialogue" across disciplines or to "apply" the insights of one to the other. I will describe a specific instance of this phenomenon: the deployment of "theory" by those engaged in the new critical rereading of international legal history.

If we wanted to categorize the wide variety of historical projects now being pursued in light of their relation to "theory," we could divide them in two: those devoted to the "pluralization of international legal history" and those focused on the "identity-constitutive" role of international law. The "pluralization" projects reject linear progress narratives and focus on disparate and conflictual genealogical lines. The mainstream account of international legal history is the story, if not of a smooth organic development, then of a limited set of dramas with a predetermined dénouement. This telling often begins with the "Grotian moment" of the seventeenth century, in which a small number of European states recognized each other as sovereign equals. It then describes the subsequent challenges to this restricted "international community" and asserts that the "community" has gradually become more and more inclusive.

The two most important sites from which the critique of this linear narrative has emerged have been those of postcoloniality and feminism. Those who describe the past in terms of a genealogy of postcoloniality displace the origin of the sovereignty focus of modern international law from the seventeenth century to the sixteenth century.[7] They argue that modern international law's obsession with sovereignty may be traced as much to that earlier period of colonial encounter as to the later period of intra-European conflict. The role of intra-

European developments in the evolution of sovereignty are not necessarily dismissed, but an alternative chronology, focusing on the role of colonial crises in the periodic reconstruction of sovereignty, are given at least equal stature.

Feminist rereadings of international legal history provide another source of "pluralization," advancing very different chronologies than either the Eurocentric or postcolonial tellings.[8] The vicissitudes of self-determination provide an important site for such rereadings.[9] Mainstream legal historians usually look at the great moments in the history of self-determination—the post-World War I period, decolonization, and so forth—for their contribution to the linear narrative of ever-greater inclusiveness (limited only by considerations of "stability"). In contrast, feminist historians show the many ways these purported transitional moments form a continuous part of the perennial subordination of women. They also describe women's struggles to create ruptures in that perennial story. Finally, postcolonial feminists demonstrate the dissonance between Eurocentric and postcolonial accounts of the place of women in the international legal system.[10]

It should be clear, by now, how the deployment of "theory" has contributed to these genealogical inquiries which presume irreducible conflict between alternative accounts. At the substantive level, these writers draw on postcolonial and feminist theorists to criticize the discipline's triumphalism. At the historiographical level, they deploy Nietzschean or Foucauldian techniques for criticizing its teleological narrative.[11] At the level of disciplinary theory, their attack on international law's unitary facade constitutes a kind of "writing against the discipline" in alliance with those anthropologists who advocate "writing against culture."[12] Both reject any understanding of a cultural formation which does not highlight plurality, incompatibility, and power struggle.[13]

The second kind of rereading of international legal history focuses on the "identity-constitutive" role of international law. For example, one of the striking things about the last two decades is the way international law appeared to have absorbed the Third World challenge. The first generation of postcolonial international lawyers seemed to have given up their radicalism and to have been assimilated into the system. This individual assimilation seemed replayed on the state level, in the efforts of the Third World states to perform their identities in conformity with international stage directions. An even more complex dynamic may be found in the way that non-state groups have continually shifted the internal and external constructions of their identity. Such shifts have operated in tandem with shifts in the international projection and valorization of such identities: at various times over the past century, a single group may have presented its identity as a "religion," a "minority," a territorial "people," a transfrontier "nation," an "undeveloped" people, and so forth. Nationalists everywhere perform, transform, and deform these international legal identities in relation to those identities' cultural meetings, legal implications, or tactical consequences.

The main theoretical strategies deployed to pursue these inquiries come from the reappropriations by postcolonial[14] and feminist writers[15] of Foucauldian and psychoanalytic notions of identity. Critical legal writers often deploy insights such as those of Judith Butler, when she writes that "[t]here is no self prior . . . to its entrance into the conflicted cultural field."[16] Assimilation and resistance to the "international community" are located in the shifting ways in which the subjectivity is constituted in relation to power—power exercised, in part, through international law. This account of "subjectification" means that the focus on the "identity-constitutive" role of international law entails a rejection of reading the history of international law as a simple story of increasing inclusiveness. Like the "pluralization" projects, this focus deploys a counter-disciplinary strategy, fundamentally attacking the liberal triumphalist narrative of linear programs.

Mitchel Lasser:

Now that we have our field of references, let's move on to the second question. What is or should be the relation between "other" disciplines (whether they're literary theory, literature or the visual arts) and our "legal" scholarship?

David Kennedy:

The second question asks, "What does it mean to read law as an art form, or to read law as a cultural or literary form?" Let me describe at least two projects of this sort that have interested me. First, treating laws as literature can often counteract the tendency in many judicial opinions and other fancy legal texts to ally law with famous literary and other cultural phenomena. For example, Shakespeare sums up a lot in legal argument and is actually one of the most cited people for some legal propositions. To my mind, it can be helpful to relate law precisely to low cultural phenomena, to try to see the relationship between styles of argument that are current in law in a given moment and the styles of popular culture and entertainment that exist simultaneously. Doing so can highlight the existence of fashion in law and break the sense of law as an unfolding search for right answers without saying "its all political" or that "its all really done by people to further their motives." This sort of work highlights the elements of desire, of what's "in" and what's "out," which are also part of legal argument and the developments of legal rules and institutions over time.

A second useful way of looking at law as a cultural or literary form is actually exemplified by a very funny article that Nathaniel wrote in which he compares international law to high rather than low culture. He picked an obscure international lawyer from the 1930s who had the unfortunate name of Redslob and compared this fellow to Picasso. In Nathaniel's telling, Redslob and Picasso were actually the same person. They were influenced by the same things; they thought about things in the same way; and there was a great deal of cubism in Redslob's plan for the partition of Upper Silesia. What is interesting here is not whether Redslob and Picasso were actually the same person or influenced by one another. What is interesting is the way this juxtaposition foregrounds the role of the individual as a culture worker, the producer of legal texts and institutions. His project asks us to ask "What was Redslob's strategy?"

So two reasons to read law as literature would be to highlight the elements of culture and fashion which can't be reduced to either pragmatism or politics and to foreground the importance of particular people with particular projects. My own view is that these two things are utterly interior to law. I don't know what goes on in art history or how a reader of Picasso would understand the relationship to Redslob, and I don't know enough about contemporary cultural studies to have a sense for what they mean by "fashion." I'm sure the very idea of "fashion" has now been critiqued. My own work is completely within the discipline of law and the subdiscipline of international law, in which fashion has hardly been discovered, let alone out of style. My strategic situation is within a discipline that doesn't take itself seriously enough as a discipline, while taking other disciplines far too seriously as disciplines. My own feeling is that we should be paddling the canoe in the other direction, trying to take our own discipline more seriously as a collective project in a particular cultural space, and avoid being deflected from that task by too earnest an interpretation of what's going on in the other field.

Mitchel Lasser:

I don't think we have an argument on the disciplinary issue. I just think that it's trite to say that "law is literature." Obviously, law speaks in language and therefore uses literary media and techniques. Needless to say, the critical work on literary techniques should therefore be brought to bear in the analysis of legal texts. It's equally trite to say that "literature can be read as law." Obviously, literature operates under externally and internally imposed rules, and therefore can be read as "law."

I simply object to the separation of the two disciplines as if they were actually distinct. If you look, for example, at the relation between what literary theorists do and what legal theorists do, I think you'll find that as a matter of fact they do a lot of the same kind of work; in both academic fields, the theoretical problematics and projects are remarkably similar. Just think, for example, of how much is being done in both spheres in the way of cultural studies, postcolonial studies, feminist studies, or gay studies. A lot of the same work is being done by the same kinds of people in the two supposedly distinct disciplines.

The danger, I think, in separating out the two disciplines is that you end up in the frequently recurring and extremely frustrating predicament in which most of us have probably found ourselves on different occasions, usually in the context of assorted "Law and" situations, whether it's "law and literature" courses or *inter*disciplinary conferences. You attend a course or conference as a "law person," and, after much anticipation, you listen to a "lit person" whose work you've respected for years, have read and reread a thousand times, and have used repeatedly in your own work; and sure enough, this person elegantly sets out some incredibly complex sociolinguistic problematic, but then turns around and tries to "apply law" to the problem. This person, who is usually so wonderfully sophisticated in his or her own "literary" analyses, suddenly appears to have some blind faith that, for example, "legal rules produce determinate solutions" and can therefore be used to resolve intractable linguistic conundrums. It's as if the person has simply forgotten the most basic premises of his "own" field, and plunges headlong into a form of analysis that he would be the first to dismiss if someone were to engage in it in his own, "literary" discipline.

It seems to me that the problem of the disciplinary divide consists largely of a projection of each side's insecurities, desire for, and fear of, the other side. The key, I think, is that the decision to become a lawyer or a "lit person" is a form of social and theoretical positioning of oneself (or of various aspects of oneself) within a constellation of possible moves of Self- (or Selves-) definition. But that initial positioning doesn't end the matter, for another positioning occurs within the lit and legal spheres when one decides, say, whether to become an academic. And once again, within the respective academic spheres, there is the decision about, on the one side, whether to be, to pick a few obvious and uni-maginative possibilities, a "new historicist," a "feminist neo-Freudian," or a "De Manian deconstructionist," or on the other, whether to be, for example, a "law and econ" type, a "law and society" type, a "progressive civil libertarian," a "republican tradition" type, or some relatively novel combination thereof.

All I'm getting at is what Duncan might call "nesting," or what a "post-De Manian, post-Freudian deconstructionist" might call—ironically and with a wink—"repetition compulsion." I think that if you know each discipline well enough to know where to look in the "other" discipline, you'll find that your double is always already there, with, needless to say, the possibility of certain variations. So if you're going to go to the "other" discipline in the hope of acquiring some form of "deep" knowledge that you're going to "bring back" and "apply" in your own discipline, I suspect that you're likely to be sorely disappointed, unless, of course, you've simply failed to map out the "other" discipline sufficiently. You may get some rudimentary knowledge of some other field, but usually, when it comes down to the big questions, you'll probably find that at that point, the people have already aligned and positioned themselves within their own disciplines in a manner strikingly similar to the way they have in yours over questions and problematics that end up, once again, remarkably similar to yours.

At that point—at least in the disciplines I know something about, namely "law" and "literature"—I don't think that there is any transfer of knowledge that's going to resolve the big questions that might have sent you running to the other discipline for help in the first place. You are likely to be left with the same array of possibilities as what you've got in your own discipline.

Nathaniel Berman:

I'd like to describe the article of mine that David mentioned[17] as an example
of counterdisciplinary strategy.The juxtaposition of a legal text, doctrine, or
writer to a painting or painter may stem from a variety of motivations. Here are
the motivations that don't interest me: because painting is viewed as more interesting than law, because a painting is respected more than a legal artifact,
because artists are cherished more than lawyers. This evaluation of relative
cultural stature may or may not be accurate, but it would be irrelevant to the
strategic conception of a counterdisciplinary work. It would simply mean
valorizing some other discipline, as Mitchel noted.

In contrast, my motivation in juxtaposing the work of Robert Redslob, a
now-obscure French legal writer from the interwar period, to a Picasso painting
was precisely its counterintuitiveness. I did not base this exercise on any
supposed analogy between law and art, or on the notion that "culture" might
provide "context" for law. On the contrary, I was trying to see what kind of
surprising insight might emerge from the juxtaposition of specific, dissimilar
cultural artifacts. I tried to use this counterintuitive juxtaposition to break the
conventional theoretical and pragmatic frameworks in which international legal
history is usually analyzed. Rather than seeing the writer's contribution to the
perennial search for truth or utility, I imagined him as a historically specific
cultural innovator, whose relation to the discipline was one of rupture and
reconfiguration.

The painting to which I juxtaposed this legal writer's work was *Les
Demoiselles d'Avignon*, of which most of you probably have some image. It is
a painting of five figures, probably female (although the history of the painting
is intriguingly ambiguous on that point), whose faces appear to be masks, some
of Iberian folk art origin and some of African origin. It's also the first painting
of Cubism, initiating the distinctive Cubist fragmentation of Renaissance
representational space. The key thing about this painting for me was the way
Picasso enlisted the energy he perceived in the so-called primitive to break with
the conventions of his medium and to initiate the sophisticated technical
experimentation that inaugurated Modernism.

This painting could thus be inscribed in several different historical
trajectories. It could be inscribed in the trajectory of male fantasies about
women, in the trajectory of European fantasies about the "primitive," and so
forth. From these perspectives, one might focus on genre history, on the way
Picasso deploys these fantasies against convention to establish a new form of
high-cultural creativity.

Turning to post-World War I innovators in international law, I reimagined
them as cultural figures involved in projects of fantasy, projection, rupture,
and reconstruction, which form a series with other Modernist innovators. I

reimagined international legal artifacts as themselves constructing a "Modernist moment," in which new forms of authority were legitimated through the projection and reappropriation of a new set of fantasies about the "primitive." Legal innovation would thus be wrenched out of a linear progress narrative and be identified as one site of European self-reinvention effected through such shifting fantasies as reappropriations. Rather than seeing law as a reflection of a larger historical context, I argued that it should be seen as one site in which that context was constructed. In this recasting of writers like Redslob as constructing a Modernist moment in the "conflicted cultural field" which is international law, one vies the history of notions of theoretical truth and pragmatic utility as functions of the discontinuous history of cultural fantasies and reappropriations, rather than vice versa.

Duncan Kennedy:

I'm going to talk about another way in which one can draw a parallel. This is just a different way to do it. I said before something about my own identity and about my own mind as a politically correct leftist kind of person. But I have another idea of what I'm doing in my scholarly life besides being a leftist. I also think of myself as a boho type, as an arty boho person who comes from a very specific American cultural tradition which is committed to modernism and then to postmodernism in the arts, and to unconventional lifestyles, and blah blah blah. So my parents were arty boho type people, though they were sort of upper-middle-class arty boho type people, and they brought me up to believe that one of the most important things you should do, whatever you do, is that you should be an artist. That meant that you have to be somewhere in the history of art—you don't have a choice—so whatever you're doing, you need not only have your relationship to its politics but you also have to be pursuing an aesthetic project. You could be a formalist, a mannerist, a modern art type; you could be a postmodern art type; you could be a surrealist, a dadaist; but you need to be part of that aesthetic project as well.

This project is in deep tension with the political project. In fact, aesthetic modernism in the West has just had a tortured relationship with the more radical forms of leftism, mainly in the form of the radical leftist slaughtering cultural modernists, or in Europe, under Communism, and in the United States, earnest political leftists tending to detest arty boho types. There are only a few moments in American cultural history, resulting in the production of lots of great posters between about 1966 and 1972, when there's really been an entente between cultural or aesthetic radicalism and modernism and political radicalism.

So this aesthetic agenda is a different agenda; and the agendas are often in terrible conflict in the way that I've already sort of defined. So just as in legal scholarship, I wanted to be a participant in a left legal theory project that would split the legal academy from its spineless centrism and polarize it into left and right camps. Have a little playground sparring instead of a lot of limp 1950s nonpolitical consensus. That might be described as the political project.

The aesthetic project was more to participate in a movement of law professors who in offices, not garrets, produced law review articles—that's what we were producing—which would have at least to some extent the effect of the *salon des refusés*. That is, it would have the effect of being a collection of law review articles that would be a symbolic, aesthetic, avant-gardist rejection of the earlier generations, of their aesthetic formalism. It was a very different agenda.

It doesn't correspond to anything the three other speakers have talked about, though I don't think it's incompatible with what they've been talking about; and I think that they are all involved in doing it to one extent or another. But in this take on art, the point is that we're not studying art, and we're not studying legal discourse. We're producing legal artifacts, which could be judicial opinions, or could be briefs, but in the case of the professoriate, it's articles or deformations and inflections of the law review article form; and there are lots of ways in which the avant-gardist impulse can be incorporated into the activity of writing law review articles. In fact, as I look out into the audience, I see two people I know who have actually done it in very dramatic ways, and all three of these panelists have done it to one extent or another.

So the idea is to use the avant-garde arty boho, living in a garret, slapping the paint on in a way that will make people say, "A monkey could have done that" or "It doesn't matter which way you hang it: There are four possibilities, and it makes about as much sense when we hang it this way as that way," in order to arouse a response. In my sort of lexicon, this is called the longing to *épater les bourgeois*, to shock the bourgeois art audience. *Épater les bourgeois*, shocking the bourgeois cultural audience, is different than appropriating, on behalf of the people, the bourgeois' own means of production. But there's a deep parallel between the idea of *épater*-ing them and nationalizing or socializing the means of production, as well as deep conflicts between the two projects. But there's no reason why one shouldn't try to keep the two projects alive, going back and forth at the same time.

Mitchel Lasser:

Should we go to the last question and the final round of answers? We've each, it seems to me, been propounding some version of what might be called "counterdisciplinarity" or "antidisciplinarity" (as opposed to "interdisciplinarity"). But what might such terms really mean? Let's take this opportunity, then, to refine our answers and flush out certain subsidiary issues. For example, what is meant by the terms *eclectic borrowing* or *ruthless appropriation*? Furthermore, do you, or should one, feel some sort of responsibility to the projects of the "other" discipline or to the projects or boundaries of our "legal" discipline?

Nathaniel Berman:

I would like to confront a common question that comes up in discussions of "interdisciplinarity." What is the responsibility of the legal theorist to the disciplines from which he or she draws? In a variety of ways we've all been advocating a strategic use of other disciplines. That strategic focus means that what we are really aiming at is a deconstruction of our own discipline, a deconstruction to which conventional "interdisciplinarity" sometimes constitutes a quite formidable hindrance.

The relationship, therefore, of my work to "Picasso Studies" is something about which I'm utterly agnostic. I simply have no idea whether it would be a critical move in Picasso Studies to juxtapose the artist to contemporaneous international lawyers. In my own work, it has been critically useful to understand the relationship of cultural Modernists to the politics of their time. But I am not sure, given the current disciplinary situation of cultural history, these same moves would have a critical edge.

For me, the productivity of surprising juxtapositions across disciplines—such as that of a legal theorist to a painter—is measured by their ability to break the linear progress narratives that govern disciplines' self-understanding. This productivity is also measured by the quality of the inevitable debate in which the inventors of new progress narratives oppose the inventors of discontinuous and disjunctive genealogies. Counterdisciplinary strategy is a quintessentially Modernist move: the juxtaposition of dissimilar artifacts undertaken with the aspiration of reaping some unpredictable political, cultural or libidinal charge.

Duncan Kennedy:

About the question of the relation to the other discipline, I agree completely with Nathaniel's statement of agnosticism about the question of responsibility to that other discipline.

But I'd just like to describe something again. I'm proselytizing here for counterdisciplinary work, especially left-wing counterdisciplinary work. It seems to me that one of the things that's fun about it is the experience of taking the abandoned car and doing what you want with the hubcaps: That's great! My relationship to the discipline represented by the car is—by the way, the car/discipline is, after all, still there; everything that's done to it is in the imagination—very much organized around an idea that's a reaction formation. The idea is that I don't care what they think about what I do with their stuff; and I know they'll never read anything I write; and I'm just a law professor; they're in Paris; and I hope they all die soon; and I hope that no more brilliant theorists on whom I'm dependent for raw materials come into existence until I'm dead so that I'll be outside the horrible grip of their patriarchal and matriarchal influence.

I also have an exhibitionist fantasy, which is that having dismantled the car, pounded the hubcaps into Art Moderne dinner plates, and served up this great bizarre artifact inside legal scholarship that represents avant-gardism as well as theoretical sophistication therein, that they would just happen to be sitting in the toilet one day and pick up a reprint—that I hadn't sent them, but that someone else had sent them—and reading along, they'd say "*Wow*!! This kid is fucking dynamite! I'd love to have him over for dinner." I would then get from Jacques Derrida a little envelope in which there would be a round-trip airplane ticket to wherever in France he lives, with an engraved invitation-like document saying, "Please come for dinner."

So the problem here is to maintain a particular attitude. As I see it, I am just an earnest moralist trying to maintain the attitude of "I don't care, I don't care what they think," or "What they have to say about it has absolutely nothing to do with it;" but at the same time, this fantasy is still there. It's a delicious fantasy; and as a fan, I've run up to many of these people at one point or another and shaken their hand and said, "You know, Mr. Derrida, your work has had a gigantic influence on my life, and I've really gotten off on it," and then sort of walked off thinking, "You know, he doesn't even know I exist." I would describe my relationship to the other discipline that way.

David Kennedy:

Let me try to bring together some strands suggested by this slogan "counterdisciplinarity." One would be not looking in other disciplines for canonical texts. This is the hubcap idea. A second strand would be building on the whole education of the person who is doing the work rather than on the particular disciplinary claims of the field from which the person has imported a text. This avoids the tendency to stereotype the field from which one imports, as in "Anthropology tells us. . . ." The idea here is to understand oneself as an interdisciplinarily influenced artisan of legal culture rather than as an insight importer. A very important text in my own upbringing was the Boy Scout oath; more important to me even than Derrida. I try to remember to think of myself as coming to the law with everything I've got, which is some knowledge of a variety of different texts from different places. My job is to mobilize them in a project.

Third, the slogan "counterdisciplinarity" suggests to me an emphasis on the critical rather than the reinforcing impulse in turning to another field. I'm more interested in the attempt, within law, to look to the other discipline as a way of unsettling law's special claims to be related to either pragmatics or politics. We've talked about a number of different ways of doing that, such as heightening the analogies to low cultures, seeing law people as artists, and trying to understand the legal production as a broader kind of cultural or social project.

I don't see the alternative strand of interdisciplinary work suggested by the slogan "counterdisciplinarity" having as its project the attempt to break down the barrier between disciplines, or to compensate for law's lack of a sophisticated understanding of how language is all put together, or as an attempt to account for law's lack of awareness of its context or to account for law's lack of something else. I see this as a project that's within the discipline and tradition of law. In the discipline of law, interdisciplinarity is one of our things. So the question is not whether to be interdisciplinary, but how to be interdisciplinary. What kinds of interdisciplinarity does one validate, what interdisciplinary projects are interesting to pursue?

Mitchel Lasser:

I think, as a final tidbit, that I'd like to tell a story. It was a delightful moment at a conference that we had on comparative law in Utah two or three weeks ago. It happened on a panel on law and interdisciplinarity that I listened in on from the audience. One of the panelists ended his intervention by reading a passage from a book, which was clearly a very "theoretical" text, and then rereading the passage with a little twist. The gist of the passage was that literary theory had for too long stood in the shadow of philosophy; that literary theory was a discipline in its own right, and was worthy of study; that, actually, lit theory was perhaps more pragmatic in its knowledge than was philosophy; and that literary theory, therefore, might well be able to teach philosophy a thing or two. Then came the rereading. The rereading substituted literary theory for philosophy, and legal theory for literary theory. What had therefore been a critique of the proposition that philosophy is somehow superior to literary theory became a critique of the proposition that literary theory is somehow superior to legal theory.

I thought it was a terrific moment, especially since the panclist neglected, to the best of my recollection, to mention the source of the original passage. The source of the original passage, which was made to read as "legal theory is at least as good as lit theory," was actually the ultimate "lit theory" person. It was Paul De Man. The passage was from *The Resistance to Theory*.[18] The panelist, by the way, was Duncan. I find it amazing that David seems to have made the same point just now, namely, that legal theory shouldn't turn to lit theory because of some undeserved inferiority complex.

I have no position on the relative merits of disciplines. The move was nonetheless worth something because it added something to the disciplinary question which hadn't been there before. The effectiveness of the move, furthermore, was only heightened by the fact that it was originally coming from another discipline's talking about it's relation to yet another discipline.

Now, I don't know how many people attending the conference actually caught the reference. To some extent, I'm not sure that it really matters. Either way, it was both enlightening and encouraging to hear a "lit theory" person standing up to "philosophy" in the way that many "legal theory" people would like to stand up to "lit theory." Although I don't believe that philosophy is any more distinguishable from lit theory than lit theory is from legal theory, I still think that the move (the reading and rereading of this passage) was tactically and situationally effective. It was something that we all seem to be fond of, which is the recasting of questions in such a way that they suddenly acquire some new impetus. The questions don't really change, but the perspective does.

In terms of what I do, for example, I find it relatively tiresome to talk about judicial decisions in terms of realism versus formalism, pragmatism versus conceptualism, or judicial activism versus judicial restraint. I find those terms to be stale conceptual constructs; they're played out. I've found, on the other hand, whether in my written work or in my class, that if I recast the questions in terms in which they're not currently asked, the results are amazingly better, even though the questions may not actually be all that different. So that if I ask, "How does this judicial decision present itself? Does it present itself as a metaphor for the primary legal source, that is, does the decision claim to be standing in for that primary source on the basis of the decision's inherent similarity to that source? Or is it presenting itself as a metonym which stands in for the primary legal source on the basis of some claim that it's meaningfully related—but not inherently similar—to that primary source?" I've found, as an empirical matter, that the answers to such questions tend to be infinitely more powerful and insightful than those that I've gotten by asking whether a given judicial decision is "formalist" or "realist."

So the recasting of questions in the terms used by another discipline may accomplish no more than that; but it's something. I'm reluctant to say what the actual force of the move really is, except that it reinvigorates me as I ask a series of questions that legal academics have, I think, been asking for a very long time.

Maybe it's time to pass the buck to our respondents.

Norman Silber:

First I want to thank everybody who has spoken so far. It has been an extremely interesting conversation. Larry Kessler and I are new guests arriving late to the dinner table. We didn't know the structure the panelists would choose or the questions they would be posing. Nonetheless, there are a lot of different places to start from.

When Mitch was just talking, he said something like he takes "no position on the relative merit of the various disciplines." I think that's an interesting comment, because having no position about them *is* a position. It implies a certain relativism about discipline. It implies a certain egalitarianism about interdisciplinarity, which in itself carries with it certain problems. One problem is that—continuing Duncan's car metaphor—it allows you to steal the hubcaps from whatever car happens to be sitting at whatever street corner you've ended up at. The car might be a Yugo, or it might be a Mercedes—to push the analogy too far.

An example: I personally came to law with a Ph.D. in history. While I was a historian, but not a lawyer, I had completed an oral history with Herbert Wechsler about a number of subjects including the Nuremberg trial and the internment of the Japanese.[19] Roughly ten years later, after having been through law school, I decided to reedit as a law review article the interview I had done essentially as a historian.[20] Adopting the lens of a lawyer, suddenly a lot of the questions that I had asked as a historian I now dismissed—in much the same way my first year law professor dismissed me, when I was a student and raised a question and the law professor said "That's not the point" or "You haven't addressed the question" or "That's not the legal issue involved." And every time I picked up the lawyer's lens with the interview and looked at my own work, I was sitting smugly in judgment of myself. I knew exactly what discipline I was in. I was a trained lawyer now. I was going to analyze those other disciplines from the prism that I had obtained while I was a law student.

That attitude says to me something about what "interdisciplinarity" can mean to lawyers. Nathaniel Berman wrote something about the reasons why he had done his work—in a piece that I read of his, which I would like to read here. Not the piece in which Berman compares Picasso to Redslob,[21] but a piece about modernism in interwar Europe.[22] Berman gets to the end of the piece and states that "unlike traditional practitioners of American Law and Humanities studies, I'm not trying to enrich the law with cultural sophistication, rather I'm trying to show how the juxtaposition of law and other cultural domains can shed light on both, and in particular highlight the promises and dangers that are implicit in all forms of modernism."[23] If one asks the question, what is the purpose of Berman's exercise comparing Picasso to Redslob,[24] or comparing interwar political statements with artistic movements, it seems to me there is some ambiguity in the answer.

One purpose might be just to adorn and to ornament. Presumably a lot of law review literature is so intended because law reviews are anxious to have something that broadens their scope and makes them appear eclectic. I don't think that's what Berman is about. His task appears to be connecting legal theory to cultural preoccupations. To be frank, I see that the "juxtaposition of the law and other cultural domains" does "shed light on both and in particular highlight the promises and dangers implicit in all forms of modernism," but I personally would hope for more—for him to enlarge his stated purpose to include the identification of particular legal arguments that can or should be rejected or accepted.

This line of reflection leads me to ask what the purposes and dangers of interdisciplinary work are. I mean, I can rattle off a lot of reasons why I am a historian. I like to bring history to law because it might wake up the legal community by making it less insular and more self-aware. The students here in the audience have been to law school where we've trained them in Karl Lewellyn's way—you know, the *Bramble Bush* way; we've trained you to think "like a lawyer" and not to think in other ways. One wonderful thing about much interdisciplinary work is that it is taking those few who may be reading a law review article and shaking them up, saying "Think again about where you came from." It is providing creative insight to tell us the way the legal system really operates, to destroy its myths, to advocate particular paths of political change, to destablize texts. Some of the work has been terribly important and meaningful to me. But there remains too much of a gap between the abstract and the concrete in some of this work.

What has kept running through my mind as I was reading a number of these articles and preparing for this talk and listening here today is a Woody Allen movie (sorry to bring in a Woody Allen film). Woody Allen is around age twelve and he's sitting on a couch and he can't get any work done. His mother has taken him to a child psychologist. He is sitting there and he just can't act like a normal kid. He's terribly troubled because he reads in the paper that *the universe is expanding*, and he can't do any of his work, and his mother keeps shouting at him; she says, "*but it's not expanding in Brooklyn!*"

Allen could be critiquing us. We work in the world of law, and we have a world of lawyers who we need to speak to and learn from. Communication between theorists and lawyers who are practitioners is poor. As it is, practitioners are terribly suspicious of legal theory—whether it is about jurisprudence or fact finding or whatever. How much more, I mean, how much more suspicious not of legal theory but of advanced social theory out of a strange world that we're not even vaguely familiar with. It seems as though interdisciplinarity may be seen as the guerrilla assault on students and practitioners who, to choose for example, God knows, have no education in semiotics. I mean, our law students if they had semiotics as undergraduates are at least one step ahead of their faculty. So it is threatening to practitioners and to law students because interdisciplinary rhetoric is not in a vernacular—not in a special vocabulary—that they're trained in. Perhaps they should be, but the case must be made.

Which brings me to another problem with interdisciplinarity: the intrinsic difficulty of envisioning falsification of the views that are expressed by the people who are reading it. I mean somebody comes to you and says, "Read Clausewitz." Maybe we can read Clausewitz and enjoy it and profit from it, but our capacity for judging is taxed and impoverished when somebody comes and brings a foreign discipline to us and we're not accustomed to the new media or methodology. I'm reminded of the fact that in the 1930s when radio actually became universal, commercials were incredibly powerful. People had been accustomed to salesmanship in print, but they weren't accustomed to radio. The new coin of the realm assigned an exaggerated importance and commercial impact in the period in which people were adjusting to it. I think some interdisciplinarity has a lot of unwarranted shock value for the reason that it amounts to a new form of salesmanship. Well, that's my reaction to a very provocative conversation.

Lawrence Kessler:

I'm sort of at the end of the table, and I wasn't sure whether my placement here was to protect you from me or me from you. Of course, we've never met before, so you are certainly not familiar with me though I'm familiar with much of your works. I'm a trial lawyer who got to be a law professor; and when you talked about the relation between the arts and the law, I must say that my initial take was that you were talking about me. That is, I'm the artist; I'm the actor; I'm the person who looks interdisciplinarily to the psychologists for help with jury selection, to manipulate and influence the trier of fact; and I've been doing that for a couple of hundred years, though I look younger. When I was asked to participate as a commentator, I wasn't exactly sure what I was doing here since I am a teacher of, and someone who is much involved in, the area of trial advocacy, and I'm not, other than as someone who's come across your work in general reading, a student or a follower. I therefore thought it was peculiar to have been selected, and I figured they needed somebody else and that they were pretty desperate.

However, as I listen to you talk, and indeed as I read some of your works, it seemed to me that you were more the trial lawyer than I had initially thought. Indeed, as we talked about the strategy of using the external doctrines from other fields for the purpose of enhancing the political agenda that you have within the legal field, I was very comfortable with that. I mean, that's what I've been doing all the time, and that's what I do with juries, and that's what I do with judges as much as I possibly can.

Obviously, I can't be as comfortable in using the language of the other disciplines as you are because it is critically important for me to be immediately understood. I must tell you that since I felt I should prepare myself by reading as much of your works as I could, there certainly is a barrier constructed to communicating with people like me. I was absolutely delighted, however, as I sat here and listened to you, to find that many of the same ideas can be expressed without interposing that barrier. There was very little multisyllabic jargon that I wasn't familiar with; I understood all of the ideas. I must say that as I listen to you here and as I read your work, I wish that you would make more of an effort to make it accessible to me because I feel that I am part of your audience, and I'm not sure that I'm being appropriately coddled: I'm the jury.

But I did feel quite comfortable in listening to you, and I also felt that much of the problems I had reading some of the works were answered. That is, there had not seemed to be an exploration of the other fields. There tended to be a selection of a particular thinker, a distillation of his thought, and then the application of that thought to particular legal position. Of course, now that I see that it is persuasive argument, it certainly makes a great deal of sense. But it does lead me to ask the question, in terms of theoretical legal analysis, whether or not there isn't a separate role for understanding the legal system by reference to these other fields, as distinguished from just using these fields as the swords to destroy one's opponent in an argument involving nothing but the political left and right in the law.

Duncan Kennedy:

Seeing that I'm the one who has made the most of the political agenda, maybe I should respond. Thank you for the comments; they're really helpful and interesting. Let me put it this way. The question about the role for understanding is an interpretation of the abandoned car/hubcap image which is perfectly plausible. But I make a distinction, in my own mind, between two different activities. As I said before, there's a first activity which is policy-oriented advocacy. It's focused on trying to figure out both what legal rules ought to be and how they ought to be changed, and to intervening in actual legislative or judicial or academic policy debates. Then there's also the attempt to figure out, at least in my case, how legal argument works.

I'm starting from the idea—it's a very strong intuition—that legal argument is enormously flexible, open ended, and plastic. This is a perception that I'm sure you fully share. It's very hard to imagine that you could be both a practitioner and a professor who teaches in the field of trial advocacy without a very strong sense of the flexibility and malleability of legal discourse.

So the question is: How to account for the combination of that property of legal argument, as experienced by the practitioner and by the professor of trial advocacy, with the very common experience of compulsion produced by legal reasoning? This experience of compulsion is everywhere in the culture; a constant aspect of the culture is the belief that particular rules—whether they're rules that flow from constitutional rights or from property rights or whatever— are legitimate because they are the correct rules of law.

In approaching this question, I see the borrowing from other disciplines as borrowing for purposes of constructing a theory of legal argument, a theory of legal indeterminacy and of legal determinacy. In this respect, what Robin West said this morning about Robert Cover might be true of him, but it's certainly not true of the "crit" strand of the indeterminacy critique, which has put an enormous emphasis from the beginning on the experience of closure and determinacy as well as on the experience of indeterminacy. So there I see the borrowing as not "politically" motivated in any straightforward way. The borrowing is to try to get elements from the other theories that will be helpful in understanding legal discourse as something that's flexible but that also constantly generates intense feelings of determinacy and boundness. Methodological eclecticism or the scavenging approach isn't done piece by piece for political effect; it's done out of a very straightforwardly scientific curiosity about how to construct a good theory for understanding the relationship between advocacy and boundness as two different aspects of the experience of law.

So in my own case, I don't see myself as having, so to speak, reduced everything to the "political," partly because it seems to me to preserve the moment of cultural radicalism which can totally crosscut and indeed explode or under-mine "the political," and partly because it seems to me that the basic scientific endeavor—to figure out the most powerful way to conceptualize the relationship between a legal argument and a sentence, using these literary theoretical docu-ments—can all go on at the same time. I think it should be highly ambiguous when one is in the domain of political advocacy and when one is in the domain of science, and I know that I hope it will be.

Lawrence Kessler:

It certainly helps persuasiveness. If I might, I did have another thought and another question. It actually focuses more on a substantive notion and it relates back to something that Mitchel Lasser said, which is that "you're dealing with a car that I have some relationship to." I wonder if there isn't a relationship between the necessity for a myth of legitimacy and the legitimacy of the legal system, and whether or not a consistent attack on the myths isn't essentially nihilistic and does not, if accepted as a legitimate analysis of the system, eventually destroy or prevent the existence of the system.

Mitchel Lasser:

I think I'll give this question a quick answer. The answer, I guess, is that I don't understand the premises of the question, in that it ends up sounding dangerously similar to questions that were once addressed to, say, Copernicus. I think that most legal academics are totally into the analysis of a legal system's myths. I would personally say that I'm totally into that form of analysis, and totally into exposing the results of that analysis. Why this would have to be nihilistic escapes me. To the charge that the analysis might have, or that one might even hope that it would have, some result on the system, I would answer that having such an effect would be terrific. That's absolutely what I see myself as being in the business of trying to do.

I don't see, however, why such a project must lead to nihilistic results. One could run all sorts of specific analogies. Does the question imply that going after or exposing the myths of *any* legal system is necessarily nihilistic? What if the legal system is not one that you would particularly endorse; so that, for exam-ple, one would be running the myths on, say, assorted totalitarian Eastern Bloc or Latin American legal systems? If the analysis were actually to have some effect on such regimes, would this be a nihilistic or a reconstructive event? The same, I think, holds true of anything that one analyzes in any way. It depends on a whole bunch of factors, not the least would be the circumstances under which one engages in the project, the sense of responsibility that one feels towards one's analysis and the object of that analysis, and the ethics with which one engages in the project. I'm an optimist, so such projects sound reconstruc-tive, and not nihilistic, to me.

David Kennedy:

My own response to the nihilism question combines some testimony about my own state of mind with some sense for the situation within which critique of this sort occurs. One time when I worked as a duty lawyer in a child's court, I represented this kid who had broken into a lot of homes in a suburban neighborhood and had stolen all sorts of stuff. He was charged with breaking into three particular homes. When he was shown pictures of the three homes he was charged with having broken into, he defended himself by claiming that he'd broken into so many homes that he couldn't remember whether or not he'd actually broken into those particular ones. That seemed nihilistic to me; he had no relationship to any of the cars he was cannibalizing. For what it's worth, my own internal experience is quite different. I feel like a person living in a culture, meshed in a particular situation arising out of my relationship with lots of different texts, in which I am trying to do things and make arguments. It doesn't have that random or nihilistic feeling for me.

At the same time, I suppose I am less worried about nihilism because of my sense of the relative stability of our legal culture. If I thought that the situation was very unstable, that at any moment the legal system might unravel or people might stop believing in its myths, then I might get worried. I think our situation is rather one in which too many professionals who are part of my small corner of the culture, lawyers and law students, are believed too much and should be believed less. So this is a marginal nihilism.

The final thing I would like to say about nihilism would return to Duncan's point about the determinacy, as well as, the indeterminacy of legal discourse. In my own field of international law, for example, once one has shown that "sovereignty," is, say, contradictory or mythological, everything doesn't just collapse. On the contrary, the very next day they go out and invent another sovereignty while reminding you that they understood all along it was a myth. It's not just that the critique has been ineffective—it's that there is also a desire for sovereignty, a desire for closure, for formalism, and so forth, which can be obscured by the discipline's own posture of flexibility. We're talking about a legal culture of ambivalence, as much as contradiction. Part of the work is to explain the moments in which the culture takes a particular direction towards closure. As a result, the interdisciplinary borrowing is not always in the service of opening up—often it is in the service of explaining those moments when we feel resistance from the legal culture, a movement to closure that feels less rational or pragmatic than simply right.

Nathaniel Berman:

Let's directly address the frequent charges of the "nihilism" of "fancy theory." One of the reasons that much theoretical writing of the last two decades seems "fancy" is that it breaks with the notion that the only alternative to a linear account of history or legitimacy is an amoral nihilism. This break often requires complicated theoretical maneuvers. Yet, it is often those who seek to maintain linear accounts who may most properly be accused of diverting attention from moral responsibility.

International legal history provides very clear illustrations of this point. Postcolonial and feminist critics demonstrate that historical or political unity is usually the product of struggles in which competing stories and legitimacy's have been defeated, suppressed, or otherwise assimilated. Far from diverting us from theoretical or political responsibility, attention to "plural" histories and to the "identity-constitutive" role of power serves to deepen the gravity of the moral context of our work. If international legal history is not a linear progressive narrative, if the appearance of its historical and political unity is a product of struggle, then one cannot simply proceed with the naive faith that one is pushing forward "the project" of world order. Rather, one is always already situated in a situation of struggle between competing stories and legitimacies— in which every act, whether in scholarship or practice, constitutes a moral choice. From this perspective, it is the linear progress narratives which obscure the moral situatedness of the discipline.

Mitchel Lasser:

Professor Kessler?

Lawrence Kessler:

Thank you. I asked the question of you because I was interested in the answer. I must say that it's your most recent work that led me to think about the issue, when you wrote about the degree to which the French and American systems have managed essentially to maintain legitimacy and flexibility at the same time.[25]

Norman Silber:

I wanted to ask a question about responsibility. History is one discipline which is very easy for lawyers to poach upon. Probably for that reason there have been a large number of interdisciplinary attempts to write history by lawyers, discussions about inderdisciplinarity. Marty Flaherty has written a piece in the *Columbia Law Review*. The title of the piece is "History Lite."[26] He proceeds to sort of pass upon the way in which a number of leading scholars had all used history. I think it's not unfair to say that he basically comes down hard on several leading scholars and basically said that few, if any of them, took a historian's approach to history. To their fellow lawyers they might be a historian, but to a historian they are not conducting themselves as historians.

The question that I would ask would be, "Isn't there a responsibility for people who profess interdisciplinarity to vet or otherwise to go through some process which tests the quality of their work by norms of the discipline they're leaning on?" I mean when you submit these things to a law review editor at a student law review, one wonders whether or not they would be sufficient. How do we all make sure that what we're doing is respectable in the eyes of the people who are in the profession? This would be a question to Duncan, because you said you hoped these people you're borrowing from would die soon. I mean you don't want to know about the way other professions evolve? You're going to grab a scholar A and hope that B, C, D, and E pass on because you don't really want to know what is the latest?

Duncan Kennedy:

History is a good example. I'll start out with the question of vetting. I've actually written quite a bit of history of legal thought, and I dared publish a certain amount of it, moreover. So, how do you make sure that you're performing in a way that the people in their discipline would consider to be respectable, as opposed to "just not a historian's work"? My most basic reaction to that is, what do I care? I do have a profoundly contemptuous attitude toward the professional ethos of modern historians, just as I have a very contemptuous attitude toward the basic ethos of modern law review scholarship. I don't see them as any better. How do I know what that ethos is like, and what particular critique would I make of that ethos? I took courses in college; I read books, history books; I know some historians; I know quite a few of the people who do interdisciplinary legal history, most of whom went to graduate school and are intensely proud of the fact that although they are law professors, the legal history that they use in their law articles is "of the highest standards of their doctoral program." So although they aren't teaching history, they were trained in it; and their training is very important to them; and they would be profoundly humiliated if people with whom they went to graduate school, and who are now teaching history, were to treat their work as not living up to the standards that they were trained into.

My reaction to this group of people, of whom there are rather a large number—and I've had them both as students and as contemporaries in law schools—is that the unbelievably important aspects of their ethos could be summed up in a set of ideological propositions like "the worst thing you can be is presentist;" that's an unbelievably important part of the training. It's very like the law school training that you described as having taken something away from your own reaction to your own historical work, although it's a different deformation than the idea that, for example, all that's relevant is "What should the judge do? Everything else is irrelevant."

The antipresentist bias among historians produces a kind of ethic of not thinking about the past in terms of the present. "History might have an indirect effect, which might be the teaching effect or political effect you might achieve in the present; but you must maintain the discipline of not allowing your current objectives to distort the utter otherness of the past or to distort the at least hypothetical and completely exotic character of past light and past consciousness," and so on. I mean, "Give me a break!" is my basic reaction to that. Get to the end of the book! And it's done under the aegis of unbelievably tense and desperately serious presentism. You can figure out on page 50 that the guy's a moderate liberal who's arguing that *Roe v. Wade* is actually constitutional. It seems about as convincing as any other such argument.

Another one of the historian's ideological propositions is the fetishism of original sources; it's incredibly important to being a serious historian. It's like fieldwork for anthropologists. Original materials for historians is utterly central in their experience of their dignity as members of their profession, and the guy who goes and finds in New Jersey a building with 1 million documents that no one had ever found before, which were produced for an occasion a long time ago, this guy thinks, "They're utterly primary!" It's sort of like an associate at Cravath finding a treasure trove of all the IBM internal memos at the moment that the antitrust suit is getting hyped up. That's an *associate*, you know. Again, give me a break. I basically don't care about whether the person is great at finding primary sources. I'm interested in whether she has some interpretation of the past that seems like it's going to have a plausible impact on me in the present. This is the hubcap stealer's approach. No loyalty at all.

Norman Silber:

The problem once again may be that over time that approach can have a dangerous effect on the way in which the other discipline sees the legal profession's work and on profession's esteem in the eyes of the other discipline.

Duncan Kennedy:

We're starting from a low base, though.

Mitchel Lasser:

I have the feeling that, once again, we've set up a false dichotomy. I actually don't know the first thing about history, but I would absolutely bet dollars to doughnuts that there are three historians out there—make it four—who are more or less situated to the field of history in about the same way as we are to the field of law. It's not as if the field of history, as an academic discipline, is a monolithic mode of thought in which there's a single take on what's the appropriate methodology for, or subject of, historical work. I'm sure that there are people who are coming up with just the kinds of variance that we're coming up with. I really think that if one only knew the field well enough, it would be fairly easy to locate those people.

Now here's my reservation about the hubcaps. My reservation is that if you take the hubcaps, I wonder whether you're really taking them from your counterparts in the other field. Furthermore, I wonder about the transferability of the hubcap's resonance. You think you're getting a critical edge by taking it, but who knows? I had an interesting experience in France a little ways back. I was taking Bourdieu and doing something I thought new and nifty with his old stuff. So I found myself in France, in Paris as a matter of fact, and I was suddenly hit by the fact that the Bourdieu followers are actually an incredibly monolithic blob in French legal thought. And it turns out that these Bourdieu types are all "enlightened Eurotechnocrats," as the French press would call them. Now what do you do with that? If you feel a responsibility toward some project, the problem is to "vet" the person from whom to take the hubcap and to watch out about taking that hubcap—with all its resonances, connotations and associations—from someone you think is your double, but is not. The concern is: What does the hubcap take with it?

David Kennedy:

I want to agree with Norm's statement of the last problem. I think that there is a reputational issue that's also a strategic challenge. You don't want to put yourself in the situation of having somebody say your economics is bad if you're relying on economics as a theory for your argument. If somebody else has relied on economics in their article to prove some proposition or to open some particular strategy toward some legal doctrine, it's great if you can say, like in another Woody Allen movie: "Really? I have an economist right here! And it's Marshall McLuhan; and Marshall McLuhan says that philosophy is as slippery as a rock." I think the vulnerability to this sort of challenge is a problem with borrowing, which needs to be managed in an advocacy mode. You can't effectively keep borrowing if you adopt too aggressively the posture "Here's what the historians say. . . ." The parallel problem would be to say "This article is an application of Derrida's Third Principle that e = mc^2 backwards" when all the Derrida people would say "That's not his formula" and everyone else would say "Oh, Derrida, we know what's wrong with him." My own strategy for this is simply not to mention the guy. It also is in the jargon department. When students come to me with papers deducing something from their favorite college theorist, I often find myself saying "If you just eliminate the theorist on whom you feel the whole thing is based, your analysis is great."

Mitchel Lasser:

I'm going to step in for a second to ask the audience whether there are any questions you'd like to ask, if only for just a couple of minutes.

Audience Member:

I'm a communications professor with a very critical position toward my own field and toward the nature of my own discipline. I'm very concerned that scholars create little boxes for themselves in which it's very comfortable to operate, which allows them then to clone other scholars in the same form and shape. In other words, I wondered what you do in the classroom. I wondered, might you be able to translate what you've been saying into a kind of a very short philosophy of what you do to students, and do you wish to create those students in your own image?

David Kennedy:

Here's my short story. I want to take the class and divide it in half, with a remainder. The class should be divided on an important question and experience, the subject is open to broad debate, in which they feel the pull of both sides. The remainder should be two or three people out of the hundred and fifty who will be interested in working with me academically and might become graduate students.

Duncan Kennedy:

In other words, here is David's and my philosophy. There's a legal question. The students in the class argue opposite sides of it, and they experience that not as a merely technical debate but a debate in which the two sides represent larger commitments of their own, which might be liberal against conservative on the legal issue or it might be men against women on the legal issue or it might be North against South. But the classroom experience is designed to cut through their impulse to believe that the law is the law and that they're there to learn it, and to replace this impulse with an experience of legal discourse as something that they can learn to do argumentatively in a way that's deeply connected with their substantive ethical and political views.

David Kennedy:

So I always ask them to vote. We sometimes vote two or three times a day, and I feel that I've failed if I haven't generated a question on which the students are more or less evenly divided, in which both sides of the question have a force that the students are feeling. Across the course, they find themselves, individually and as a group, making commitments.

Susan Tiefenbrun:

I wish we could go on. I sense that we all could go on, and maybe we will at dinner. After dinner, we will all hopefully reconvene in the moot court room for *The Merchant of Venice* and the retrial of Shylock.

NOTES

1. *See* Duncan Kennedy, *A Semiotics of Legal Argument*, 42 SYRACUSE L. REV. 75 (1991).

2. GERARD GENETTE, FIGURES OF LITERARY DISCOURSE (Alan Sheridan, trans., 1982).

3. *See* ROMAN JAKOBSON, LANGUAGE IN LITERATURE (Kristina Pomorska and Stephen Rudy, eds., 1987).

4. *See* ROLAND BARTHES, MYTHOLOGIES (Annette Lavers, trans., 1972).

5. *See* PAUL DE MAN, ALLEGORIES OF READING (1979). *See also* PAUL DE MAN, THE RESISTANCE TO THEORY (1986).

6. *See* Wesley Hohfeld, *Some Fundamental Legal Conceptions as Applied in Judicial Reasoning*, 23 YALE L.J. 16 (1913).

7. *See e.g.*, David Kennedy, *Primitive Legal Scholarship*, 27 HARV. INT'L. L.J. 1 (1986); Anthony Anghie, *Franciso de Vitoria and the Colonial Origins of International Law*, 5 SOCIAL AND LEGAL STUDIES 321 (1996).

8. For an overview on feminist work in international law, *see* Karen Engle, *International Human Rights and Feminism: When Discourses Meet*, 13 MICH. J. INT'L L. 517 (1992).

9. *See, e.g.*, Karen Knop, THE MAKING OF DIFFERENCE IN INTERNATIONAL LAW: INTERPRETATION, IDENTITY AND PARTICIPATION IN THE DISCOURSE OF SELF-DETERMINATION (1997).

10. *See, e.g.*, Vasuki Nesiah, *Toward a Feminist Internationality*, 16 HARV. WOMEN'S L.L.J. 189 (1993).

11. *See, e.g.*, Michel Foucault, *Nietzche, Genealogy, History, in* LANGUAGE, COUNTER-MEMORY, PRACTICE 139 (Donald F. Bouchard & Sherry Simon trans., 1977).

12. Lila Abu-Lughod, *Writing against Culture, in* WRITING AGAINST CULTURE 137 (Richard Fox, ed., 1991).

13. *See, e.g.*, JAMES CLIFFORD, THE PREDICAMENT OF CULTURE (1988).

14. *See, e.g.*, HOMI K. BHABHA, THE LOCATION OF CULTURE (1994).

15. *See, e.g.*, JUDITH BUTLER, GENDER TROUBLE; FEMINISM AND THE SUBVERSION OF IDENTITY (1990).

16. *Id*. at 145.

17. Nathaniel Berman, *Modernism, Nationalism, and the Rhetoric of Reconstruction*, 13 CURRENT LEGAL THEORY 3 (1995).

18. *See* DE MAN, *supra* note 5.

19. *See* Norman Silber & Geoffrey Miller, *Towards "Neutral Principles" in the Law Selections from the Oral History of Herbert Wechsler*, 93 COLUM. L. REV. 854 (1993).

20. *Id*.

21. Nathaniel Berman, *Between "Alliance" and "Localization,"* 26 N.Y.U.J. INT'L L. & POL. 449 (1994).

22. Berman, "Modernism, Nationalism, and the Rhetoric of Reconstruction," *supra* note 17.

23. Berman, *"Alliance" and "Localization,"* *supra* note 21.

24. Berman, *"Modernism, Nationalism, and the Rhetoric of Reconstruction, supra* note 17.

25. Mitchel de S.-O.-l'E. Lasser, *Lit. Theory Put to the Test*, 111 HARV. L. REV. (1998).

26. Martin Flaherty, *"History Lite"* in *Modern American Constitutionalism*, 95 COLUM. L. REV 523 (1995).

Part V

Law and Shakespeare

11
Introduction to Interdisciplinarity and the Retrial of Shylock

Susan Tiefenbrun

You are about to embark on a fantastic voyage into the land of interdisciplinarity. This voyage leads to a crossroads of two ancient and well-traveled highways. The first of these highways is Literature with its many twists and turns, rules and regulations, which, if followed, may or may not lead to a work of art, a masterpiece like Shakespeare's *Merchant of Venice*. The other highway is Law, with its rules, its Constitution, its statutes, treaties, cases, which, if followed, may or may not lead to truth and justice. Where the two highways cross is the famous and disturbing trial of *Shylock v. Antonio*. By revisiting this trial, we are asking you who are gathered here tonight—lawyers, literary scholars, and lovers of Shakespeare—to think about the trial from two different points of view: that of the law and that of literature.

During the retrial of Shylock, you might want to think about the substantive and procedural legal issues that are reflected so artfully in the play. *Shylock v. Antonio* on appeal is a perfect case for a conflicts of law professor to use on an exam, but the law school student would probably classify it as a nightmare. What law applies in this case? Is it medieval Venetian law, Roman civil law, English common law, English law of equity, or is it New York law? Do we apply civil law or criminal law?

This trial is, above all, a literary work about the difference between appearances and reality, about duplicity, about revenge. The trial is set in the context of a romantic comedy—romantic because the play tells about love and marriage in the most romantic of all cities, Venice. Shakespeare captured the romantic quality of Italy when he carefully chose Italian names providing local color like Antonio, Bassanio, Lorenzo, Italian cities and places like Padua, Genoa, Rialto, and Italian words like *gondola*. The very sound of these names and words breathes romance into the play situated in *la bellissima Venezia*. And yet Antonio is not Antonio but Antonio, pronounced in the British manner, because this is a play written by an English playwright and infused with the beauty of the English language of the Elizabethan era.

The Merchant is a comedy because it ends happily for some, but tragically for others, like Shylock who is sentenced to convert to Christianity, forced into poverty and death by the inimical Alien Statute—which is nothing less than a racial law like the laws of Nuremberg and Vichy or our own Jim Crow laws. Shylock must give up all his property and goods by giving half his property to the state and the other half as a gift to his daughter, Jessica. All her life Jessica hated her father and was ashamed of her Jewishness, and she ultimately robbed her own father of his money and jewels to marry the Christian, Lorenzo, and to leave the Jewish faith. Shylock is subject to the Alien Statute because as a Jew Shylock is not permitted to be a Venetian citizen and is, therefore, classified as an alien. Because he is Jewish, throughout his life Shylock is forced to endure constant racial and religious slurs. He is called a "dog," a "demon," a "member of the Hebrew tribe," a "faithless Jew" by Antonio, the "good Christian," by Lorenzo, his soon to be Christian son-in-law, and by his slave, Launcelot, the Clown. Launcelot ultimately abandons his hated master, Shylock, because Launcelot fears he will himself become a Jew by mere association with a Jew. So Launcelot runs away to be the slave of a more humane Christian master.

This trial is, like many other great works of law and literature, a play about revenge, about the personal and lawful revenge of Shylock, the creditor, who inexplicably refuses to accept a pretrial settlement offer of twice and later three times the principal of the interest-free loan. Shylock, the moneylender, wants revenge from the debtor, Antonio, for several reasons. Shylock hates Antonio and hates the whole Christian community which has shunned Shylock all his life. Moreover, Shylock is mad with rage at his daughter who has just deceived him, stolen his money and jewels, and run off to marry and become, of all things, a Christian! It is these very Christians, Shylock claims, who call him a "cut-throat dog" simply because he is a Jew. It is the good Antonio who spat on Shylock. And now Shylock wants Antonio's "pound of fair flesh." Shylock claims he has the right to cut off Antonio's pound of flesh in accordance with the terms of a bond that the two contracting parties entered into legally.

Yes, believe it or not, this is a Shakespearean comedy, but it is like all great high comedies, close to tragedy, full of seriousness, and full of weighty legal issues like the legality of usury, the relative values of law and equity, the quality of mercy in justice, the liberty of contract, the folly of revenge, the proper use of wealth, the freedom to associate and to marry, and above all, it is about racial and religious discrimination.

Shylock represents the minority member who seeks protection in the clear, precise, written letter of the law, and who seeks comfort in the sanctity of contract. The play is about what happens when this good idea is carried too far. And Portia represents the judicial activist whose eloquent insistence on mercy underscores the power of judicial discretion. The play is about what happens when this good idea is carried too far. Shylock wants deadly specific performance for nonpayment of his contract—a pound of flesh—and insists on a literal interpretation of the law. He aligns himself with the rule of law: "I stand here for law," he cries (IV.i.145), "I crave the law," (IV.i.211). "If you deny me, fie upon your law!" (IV.i.103). Portia's ruling resides on an ironic dramatic reversal of Shylock's own belief in the justice of following black letter law. Portia's ruling is harsh. She is an imposter acting duplicitously as a judge with a conflict of interest. With power and authority, she turns Shylock's world topsy-turvy and arguably engineers the conviction of a member of the oppressed class. Some will claim that she is in flagrant violation of the Code of Judicial Conduct. But she and her passionate plea for mercy illustrate the tension between a rigidly literal interpretation of the law and the power of judicial discretion.

This play, as timely as it is today, was written in 1598 in response to a sensational trial that took place in Shakespeare's London in 1594. In that trial, the defendant was Roderigo Lopez, a converted Portugese Jew and the physician in chief to Queen Elizabeth herself, a very distinguished man, indeed. He unfortunately entangled himself in a Spanish plot to poison his mistress. He was tried and convicted despite his protestations of innocence, and on June 7, 1594, he was hanged, drawn, and quartered at Tyburn. Another source is Marlowe's earlier play written between 1589 and 1590, *The Jew of Malta*, which is about a wicked Jew who plotted, poisoned, and murdered, and who came to a horrible end, shrieking out curses as he was sentenced to die a slow death in a boiling cauldron of oil. Let us see tonight if our modern-day judges decide the case of *Shylock v. Antonio* on appeal any differently from Portia or from Marlowe's judge.

But before I turn the stage over to our actors, I just want to tell you that this play is so controversial, so racially sensitive, that it is no longer read by most high school students and is off the core list of great works in most colleges. Perhaps the retrial of *Shylock v. Antonio* tonight will whet your appetite to reread *The Merchant*—not for the same reasons of revenge that Shylock earnestly whet his knife—but for reasons of pleasure and inspiration. We hope that the retrial of Shylock will encourage you to think about the laws of literature and the literature of law.

12
The Trial of Shylock from *The Merchant of Venice*

Peter M. Sander

Act I, Scene 3, lines 100–177; Act IV, Scene 1, lines 16–103, 172–260, 294–393.

Peter M. Sander (Narrator)

Actors

Arlene Sterne, as Portia

Peter M. Sander, as Shylock

Jason O'Connell, as Antonio

Laura Cohen, as Bassanio

Richard H. Weisberg, as Duke

William Ginsberg, as Gratiano

The Trial of Shylock from
The Merchant of Venice[1]

NARRATION

Bassanio, a young lord, wants to woo the rich heiress Portia, but he is short of
cash. He begs his friend Antonio, a Venetian merchant, to bankroll him. Antonio's money, however, is tied up at sea, so the merchant agrees to borrow funds
from Shylock, a Jewish moneylender, for Bassanio's expedition.

(ACT I, Scene 3, 100–177)

ANTONIO

Well, Shylock, shall we be beholding to you?

SHYLOCK

Signior Antonio, many a time and oft
In the Rialto you have rated me
About my moneys and my usances:
Still have I borne it with a patient shrug,
(For suff'rance is the badge of all our tribe)
You call me misbeliever, cut-throat dog,
And spet upon my Jewish gabardine,
And all for use of that which is mine own.
Well then, it now appears you need my help:
Go to then, you come to me, and you say,
"Shylock, we would have moneys," you say so:
You that did void your rheum upon my beard,
And foot me as you spurn a stranger cur
Over your threshold, moneys is your suit.
What should I say to you? Should I not say
"Hath a dog money? Is it possible
A cur can lend three thousand ducats?" or
Shall I bend low, and in a bondman's key
With bated breath, and whisp'ring humbleness
Say this:
"Fair sir, you spet on me on Wednesday last,
You spurn'd me such a day, another time
You call'd me dog: and for these courtesies
I'll lend you thus much moneys"?

ANTONIO

I am as like to call thee so again,
To spet on thee again, to spurn thee too.
If thou wilt lend this money, lend it not
As to thy friends, for when did friendship take
A breed for barren metal of his friend?
But lend it rather to thine enemy,
Who, if he break, thou may'st with better face
Exact the penalty.

SHYLOCK

Why look you how you storm!
I would be friends with you, and have your love,
Forget the shames that you have stained me with,
Supply your present wants, and take no doit
Of usance for my moneys, and you'll not hear me,—
This is kind I offer.

BASSANIO

This were kindness.

SHYLOCK

This kindness will I show,
Go with me to a notary, seal me there
Your single bond, and (in a merry sport)
If you repay me not on such a day
In such a place, such sum or sums as are
Express'd in the condition, let the forfeit
Be nominated for an equal pound
Of your fair flesh, to be cut off and taken
In what part of your body pleaseth me.

ANTONIO

Content in faith, I'll seal to such a bond,
And say there is much kindness in the Jew.

BASSANIO

You shall not seal to such a bond for me,

I'll rather dwell in my necessity.

ANTONIO

Why fear not man, I will not forfeit it,—
Within these two months, that's a month before
This bond expires, I do expect return
Of thrice three times the value of this bond.

SHYLOCK

O father Abram, what these Christians are,
Whose own hard dealings teaches them suspect
The thoughts of others! Pray you tell me this,—
If he should break his day what should I gain
By the exaction of the forfeiture?
A pound of a man's flesh taken from a man,
Is not so estimable, profitable neither
As flesh of muttons, beefs, or goats,—I say
To buy his favor, I extend this friendship,—
If he will take it, so,—if not, adieu,
And for my love I pray you wrong me not.

ANTONIO

Yes Shylock, I will seal unto this bond.

SHYLOCK

Then meet me forthwith at the notary's,
Give him direction for this merry bond—
And I will go and purse the ducats straight,
See to my house left in the fearful guard
Of an unthrifty knave: and presently
I'll be with you.

ANTONIO

Hie thee gentle Jew.
The Hebrew will turn Christian, he grows kind.

BASSANIO

I like not fair terms, and a villain's mind.

ANTONIO

Come on, in this there can be no dismay,
My ships come home a month before the day.   *Exeunt.*

NARRATION

Antonio's goods are reported lost at sea, and he defaults on Shylock's loan.
In the meantime, Shylock's daughter Jessica elopes with one of Antonio's
friends, stealing most of her father's valuables. This is the final straw for
Shylock, who has long borne abuse from Antonio and his circle. He brings
Antonio to court and demands that the Duke honor the terms of the bond.

(ACT IV, Scene 1, 16–103)

DUKE

Make room, and let him stand before our face.
Shylock the world thinks, and I think so too,
That thou but leadest this fashion of thy malice
To the last hour of act, and then 'tis thought
Thou'lt show thy mercy and remorse more strange
Than is thy strange apparent cruelty;
And where thou now exacts the penalty,
Which is a pound of this poor merchant's flesh,
Thou wilt not only loose the forfeiture,
But touch'd with human gentleness and love,
Forgive a moiety of the principal,
Glancing an eye of pity on his losses
That have of late so huddled on his back,
Enow to press a royal merchant down,
And pluck commiseration of his state
From brassy bosoms and rough hearts of flint,
From stubborn Turks, and Tartars never train'd
To offices of tender courtesy:
We all expect a gentle answer Jew!

SHYLOCK

I have possess'd your grace of what I purpose,
And by our holy Sabbath have I sworn
To have the due and forfeit of my bond,—
If you deny it, let the danger light
Upon your charter and your city's freedom!

You'll ask me why I rather choose to have
A weight of carrion flesh, than to receive
Three thousand ducats: I'll not answer that!
But say it is my humour,—is it answer'd?
What if my house be troubled with a rat,
And I be pleas'd to give ten thousand ducats
To have it ban'd? what, are you answer'd yet?
Some men there are love not a gaping pig!
Some that arc mad if they behold a cat!
And others when the bagpipe sings i'th'nose,
Cannot contain their urine—for affection
(Master of passion) sways it to the mood
Of what it likes or loathes,—now for your answer:
As there is no firm reason to be rend'red
Why he cannot abide a gaping pig,
Why he a harmless necessary cat,
Why he a woollen bagpipe, but of force
Must yield to such inevitable shame,
As to offend himself being offended;
So can I give no reason, nor I will not,
More than a lodg'd hate, and a certain loathing
I bear Antonio, that I follow thus
A losing suit against him!—are you answered?

BASSANIO

This is no answer thou unfeeling man,
To excuse the current of thy cruelty.

SHYLOCK

I am not bound to please thee with my answers!

BASSANIO

Do all men kill the things they do not love?

SHYLOCK

Hates any man the thing he would not kill?

BASSANIO

Every offence is not a hate at first!

SHYLOCK

What! wouldst thou have a serpent sting thee twice?

ANTONIO

I pray you think you question with the Jew,—
You may as well go stand upon the beach
And bid the main flood bate his usual height,
You may as well use question with the wolf,
Why he hath made the ewe bleak for the lamb:
You may as well forbid the mountain pines
To wag their high tops, and to make no noise
When they are fretten with the gusts of heaven;
You may as well do anything most hard
As seek to soften that—than which what's harder:—
His Jewish heart! Therefore (I do beseech you)
Make no more offers, use no farther means,
But with all brief and plain conveniency
Let me have judgment, and the Jew his will!

BASSANIO

For thy three thousand ducats here is six!

SHYLOCK

If every ducat in six thousand ducats
Were in six parts, and every part a ducat,
I would not draw them, I would have my bond!

DUKE

How shalt thou hope for mercy rend'ring none?

SHYLOCK

What judgment shall I dread doing no wrong?
You have among you many a purchas'd slave,
Which (like your asses, and your dogs and mules)
You use in abject and in slavish parts,
Because you bought them,—shall I say to you,
Let them be free, marry them to your heirs?
Why sweat they under burdens? let their beds

Be made as soft as yours, and let their palates
Be season'd with such viands? you will answer
"The slaves are ours,"—so do I answer you:
The pound of flesh which I demand of him
Is dearly bought, 'tis mine and I will have it:
If you deny me, fie upon your law!
There is no force in the decrees of Venice:
I stand for judgment,—answer, shall I have it?

NARRATION

Portia, now engaged to Bassanio, is determined to rescue Antonio. She gives
her fiancé three times the value of the bond to pay Shylock off, disguises
herself as a young man, the lawyer Bellario, and arranges to act as judge in
the proceedings.

(ACT IV, Scene 1, 172–260)

DUKE

Antonio and old Shylock, both stand forth.

PORTIA

Is your name Shylock?

SHYLOCK

Shylock is my name.

PORTIA

Of a strange nature is the suit you follow,
Yet in such rule, that the Venetian law
Cannot impugn you as you do proceed.
You stand within his danger, do you not?

ANTONIO

Ay, so he says.

PORTIA

Do you confess the bond?

ANTONIO

I do.

PORTIA

Then must the Jew be merciful.

SHYLOCK

On what compulsion must I? Tell me that.

PORTIA

The quality of mercy is not strain'd,
It droppeth as the gentle rain from heaven
Upon the place beneath: it is twice blest,
It blesseth him that gives, and him that takes,
'Tis mightiest in the mightiest, it becomes
The throned monarch better than his crown.
His sceptre shows the force of temporal power,
The attribute to awe and majesty,
Wherein doth sit the dread and fear of kings:
But mercy is above the sceptred sway,
It is enthroned in the heart of kings,
It is an attribute to God himself;
And earthly power doth then show likest God's
When mercy seasons justice: therefore Jew,
Though justice be thy plea, consider this,
That in the course of justice, none of us
Should see salvation: we do pray for mercy,
And that same prayer, doth teach us all to render
The deeds of mercy. I have spoke thus much
To mitigate the justice of thy plea,
Which if thou follow, this strict court of Venice
Must needs give sentence 'gainst the merchant there.

SHYLOCK

My deeds upon my head! I crave the law,
The penalty and forfeit of my bond.

PORTIA

Is he not able to discharge the money?

BASSANIO

Yes, here I tender it for him in the court,
Yea, twice the sum,—if that will not suffice,
I will be bound to pay it ten times o'er
On forfeit of my hands, my head, my heart,—
If this will not suffice, it must appear
That malice bears down truth. And I beseech you
Wrest once the law to your authority,—
To do a great right, do a little wrong,—
And curb this cruel devil of his will.

PORTIA

It must not be, there is no power in Venice
Can alter a decree established:
'Twill be recorded for a precedent,
And many an error by the same example
Will rush into the state,—it cannot be.

SHYLOCK

A Daniel come to judgment: yea a Daniel!
O wise young judge how I do honour thee!

PORTIA

I pray you let me look upon the bond.

SHYLOCK

Here 'tis most revered doctor, here it is.

PORTIA

Shylock there's thrice thy money off'red thee.

SHYLOCK

An oath, an oath. I have an oath in heaven,—
Shall I lay perjury upon my soul?
No not for Venice.

PORTIA

Why this bond is forfeit,
And lawfully by this the Jew may claim
A pound of flesh to be by him cut off
Nearest the merchant's heart: be merciful,
Take thrice thy money, bid me tear the bond.

SHYLOCK

When it is paid, according to the tenour.
It doth appear you are a worthy judge,
You know the law, your exposition
Hath been most sound: I charge you by the law,
Whereof you are a well-deserving pillar,
Proceed to judgment: by my soul I swear,
There is no power in the tongue of man
To alter me,—I stay here on my bond.

ANTONIO

Most heartily, I do beseech the court
To give the judgment.

PORTIA

Why then thus it is,—
You must prepare your bosom for his knife.

SHYLOCK

O noble judge! O excellent young man!

PORTIA

For the intent and purpose of the law
Hath full relation to the penalty,
Which here appeareth due upon the bond.

SHYLOCK

'Tis very true: O wise and upright judge,
How much more elder art thou than thy looks!

PORTIA

Therefore lay bare your bosom.

SHYLOCK

Ay, his breast
So says the bond, doth it not noble judge?
"Nearest his heart," those are the very words.

PORTIA

It is so,—are there balance here to weigh
The flesh?

SHYLOCK

I have them ready.

PORTIA

Have some surgeon Shylock on your charge,
To stop the wounds, lest he do bleed to death.

SHYLOCK

Is it so nominated in the bond?

PORTIA

It is not so express'd, but what of that?
'Twere good you do so much for charity.

SHYLOCK

I cannot find it, 'tis not in the bond.

PORTIA

You merchant, have you any thing to say?

ANTONIO

But little; I am arm'd and well prepar'd,—

(ACT IV, Scene 1, 294–393)

SHYLOCK

We trifle time, I pray thee pursue sentence.

PORTIA

A pound of that same merchant's flesh is thine,
The court awards it, and the law doth give it.

SHYLOCK

Most rightful judge!

PORTIA

And you must cut this flesh from off his breast,
The law allows it, and the court awards it.

SHYLOCK

Most learned judge! a sentence, come prepare.

PORTIA

Tarry a little, there is something else,—
This bond doth give thee here no jot of blood,
The words expressly are "a pound of flesh":
Take then thy bond, take thou thy pound of flesh,
But in the cutting it, if thou dost shed
One drop of Christian blood, thy lands and goods
Are (by the laws of Venice) confiscate
Unto the state of Venice.

GRATIANO

O upright judge!—
Mark, Jew,—O learned judge!

SHYLOCK

Is that the law?

PORTIA

Thyself shalt see the act:
For as thou urgest justice, be assur'd
Thou shalt have justice more than thou desir'st.

GRATIANO

O learned judge!—mark Jew, a learned judge.

SHYLOCK

I take this offer then,—pay the bond thrice
And let the Christian go.

BASSANIO

Here is the money.

PORTIA

Soft!
The Jew shall have all justice,—soft, no haste!
He shall have nothing but the penalty.

GRATIANO

O Jew! an upright judge, a learned judge!

PORTIA

Therefore prepare thee to cut off the flesh,—
Shed thou no blood, nor cut thou less nor more
But just a pound of flesh: if thou tak'st more
Or less than a just pound, be it but so much
As makes it light or heavy in the substance,
Or the division of the twentieth part
Of one poor scruple, nay if the scale do turn
But in the estimation of a hair
Thou diest, and all they goods are confiscate.

GRATIANO

A second Daniel, a Daniel, Jew!—

Now infidel I have you on the hip.

PORTIA

Why doth the Jew pause? take thy forfeiture.

SHYLOCK

Give me my principal, and let me go.

BASSANIO

I have it ready for thee, here it is.

PORTIA

He has refus'd it in the open court,
He shall have merely justice and his bond.

GRATIANO

A Daniel still say I, a second Daniel!—
I thank thee Jew for teaching me that word.

SHYLOCK

Shall I not have barely my principal?

PORTIA

Thou shalt have nothing but the forfeiture
To be so taken at thy peril Jew.

SHYLOCK

Why then the devil give him good of it:
I'll stay no longer question.

PORTIA

Tarry Jew,
The law hath yet another hold on you.
It is enacted in the laws of Venice,
If it be proved against an alien,

That by direct, or indirect attempts
He seek the life of any citizen,
The party 'gainst the which he doth contrive,
Shall seize one half his goods, the other half
Comes to the privy coffer of the state,
And the offender's life lies in the mercy
Of the Duke only, 'gainst all other voice.
In which predicament I say thou stand'st:
For it appears by manifest proceeding,
That indirectly, and directly too,
Thou hast contrived against the very life
Of the defendant: and thou hast incurr'd
The danger formerly by me rehears'd.
Down therefore, and beg mercy of the duke.

GRATIANO

Beg that thou may'st have leave to hang thyself,—
And yet thy wealth being forfeit to the state,
Thou hast not left the value of a cord,
Therefore thou must be hang'd at the state's charge.

DUKE

That thou shalt see the difference of our spirit
I pardon thee thy life before thou ask it:
For half thy wealth, it is Antonio's,
The other half comes to the general state,
Which humbleness may drive unto a fine.

PORTIA

Ay for the state, not for Antonio.

SHYLOCK

Nay, take my life and all, pardon not that,—
You take my house, when you do take that prop
That doth sustain my house: you take my life
When you do take the means whereby I live.

PORTIA

What mercy can you render him Antonio?

GRATIANO

A halter gratis, nothing else for Godsake!

ANTONIO

So please my lord the duke, and all the court,
To quit the fine for one half of his goods,
I am content: so he will let me have
The other half in use, to render it
Upon his death unto the gentleman
That lately stole his daughter.
Two things provided more, that for this favour
He presently become a Christian:
The other, that he do record a gift
(Here in the court) of all he dies possess'd
Unto his son Lorenzo and his daughter.

DUKE

He shall do this, or else I do recant
The pardon that I late pronounced here.

PORTIA

Art thou contented Jew? what dost thou say?

SHYLOCK

I am content.

PORTIA

Clerk, draw a deed of gift.

SHYLOCK

I pray you give me leave to go from hence,
I am not well,—send the deed after me,
And I will sign it.

DUKE

Get thee gone, but do it.

Exit [Shylock].

NOTE

1. *The Arden Shakespeare*, ed. by John Russell Brown, London & New York: Methuen, 1955.

13
Appellant's Brief

SPECIAL COURT OF APPEALS

———————————————————————— x

SHYLOCK,

      Appellant

   -against-

ANTONIO,

      Appellee

———————————————————————— x

DANIEL J. KORNSTEIN[1]
Attorney for Appellant
757 Third Avenue
New York, N.Y., 10017
(212) 418-8600

TABLE OF CONTENTS

Prejudice is never pretty, particularly when it infects a legal proceeding. Yet such ugly prejudice—in the form of virulent anti-Semitism—irreparably marred the trial below. The facts in this simple breach of contract case are undisputed. Appellant Shylock loaned money to appellee Antonio, a wealthy importer, who failed to repay on time. Shylock sued to enforce a written loan agreement. Their contract stated that if the borrower missed his payment, then the lender was entitled to a penalty.

At least it was a simple contract case until the biased impostor of a trial judge complicated matters unnecessarily and, in a fit of raw judicial activism, decided in Antonio's favor. The trial court in effect declared the penalty clause void against public policy, which by itself was unremarkable. But then the lower court went on to nullify the entire contract, subvert stability and certainty in commercial transactions, and, relying on an unconstitutional law, impose cruel and unusual punishments on appellant, who had merely kept his part of the bargain.

Invoking the notorious Alien Statute, the trial judge awarded half of appellant's assets to the State and half to Antonio, who said he would only "use" his half as long as Shylock lived. But, on Shylock's death, all Shylock owned had to pass to appellant's estranged daughter. The trial judge, at Antonio's specific request, also compelled appellant, a Jew, to convert to Christianity or die. (4.1.359-405).

No wonder appellant, in understandable disbelief, asked, "Is that the law?" (4.1.311). Now this court has the chance to tell him and the rest of the world: It is not.

ARGUMENT

I. SINCE ANTI-SEMITISM TAINTED THE TRIAL, THE LOWER COURT DECISION VIOLATED THE EQUAL PROTECTION CLAUSE

Rampant anti-Semitism ruined the trial below. The community in general, the witnesses, and even the trial judge were all blinded by religious prejudice. The judge herself more than once referred to appellant not by name but by the epithet "Jew." This prejudice is indisputable. *See, e.g.*, James Shapiro, *Shakespeare and the Jews* (1996); John Gross, *Shylock* (1993); Harold Bloom, "Operation Roth," *N.Y. Rev. of Books* (Apr. 22, 1993) 45, 48 ("an anti-Semitic masterpiece, unmatched in its kind"). Amid such deep and widespread prejudice, appellant could not and did not get a fair trial. *See Moore v. Dempsey*, 261 U.S. 86 (1923) (reversal where legal proceeding is a "mask" and judge is swept away by "an irresistible wave of public passion").

The general pall of thick prejudice became specific when the trial court relied on an outrageous and obviously unconstitutional law, the Alien Statute. That statute provides, in pertinent part:

> If it be prov'd against an alien
> That by direct or indirect attempts
> He seek the life of any citizen,
> The party 'gainst the which he doth contrive
> Shall seize one half his goods; the other half
> Comes to the privy coffer of the state;
> And the offender's life lies in the mercy
> Of the duke only, 'gainst all other voice.
>
> (4.1.360–67)

The Alien Statute, on its face and as applied, unlawfully discriminates against appellant by deeming him an alien by virtue of his religion and by treating him differently for that impermissible reason.

By singling out aliens for such treatment, and by using appellant's religion as a badge of alienage, the Alien Statute denies equal protection of the laws. *See Romer v. Evans*, 116 S. Ct. 1620 (1996) (voiding, on equal protection grounds, state constitutional amendment prohibiting laws protecting homosexuals against discrimination); Peter J. Alscher, "Staging Directions for a Balanced Resolution to the Merchant of Venice Trial Scene," 5 *Cardozo Studs. in Law & Lit.* 1 (1993). The statute is subject to strict scrutiny and cannot be justified by any possible governmental interest, much less a compelling one. It raises "the inevitable inference that the disadvantage imposed is born of animosity toward the class of persons affected," which "cannot constitute a *legitimate* governmental interest." *Romer, supra*, at 1628, *quoting Department of Agriculture v. Moreno*, 413 U.S. 528, 534 (1973).

By virtue of this law, a Jew does not have the same rights as a citizen of Venice. It constitutes unequal treatment by the State, takes away the civil rights of Jews, and deprives Jews of the rights to private property. The obnoxious Alien Statute thus joins the Nuremburg laws, Jim Crow laws, and South African apartheid laws as repugnant to basic notions of decency.

II. SINCE THE TRIAL "JUDGE" WAS MARRIED TO ANTONIO'S BEST FRIEND (FOR WHOM THE LOAN WAS MADE) AND WAS NEITHER A LAWYER NOR A JUDGE, SHE WAS BIASED AND INCOMPETENT

Appellant was entitled to an impartial judge, and Portia was neither impartial nor a judge. A party is deprived of due process of law when his or her liberty or property is subject to the decision of a judge who has a personal or pecuniary interest in the outcome. *Tumey v. Ohio*, 273 U.S. 510 (1927). Portia violated Canon 2B of the *Code of Judicial Conduct* by allowing her "family, social or other relationships to influence" her judicial conduct or judgment. She should have recused herself under Canon 3 C(1)(a) of the *Code of Judicial Conduct*, because her impartiality "might reasonably be questioned" inasmuch as she "has a personal bias or prejudice concerning a party, or personal knowledge of disputed evidentiary facts concerning the proceedings."

And of course Portia committed a crime by impersonating a judge and practicing law without a license. *N.Y. Judiciary L.* §478 (unlawful practice of law); §484 (same); §492 (use of attorney's name—Balthasar—by Portia).

III. SINCE APPELLANT WAS ORDERED IN A CIVIL CASE TO PAY OVER ALL HIS PROPERTY AND CONVERT TO ANOTHER RELIGION, THE JUDGMENT BELOW CONSTITUTED CRUEL AND UNUSUAL PUNISHMENT AND VIOLATED DUE PROCESS

Appellant's civil suit on a loan agreement should never have ended up in severe criminal penalties against him. He received no prior notice of any criminal charges. The trial judge trotted out the criminal statute for the first time in the middle of the trial. This alone violates due process.

By any measure, the severe penalties actually imposed on appellant constitute cruel and unusual punishment. They degrade the dignity of humans beings, they are arbitrary, they are unacceptable to contemporary society, and they are excessive. *See Furman v. Georgia*, 408, U.S. 238, 270–82 (1972) (Brennan, J. concurring).

IV. SINCE THE TRIAL "JUDGE" IMPROPERLY REQUIRED PLAINTIFF TO CONVERT TO CHRISTIANITY, THE COURT VIOLATED THE FIRST AMENDMENT'S FREE EXERCISE AND ESTABLISHMENT CLAUSES

Freedom of religion means that the trial court's order to appellant that he convert to another religion is null and void. That order simultaneously violates both aspects of the Religion Clause. It abridges appellant's freedom to worship in the religion of his own choice and it "force[s] him to profess a belief" in a particular religion. *Everson v. Board of Education*, 330 U.S. 1, 15 (1947).

V. SINCE APPELLANT WAIVES SPECIFIC PERFORMANCE OF THE PENALTY CLAUSE, THE REST OF THE CONTRACT IS ENFORCEABLE AND APPELLANT IS ENTITLED TO PRINCIPAL PLUS INTEREST

Appellant no longer seeks his pound of flesh. Even during the trial, appellant stated: "Give me my principal, and let me go" (4.1.348). With that controversial issue waived and therefore out of the case, appellant is entitled to principal and interest.

The whole controversy over the equitable remedy of specific performance of the penalty clause could have been easily avoided. All the trial judge had to do was find that Shylock had an adequate remedy at law for damages (*i.e.*, principal and interest) and award those damages, while denying specific performance. In not doing so, the court below erred by failing to enforce the contract, thereby jeopardizing stability and certainty in commercial law, a point conceded by both Antonio and Portia (3.3.26-31; 4.1.215-19).

To deny appellant principal and interest would, moreover, give appellee a tremendous windfall. Three of his ships did return safely, after the trial, with huge profit to Antonio (5.1.295-96). In such circumstances, it would be unjust in the extreme to deny appellant recovery. The safe return of Antonio's three ships supplies a basis for mutual mistake—everyone was under the misimpression that they were lost. Now Antonio can pay the debt.

CONCLUSION

Appellant was victimized and degraded in the trial court. The decision below, as many have noted, embodies raw anti-Semitism and encourages persecution against Jews. This court, however, should assert itself and strike a blow for freedom of religion, liberty of contract, and equal protection of the laws.

At one point during the proceedings, Shylock movingly asked: "Hath not a Jew eyes?" (3.1.52). On behalf of him and all other minority members, we now ask this court: Hath not a Jew (or any other minority member) rights?

For the reasons given, the Alien Statute should be declared unconstitutional, the judgment below should be reversed, appellant should be awarded principal plus interest, and the court should make a criminal reference to the attorney general about Portia impersonating a judge and practicing law without a license. *N.Y. Judiciary L.* §476–a.

As appellant rightly exclaimed below: "If you deny me, fie upon your law!" (4.1.100).

Dated: New York, New York
September 9, 1996

Respectfully submitted,

DANIEL J. KORNSTEIN
Attorney for Appellant
757 Third Avenue
New York, N.Y. 10017
(212) 418-8600

NOTES

Material from this chapter is based on an earlier work by Daniel Kornstein, *Kill All the Lawyers* (Princeton: Princeton University Press, 1984).

1. Although Shylock naively represented himself *pro se* at trial, on appeal he is aided by the guiding hand of counsel.

14
Appellee's Brief

HOFSTRA LAW AND THE ARTS SYMPOSIUM
SPECIAL COURT OF APPEALS

———————————————————————— x

SHYLOCK,

                              Appellant

            -against-

ANTONIO,

                              Appellee

———————————————————————— x

FLOYD ABRAMS
Attorney for Appellee
Cahill Gordon & Reindel
(a partnership including
a professional corporation)
80 Pine Street
New York, N.Y., 10005
(212) 701-3000

This article is reprinted with permission from the October 30, 1996 issue of the *New York Law Journal* © 1996 NLP IP Company.

TABLE OF CONTENTS

INTRODUCTION

Shakespeare's *The Merchant of Venice* bears the Bard's allegorical flourish. One commentator has called the play the "most ingenious satire on justice and the courts of law in the literature of the world." H. Sinsheimer, Shylock 139 (1947). Another observed that the play was a "fairy tale" with "no more reality in Shylock's bond and the Lord of Belmont's will than in Jack and the Beanstalk." John Russell Brown, Introduction to *The Merchant of Venice* 1 (John Russel Brown ed., 1994) *quoting* Granville-Barker, Prefaces 67 (2d series 1930).

Shakespeare's characters and words vividly remind readers of the difference between appearance and reality. His characters themselves caution readers against accepting appearances as truth. Antonio speaks such a warning to friend Bassanio:

> The devil can cite Scripture for his purpose,—
> An evil soul producing holy witness
> Is like a villain with a smiling cheek,
> A goodly apple rotten at the heart.
> O what a goodly outside falsehood hath! (II. iii.92-97).

Similar warnings are present elsewhere in the text: "[a]ll that glisters is not gold" (II. vii.65) and "[g]ilded tombs do worms infold" (II. vii.69). So we must take care not to engage in any reading of *The Merchant of Venice* that is too literal—or too contemporaneous. The Venetian trial described—replete with the "male judge" played by a disguised woman who was a close friend of the witness Bassanio—could not even had occurred in sixteenth-century Venice, let alone in near-twenty-first-century United States.[1] Shakespeare was a genius, not a lawyer.

It is thus error, appellee Antonio respectfully asserts, to accept the text or the play's happenings too much at face value. It would also be a mistake to examine the trial court's decision through the unforgivingly politically correct lens of contemporary legal and social mores as appellant does when he goes so far as to object to Portia's making believe she was a judge. Appellant's Brief at 3-4. Are we next to be told that Hamlet was played by an actor and was not actually a prince?

In the end, however, Shylock's problems stem not from his brief but his conduct. One could read appellant's papers in vain without the slightest perception of what Shylock intended to *do* to Antonio: cut off "an equal pound of [his] fair flesh . . . taken/In what part of [his] body pleaseth me" (I.iii.145-47). Or, to put it a bit more concretely, to murder Antonio simply because he repaid a loan a bit late. As we recall, the Shakespearean image of Shylock earnestly whetting his knife (IV.i.121), we must not forget what he intended to do with it.

ARGUMENT

I. THE ANTONIO-SHYLOCK CONTRACT IS UNENFORCEABLE AS A MATTER OF PUBLIC POLICY AND NO PROVISION IS SEVERABLE

The contract at issue stated:

> If you repay me not on such a day,
> In such a place, such sum or sums as are
> Exprest in the condition, let the forfeit
> Be nominated for an equal pound
> Of your fair flesh, to be cut off and taken
> In what part of your body pleaseth me.
> (I.iii.144)

A contract based on an unlawful promise is unenforceable. 22 John D. Calamari & Joseph M. Perillo, *Contracts* 889 (3d ed. 1987). At common law, it was said "[n]o court will lend its aid to a man who founds his cause of action upon an immoral or an illegal act." E. Allan Farnsworth, 2 *Farnsworth on Contracts* §5 (1990), *quoting Holman v. Johnson*, 1 Cowp. 341, 343, 98 Eng. Rep. 1120, 1121 (1775).

Similarly, it is well established that a court will not enforce a contract which contains two promises, one lawful and one unlawful, if the unlawful promise is so "heinous in character" such that it colors the whole. Arthur Linton Corbin, *Corbin on Contracts*, §1522, 762 (1962). As Corbin explained through example:

> One who pays $1,000 in good money for another's promise to
> cut cord-wood for a month and to shoot a feuding neighbor if
> he appears can get no judgment for damages for failure to cut
> the wood, or to recover the money paid, whether the promised
> shooting occurs or not. The court may say no more than that
> such a bargain is "not divisible" or that the illegality is such
> as to "taint" the whole consideration. . . . What the court is
> in fact doing is to measure the degree of the illegality
> involved, to charge it against the promisee who paid the "good
> money" as well as against the [one] . . . who made the bad
> promise. *Id.* at n.32

A court's refusal to sever an unconscionable provision and enforce the remainder of a contract may properly be based on a public policy rationale. *Id.* at 763. Thus, a party who enters into a contract with an illegal component must bear the risk that a court will refuse to enforce the entirety of the contract and leave that party without any recourse at law. *See, e.g., Smith v. National Super*

Markets, Inc., 876 S.W.2d 785, 791 (Mo. App. 1994) (where minor signed agreement releasing supermarket of claims relating to her detention by store and store agreed not to press shoplifting charges, agreement was void and unenforceable as contrary to public policy).

Such is the case here. The Antonio-Shylock contract is as contrary to public policy as would be any contract countenancing murder. No court of law would find a contract lawful whereby one party offers a promise to pay a fixed sum in consideration for a loan and pledges his own death if he fails to make timely repayment. As one court has remarked, "The law does not and should not permit private persons to submit themselves to punitive sanctions of the order reserved to the State. The freedom of contract does not embrace the freedom to punish, even by contract." *Garrity v. Lyle Stuart, Inc.*, 40 N.Y.2d 354, 360, 353 N.E.2d 793, 834 (N.Y. 1976). The trial court properly construed the contract's silence regarding blood against its drafter (IV.i.301-304). As a result of the trial court's correct interpretation, the contract became a nullity.

The court below properly refused to enforce any aspect of the contract or to return any of Shylock's money. To do so would be against public policy. Shylock's willingness to enter into the contract reflects a lack of moral character which is chargeable to him. As author of the bond, its immorality leaves him with the uncleanest of hands. If the trial court had ordered Antonio to repay the principal of the loan (with interest as Shylock revealingly continues to seek, Appellant's Brief at 5-6, or without it) the court's imprimatur would have sanctioned the illegal contract.[2] Corbin, *Corbin On Contracts, supra,* at 762. This court simply should not entertain the application of a person who has behaved with such venom.[3]

II. AS APPELLANT ATTEMPTED TO MURDER APPELLEE, THE TRIAL COURT PROPERLY ASSESSED CIVIL PENALTIES IN ACCORDANCE WITH VENETIAN LAW

As for appellant's claim that the Alien Act is unconstitutional, this is largely a problem of literature not law. The Alien Act's provisions existed to protect wealthy Venetian merchants from such nomadic foreigners as the "stubborn Turks, and Tartars never train'd to offices of tender courtesy" (IV.i.32-33). In the city-state of Venice, Jews, like other outsiders, were not citizens and did not enjoy equal protection of Venetian law. The label "Jew" used by the trial court reflects the court's identification of Shylock as a foreigner, one not of "Christian blood" (IV.i.306).

Contrary to appellant's assertion that he was unaware that pressing his civil suit could have negative consequences, Appellant's Brief at 4, Shylock taunted Venetian authorities to sanction him. At the very beginning of the scene, when the Duke urged Shylock to reconsider his suit ("We all expect a gentle answer Jew!" IV.i.34) his response to the Duke was a profane mockery of religion which revealed a cold heart: "And by our holy Sabbath have I sworn/To have the due and forfeit of my bond" (IV.i.36-37). Later in the scene he demanded that the trial court stop dissuading him from his aim: "My deeds upon my head! I crave the law,/The penalty and forfeit of my bond" (IV.i.202-203). With these words Shylock accepted full responsibility for his deeds. This was not a man who was unaware that his intent to kill had attracted the attention of the court.

In light of Shylock's self-professed criminal intent, the court did not err in its application of the Alien Act.[4] Under Venetian law the court properly found that Shylock was guilty of attempted murder: "In which predicament I say thou stand'st:/For it appears by manifest proceeding,/That indirectly, and directly too,/Thou hast contrived against the very life/Of the defendant" (IV.i.353–357). Nothing in this passage suggests religious bias motivated Shylock's prosecution under the Alien Act.

The court then correctly assessed a financial penalty as punishment. A civil forfeiture is not a criminal punishment, as appellant argues, but rather a civil sanction. *United States v. Ursery*, 518 U.S. 267, 116 S. Ct. 2135, 2149 (1996). At the time of the court's assessment, Shylock had a full opportunity to be heard and the proceedings did not violate due process. He *consented* to the creation of trust in which he had a life estate (IV.i.379) and agreed to pay restitution to appellee (IV.i.389 "I am content").

It is of no significance that the court's final disposition of the civil penalty phase of the trial—which amounted to a negotiated settlement—included an agreement that Shylock convert. Shylock never uttered a word of protest regarding *Antonio's* (not the court's) suggestion in this regard. He may not now raise on appeal, that which he did not raise below. Further, appellant's acquiescence suggests only more strongly why this court should reject any equitable arguments or claims of bias asserted by appellant. As one commentator recognized:

> What professing Jew, such as Shylock pretends to be, would agree to such terms to save his life and fortune? The rabbis say that for the sake of life you may violate any of the more than 600 commandments in the Bible—except one, that prohibiting the desecration of God.

Jay L. Halio, "Portia: Shakespeare's Matlock?" *supra* at 62.

In sum, then, Shakespeare's portrayal is not one of religious bias but of evil justly rewarded. Shakespeare's Venetian court is not ours; we have learned since then; but it was justice the court meted out.

CONCLUSION

The decision of the court below should be affirmed.

Dated: New York, New York
        October 18, 1996

                        Respectfully submitted,

                        Floyd Abrams, Attorney for Appellee
                        Cahill Gordon & Reindel
                        (a partnership including
                        a professional corporation)
                        80 Pine Street
                        New York, N.Y. 10005
                        (212) 701-3000

NOTES

1. Liner notes evidence this point stating, "[t]he constitution of this court bears little relation to historical fact; the Doge [Duke] had not presided over a Court of Justice since the 14th century and magnificoes did not act as judges." *William Shakespeare, The Merchant of Venice* 103 marginal notes (John Russell Brown, ed., 1994).

2. That appellant—four centuries late—finally abandoned his quest for a "pound of flesh" is irrelevant. Appellant's Brief at 5. The trial court had earlier offered to settle the matter by encouraging Shylock to accept Bassanio's offer of double the principal (IV.i.206, 230). As in all settlement negotiations, Shylock rejected the court's suggestion at his peril for once the trial court ruled (IV.i.295-296, 300-308) the opportunity to settle had passed.

3. Shakespeare's caricature repels, "By murderously lusting after vengeance, [Shylock] shows himself . . . to be both a bad Jew and a bad human being, violating yet another commandment, Thou shall not kill" (Exodus 20:13). Jay L. Halio, *Portia: Shakespeare's Matlock?* 5 CARDOZO STUDIES IN LAW AND LIT. 57, 62 (1993).

15
Appellant's Reply Brief

SPECIAL COURT OF APPEALS

──────────────────────────────── x

SHYLOCK,

Appellant

-against-

ANTONIO,

Appellee

──────────────────────────────── x

DANIEL J. KORNSTEIN
Attorney for Appellant
757 Third Avenue
New York, N.Y., 10017
(212) 418-8600

Appellee Antonio's brief offers no good reason—much less a cogent one—for affirming the intolerable decision below. On the contrary, Antonio's brief is a curious and extraordinary document, curious in what it says and extraordinary in what it doesn't say. Unhappy with the trial record and the applicable law, Antonio vainly tries to ignore both.

Appellee's brief is an example of what one of the trial witnesses—an early and prescient champion of litigation reform—described memorably:

> In law, what plea so tainted and corrupt
> But, being seasoned with a gracious voice,
> Obscures the show of evil. (3.2.75-79)

Indeed. This court should cut through Antonio's sophistry, pull the mask off the pretense of a trial below, and reverse.

1. *What appellee's brief fails to say catches the eye immediately*. A glance at Antonio's brief shows that it says absolutely nothing in response to many of our most compelling points, and almost nothing about the rest. Such conspicuous silence is understandable, given the lack of merit in Antonio's position.

Antonio fails, for example, to rebut the indisputable evidence that the phony trial judge was biased and incompetent. He does not—because he cannot—even attempt to explain or justify Portia's gross misbehavior. As another court has held in a related case, the record here

> presents a disturbing picture of Portia's actions as a jurist. The record makes evident that Portia appeared in disguise because she, in fact, was not learned in the law, and that, having gained a position of power under false pretenses, proceeded to abuse that position at the trial by acting in a mean, prejudiced and vindictive manner toward Shylock.

David B. Saxe, "Shylock, Portia and a Case of Literary Oppression," 5 *Cardozo Studies in Law and Literature* 115, 118 (1993). In short, "Portia's actions at the trial were outrageous; she violated the most basic principles of fairness and impartiality" *Id*. at 121.

Equally unrebutted are appellant's other arguments. Antonio offers no equal protection analysis that would save the patently discriminatory Alien Statute. Nor does Antonio seriously deny the anti-Semitic tenor of the trial. He also fails to answer the arguments based on cruel and unusual punishment and due process violations. As for the massive violation of Shylock's First Amendment rights, Antonio has virtually nothing to say.

2. *Antonio's appellate silence on crucial points is matched by the hollowness of the little he does say on other issues*. A good example is Antonio's blithe but baseless assertion that Shylock "consented" to the awful punishments imposed

on him as part of a "negotiated settlement." *Appellee's Brief* at 8. Faced with a choice between death or lesser punishments, Shylock chose to live, but such a choice is hardly consent freely given. The law does not recognize a choice made under such circumstances of extreme threat and duress as legal consent.[1]

But Antonio's disingenuous argument based on Shylock's compelled consent is typical. Prejudice at trial? No, says Antonio, "it was justice the court meted out." *Appellee's Brief* at 9. Religious bias? No, argues appellee, merely "evil justly rewarded." *Id.* The Alien Statute unconstitutional? No, asserts Antonio, "largely a problem of literature not law." *Id.* at 7. These are not reasoned legal arguments, but glib one-liners designed to stifle discussion.

Even Antonio's most serious argument—lack of severability of an unconscionable contract provision—should be rejected. This Court cannot ignore the conditions out of which the loan agreement arose: the long and provocative history of religious prejudice and abuse suffered by Shylock at the hands of Antonio and his friends, the spirit of jocularity in which the penalty provision was created, and the widowed Shylock's breakdown on learning that his only daughter had run away with his money to marry out of the faith. Public policy considerations, moreover, do not all point in Antonio's favor. He has obtained a huge windfall as a result of the decision below, while Shylock has lost his principal plus interest.

Antonio's effort to blame Shylock for not accepting the principal at trial will not work either. Shylock's refusal was based on Judge Portia's misleading him about his chances of winning. The trial judge raised Shylock's expectations of success so that he rebuffed settlement. (4.1.175-76, 227-30, 244-46). Now she and her wily ways have been exposed.

Even the legal precedent relied on by Antonio—*Garrity v. Lyle Stuart, Inc.*, 40 N.Y.2d 354 (1976) (*Appellee's Brief* at 5-6)—has been seriously eroded. Earlier this month, the Appellate Division specifically held that *Garrity* will not stand in the way of private parties seeking punitive damages under a contract arbitration clause. *Mulder v. Donaldson, Lufkin & Jenrette*, 224 A.D.2d 125, *N.Y.L.J.*, Oct. 10, 1996, at 21 (1st Dep't). Thus freedom of contract does allow some scope to penalty clauses.

3. *At a loss for argument, Antonio retreats to the last refuge of appellate advocacy: wanting different facts and different law.* But the transparent attempt to rewrite the record and import inapplicable law must fail. Antonio is so unhappy with the trial record that he urges this Court *not* to accept that record "too much at face value." *Appellee's Brief* at 4. In other words, Antonio does not like the facts, dubbing them "satire" and "fairy tale." *Id.* at 3. But the facts are true facts; what happened at the trial is what we are appealing from. Antonio cannot wish them away.

Nor can Antonio wish away the applicable law. This appeal is governed by American law circa 1996. To describe such law, as Antonio does, as "the unforgivingly politically correct lens of contemporary legal and social mores," *Appellee's Brief* at 4, is to miss the point. This is not an appeal based on medieval Venetian law, whatever that may be. The purpose of the appeal, by stipulation of the parties and the Court, is to see how the case would be argued in today's legal climate, as if it arose in Venice, New York.

CONCLUSION

"Truth will come to light," one of the trial witnesses exclaimed, "in the end truth will out" (2.2.72–74). Only this court can ensure that happy result. For the reasons given here and in our main brief, the decision of the court below should be reversed. We have conservatively calculated the interest (at the legal rate of 9% simple interest annually) due since the year 1600 (that is, 396 years) on appellant's loan of 3,000 ducats to be 106,920 ducats (that is, 3,000 x .09 x 396 = 106,920).

Dated: New York, New York
        October 22, 1996

Respectfully submitted,

DANIEL J. KORNSTEIN
Attorney for Appellant
757 Third Avenue
New York, N.Y., 10017
(212) 418–8600

NOTE

1. These special circumstances, coupled with Shylock's not being represented by counsel below, excuse his failure to raise certain isuses at trial now asserted on appeal.

16
Shylock v. Antonio on Appeal: The Deliberations

Daniel J. Kornstein

Judge Pierre N. Leval:	Court will come to order please. The next case is the case of Shylock against Antonio. Are counsel ready?
Daniel J. Kornstein:	Yes, Your Honor.
Kevin Castel:	Ready for the appellee.
Leval:	We will allow twenty minutes for argument, which will be timed. Counsel for Shylock, do you request any time for rebuttal?
Kornstein:	Yes, I'll save five minutes for rebuttal.
Leval:	Five minutes saved for rebuttal.
Kornstein:	May it please the court. Never again. Never again should a trial occur like the one that happened below in this case. It is so filled with errors, riddled with errors, with problems from start to finish. But first let me clear away some underbrush so we don't get distracted. The appellant waives specific performance. He tried to waive it below twice, but the impostor of a trial judge didn't let him. There is no question about the contract penalty; the penalty is not on appeal. The decision below should be reversed. Appellant should be entitled to his principal and interest for 396 years at the statutory rate of interest. According to our calculations based on 3,000 ducats, that comes to approximately 110,000 ducats.
Leval:	Mr. Kornstein, in your reply brief on page 5 you assert that this appeal should be governed by the American law circa 1996. You say there that this is governed by a stipulation between the parties and the court. Can you direct our attention to whatever document it is that effectuates the choice of law governing

	this appeal?
Kornstein:	The stipulation is not a written document. It is an oral stipulation. But as for the document, the bond itself provides for choice of law, the American law circa 1996, and that choice of law clause should be appropriate and, of course, that's a choice of forum clause. The parties agreed on this forum. And, besides, it happened in Venice, New York.
Betty Weinberg Ellerin:	Mr. Kornstein, notwithstanding that your client now waives the forfeit, can we ignore the fact that the forfeit was at the heart of this agreement and that it was a noxious forfeit that is so against public policy that it should completely invalidate this agreement.
Kornstein:	What we have to do, Your Honor, is look at the genesis of how that clause came into being. Let's focus for a moment on how the contract arose. Remember that Antonio came to ask Shylock to lend him money. Shylock at first didn't want to do it. He recalled the history of anti–Semitism, the spitting, the kicking, the name calling and then when Antonio first mentions the notion of a penalty, Antonio says, "Treat me as an enemy. Put a penalty in there." He wasn't referring to interest; he knew that Shylock ordinarily got interest. That was the difference between Shylock and Antonio. Antonio didn't lend at interest. So, Antonio says put a penalty in and that's when Shylock says, "Look, I want to be your friend. This is kindness, I'll make you an interest–free loan." Something Shylock had never done before or since. He says "an interest free loan and as a sport and something like a joke, let's go put in this weird clause." And, in fact, this is something that there is no dispute about in the record; it wasn't until Shylock's daughter ran away with his money, with Lorenzo, and married out of the faith, that Shylock was distraught, emotionally upset, and he invoked the bond. He wasn't represented by counsel below. Now he has a chance. I think the proper way is just to discount that—the rule about severability of unconscionable provisions, and void against public policy. There has to be some effort to put things into a context here. It was Antonio who actually made a profit. Three of his ships came in so there is a mutual mistake aspect.

Leval:	Your adversary quotes from *Corbin on Contracts*, citing an example to the effect that when a contract provides for a reward that is unconscionable, the entire contract is not susceptible to enforcement by a court. And the example given by Corbin is the person who has paid good money would not recover his good money if part of the consideration was unconscionable consideration. Why is your case different? Or why do you dispute the authority of Corbin?
Kornstein:	I don't dispute the authority of Corbin, one of the great contract professors of all times. The *Weiss* case in Corbin and the cases that follow it make it a question of the particular facts and the circumstances. It's not an automatic rule. One must decide whether the clause and its genesis are so noxious, so terrible, and here we have a situation where something started out as a joke and remember the man had been provoked by a lifetime of anti-Semitism.
Leval:	It may have started out as a joke, but it became quite extreme the moment the lawsuit came to court.
Kornstein:	Well, that's something that we have to consider too. At the trial . . . there is an aspect of the trial that has been misinterpreted for centuries. It's not a scene, it happened at the trial. Shylock was scraping something off his shoe with a butter knife. It was interpreted for centuries as if he was honing the blade. There is no basis for that.
Ellerin:	Mr. Kornstein, he was offered not only the amount of the loan, thrice the loan, and he rejected it in open court and sought the court's good offices to enforce the—putting it mildly—the noxious penalty.
Kornstein:	He was misled by the fake trial judge. The fake trial judge told him, "You're going to win. Don't worry about it. You have a great case." She misled him on purpose because *she* was noxious. She talks about mercy but what she did was the very opposite. The worst hypocrite in the history of the law.
Phyllis Gangel–Jacob:	Was she a judge?
Kornstein:	No.
Gangel–Jacob:	And was there a trial? Or was she simply an expert who was called in by the judge, and this was a conference and a settlement?
Kornstein:	Let me start from the last part. As we know from the trial transcript, whatever Shylock consented to at the

end was not consent because it was under a threat of death. The duke says to him, "If you don't agree, I'll take away the pardon and you'll die right now." So there's no consent. This was not a negotiated settlement. And to say that—

Gangel–Jacob: Doesn't she say to him, "Does this satisfy you?" If it were a decision from on high, and if she was a judge (which I don't think she was), would she say, "Does this satisfy you?" "Are you content," I think the words were.

Kornstein: Your Honor, I think when the fake trial judge said those words, she was spitting them out at Shylock in sarcastic, nasty tones. She knew he had no choice, just as she had said the same thing to Bassanio earlier. There is testimony that when Portia and Bassanio were together and were talking, she says to Bassanio something like, "Do you love me?" and "How do you feel about that?" and Bassanio says, "Yes I do." And she says, "Well, of course, you're like someone on the rack, you have to say yes." And he says, "Well, if I'm threatened with death, of course, I'd be lying." The same thing that she said then was what happened at the mockery of the trial.

We're veering off the crucial issues here. The terrible anti–Semitism, with prejudice that marred this trial, the use of an unconstitutional law, the Alien Statute is exactly the sort of law we had in an earlier case today involving the laws, racial laws of Vichy France. This is part of that same stream.

Leval: Let me ask, let me ask you a couple of questions about your claim that the law is unconstitutional. You say that this law is unconstitutional because it denies equal protection to an alien party. I don't understand how you can justify that claim, because the record presents nothing with which to compare it. Surely, if a Venetian citizen plotted to murder another Venetian citizen, there would be penalties for the murder or the attempted murder. Now, you have not presented to us what those penalties are under Venetian law that permits us to conclude that the alien was illegally discriminated against. There is a severe penalty for an alien who plots murder. There surely is a severe penalty also for a citizen who plots murder.

Kornstein: Not in Venice, New York. It's a strange little town.

	Seriously, there is a negative attitude toward aliens that had led to this ridiculous statute. There is no comparable statute. There's no Citizen Law, only an Alien Law. Otherwise, why have it called an Alien Law, when you can have one law that covers everybody? That's the problem.
Ellerin:	Is there any definition of who is an alien?
Kornstein:	Well, now that's another terrible part about this law. It considers somebody an alien by virtue of religion not by their not being a citizen because they're from another country. Here they have someone who's from Venice, lives in Venice, works there, and is not considered a citizen. Now this is contrasted with another Venetian, my other client, Mr. Othello. He was given honors by the Venetians. He was allowed to command an army. He, of course, has his own trial to deal with.
Howard Kissel:	Mr. Kornstein, are you suggesting there's an equation between a civil servant, which Othello was as the commander of the army, and simply a Jewish moneylender?
Kornstein:	Well, I think, the comparison with Mr. Othello, General Othello is to Colin Powell. It's hard to say that Colin Powell is just a simple servant.
Kissel:	Civil servant.
Kornstein:	Well, civil servant, Colin Powell is a commanding general; it's a special status. I don't think the comparison is really valid. The question is what do you do at the trial. Even the fake judge talked about the danger of bad precedent. If this court affirms, the message will go forth that every other time a minority is involved in a case, the court and everybody else can run roughshod. We haven't yet talked about the forced conversion of religion. Now, that can't be allowed. It's got to be stopped here and now. Some of the docudramas portrayed this incident as some sort of a comedy. This is not a comedy. This is a very, very serious event, and it breeds intolerance. It has to stop here! It's your burden. You must send this message.
Gangel–Jacob:	Was the suggestion of the conversion to another religion, did that come from the court? Any court? Or did it come as a proposal from Antonio as a way out of losing all of his wealth and of Shylock losing

	all of his wealth?
Kornstein:	Once the court endorsed it, under the rule of *Shelley v. Kramer*, it became a state action, a government action, and entailed judicial involvement. So the answer is yes. The court was involved because it backed it up. In fact, it was right after that the duke or she said, "If you don't agree to that, then we'll enforce the death penalty; we'll lift the pardon."
Gangel–Jacob:	Oh, I don't think so. Didn't the duke say that, even without your plea for relief from the death penalty . . . ?
Kornstein:	That's the first time, Your Honor. The trial transcript, if you check the trial transcript, the first time the duke says, "I'll pardon you if you ask," and just a few pages later, after Antonio proposes this hideous conversion, the duke says: "He shall do this, or else I do recant the pardon that I late pronounced here." And then Portia, that faker, says "Art thou contented, Jew? What does thou say?" Based on that, everything below should be reversed. This man is the only loser; he lent them money. Everybody else has come out all right. Now the thing that's not been discussed really is the mutual mistake aspect. The only reason that Antonio is in this predicament is that he thought that none of the ships came in. He had six ships out there; he heard that they were lost, but they were not all lost. There were three that came in. He found out about that afterwards. The proper result is we don't need a remand, and if there is, we certainly want a different judge. This particular judge . . . I think the court ought to make a criminal reference—is impersonating a lawyer, a judge.
Leval:	All right, thank you for your time.
Castel:	May it please the court. My name is Kevin Castel. I am a member of the firm of Cahill, Gordon & Reindel, and we are local counsel to the appellee, Antonio. It's apparent to me now what the substance was that Mr. Kornstein contends Shylock was scraping off his shoes at Antonio, the hard working merchant. And Shylock is now in this court appealing from the denial of any monetary relief. It has long been the law of this state and every civilized nation that where illegality permeates an agreement, that agreement is absolutely unenforceable. Here we have

an agreement with a provision that is *malum in se*, inherently wrong: the taking of another life.

Ellerin: Okay, fine, Mr. Castel, so that means nobody owes any money whatsoever. Why shouldn't they then both go home, your client, the victor by 3,000 ducats; Shylock having lost the ducats and any possible interest. Why should the court go beyond that?

Castel: Judge Ellerin, I am in substantial agreement with you on that. After all, this is civil litigation brought by Shylock against Antonio. This is not a direct appeal from a criminal conviction. This is not a habeas petition. This court could not grant Shylock relief from the criminal sanctions that were imposed by the duke.

Ellerin: May we say this: Should those criminal sanctions have been there in the first place? I believe you're familiar with the concept of due process. I think that even made it to Venice, New York. As I understand it, before there may be any criminal trial, a defendant, and that's exactly what happened here— wasn't Shylock converted to a defendant—who is supposed to have some notice, given the opportunity for representation and what have you. How can you justify that aspect of the proceedings?

Castel: I would be delighted to do that. First of all, in terms of notice, my client was the defendant in that proceeding. Shylock hunted down the duke and desperately implored the duke repeatedly to convene this court to hear the proceeding below. As to the claim that somehow Shylock is entitled to some relief because he wasn't represented by counsel, the Sixth Amendment says you have a right to waive counsel and, in fact, it's inappropriate for a court to insist that a litigant have counsel when they have rejected it. Now I realize that it may be difficult to get this man counsel, but that's a different problem.

Leval: I am very troubled by your arguments about the applicability of the Alien Statute. The Alien Statute provides that an alien who seeks the life of a Venetian citizen will suffer the forfeitures. The circumstances under which this occurred were not an attempted murder. It was an attempt to ask the court to grant relief. For example, suppose that an alien has suffered the murder of his own wife or daughter and went to the court and said to the court: "The law of Venice provides the death penalty for one who does murder. My wife and child have been murdered. I implore the court to impose the death penalty on the murderer, the murderer being a Venetian citizen."

That person, like Shylock, is simply asking the court to impose a death sentence. If it's not appropriate under the law, the court will not impose it. If Shylock's bond were contrary to public policy under the laws of Venice, this would suffice for the judge, for the duke, to say this bond cannot be enforced. End of matter. This is not a matter that falls under essentially a murder statute that punishes one for attempted murder. How do you justify the application of this statute to these facts?

Castel:	As Your Honor is alluding, there certainly is the concept in the law as we know it in, at least, Venice, New York and Venice, California, that there is a legitimate right to petition your government for redress of grievance and that has been extended to seeking judicial relief, the *Pennington* doctrine, for example. But the *Noerr–Pennington* doctrine, which gives immunity in some instances for a litigant seeking judicial relief, has exceptions and has a sham exception. You have to look at the record here, the extra judicial conduct of Shylock. Shylock showed up through the streets of Venice with a scale to measure the pound of flesh and with a knife, and it was a vengeance attempt.
Leval:	Be it nonetheless, he merely asked the court to adjudicate the issue: "Am I entitled to a pound of flesh or not?"
Castel:	Well, your Honor, there is—
Leval:	If the judge had said no, he would have gone home.
Castel:	There is the tort of abuse of process, and it can very well be, for example, that where a party seeks judicial relief for an extrajudicial purpose, that the rules are different. Take the response that Mr. Shylock gave when he was asked why he wants the pound of flesh. He said, "To bait fish withal. If it feed nothing else, it will feed my revenge." This was a revenge attempt, and I understand Your Honor's concern here, but I think when you're dealing with the situation where outside the courtroom this man traveled through the

	streets of Venice, knife in hand, looking for this man and entered into a bond, before it came to court, which had as part of it the would–be murder of this man, is a different situation.
Ellerin:	Only if legally sanctioned, as Judge Leval so aptly put it.
Castel:	Well, Your Honor, let's look at what happened here. Is this man suffering any penalty under the criminal law at this stage of the game? You will recall that he was pardoned by the duke. Now, my client, Antonio, has nothing to do with the criminal prosecution. He was pardoned and as to the one half that was otherwise to go to the duke, my client graciously urged the duke to allow Shylock to keep that half. The other half was to go to Jessica and Lorenzo, who Shylock was going to cut out of the will anyway, because of the conversion.
Leval:	Antonio very generously gave away the part that was going to Venice.
Castel:	Yes, that's true.
Ellerin:	Mr. Castel, what authority could you point us to that brings Shylock within the definition of alien? After all, he was permitted to do business in Venice, which was a thriving commercial area, and he apparently was a very active commercial person. Within this statute, where is the word *alien* defined?
Castel:	Well, Your Honor, the definition is not in the statute and the fact of the matter is that at trial when Shylock was accused of being an alien he did not say, "Oh, no, that's not correct, I'm not an *alien* here." He didn't preserve that issue for appellate review.
Ellerin:	That goes back to due process. Perhaps had he been on notice before he walked into that courtroom, he would have consulted eminent counsel such as yourself, and he might have been counseled that that statute might not apply to him.
Castel:	Well, I think Judge Leval raised a very important point in his questioning of counsel here. What is the penalty in Venice for attempted murder of a citizen? We know that certainly in seventeenth–century England the penalty would have been forfeiture of land and goods. So it may very well have been that in Venice at the time all of your goods would have gone to the duke and, in fact, the alien could have

been the recipient of more favorable treatment. But the fact of the matter is, this is civil litigation. You know, I would think there might be a slight statute of limitations problem bringing a habeas corpus proceeding 400 years later.

I would be happy to address the mistaken point which was raised by Mr. Kornstein. The fact of the matter is that this was a situation where the bond was not dependent upon the ships coming in. The ships are not mentioned in the bond. There was an absolute obligation to pay within three months. Now if Shylock wanted to be a big sport about all this, he could have decided to forebear in bringing this litigation. But he's the guy who declared the default, and he went into court declaring the default. If he had waited and the ships had come in, it would have been a different story. But this case has to be adjudicated as of the time of trial, not on the basis of the subsequent happy discovery that the ships were not lost.

Peter J. Alscher:	Counselor, isn't it true that the wording of the Alien Statute is that "if an alien attempt the life of a citizen." Is that correct? It doesn't actually say "attempt to murder a citizen"; it says "attempt to take the life," to "seek the life of a citizen."
Castel:	Directly or indirectly?
Alscher:	Directly or indirectly. Your client on the Rialto is reported by Shylock to have repeatedly spit, kicked, verbally abused, physically harassed, treated like a dog the moneylender. Is that not correct?
Castel:	I'm happy that you raised this point.
Alscher:	I just asked, is it correct?
Castel:	Well, first of all, it's not in the trial record. This is the contention. This comes from Shylock's mouth.
Alscher:	Did your client protest the allegation that Shylock made when he said, "When on Wednesday last," I believe specifically, "you kicked me, you called me disbeliever, cutthroat dog. How is it that you asked me for money when I'm only a dog?" Did Antonio say, "When did I say that? You're my bosom buddy."
Castel:	If you will give me an opportunity to respond, I will do the best that I can for my client Antonio. I don't claim that my client is an angel, that Venice, New York, was not a place where there was bigotry, but I would like to, if I may, Your Honor, if you will just

give me a moment, to cite what Mr. Shylock had to say when he first met Antonio. He was introduced to him by Bassanio and he says, "how like a fawning publican he looks. I hate him for he is a Christian but more for his low simplicity. He lends out money gratis and brings down the rate of usury here with us in Venice." It's apparent that Shylock is an active and willing participant in the ethnic bias that was prevalent in his town. It's wrong, but it has nothing to do with the adjudication of Shylock's claim against Antonio.

Alscher: It has a great deal to do with the resolution of the court, because if it is true that Antonio was attempting to take, was attempting to seek the life of the money-lender, albeit not exactly with a pointed knife to the heart but with kicks to, let's say, kicks to the groin, and other abusive . . . in other words he was degrading the moneylender to the point that a life was metaphorically being taken out of him, and our moneylender is pleading for his life to Antonio in that first scene. In other words, to say, "Can't we come to some kind of a truce here for you will stop this kicking and beating and taking life from him." Okay, which your client denies, sorry I'll do it again. He does not make any apology whatsoever for those charges. Those are grievances brought to him out of court in which he had the opportunity to say, "Shylock, I'm sorry. What I did last Wednesday was wrong. I won't kick, and I will not do this again."

Castel: I think I understand your question. The question you ask is a very relevant one because we see it in the City of New York in 1996. We see gangs, and gangs that are formed on the basis of ethnicity, white gangs, black gangs, all different types of groups; some people are not in gangs, and there are racial taunts that go on. But it's very clear in the law that the fact that somebody is actually taunted on the basis of their race is a very wrong act but, it does not ever justify murder or attempted murder. And that I think is a pretty clear and pretty important principle that this court uphold.

Alscher: Well, in that case, counselor, I'm going to make a point to you that there was no attempted murder in the courtroom. You tell me; what is the evidence that

	Shylock would—since your client is very much still alive—you tell me what the evidence was that he attempted to murder him.
Castel:	Well, Your Honor, let's think of why we are here today. Are we here to review the criminal conviction of Shylock? Absolutely not. Is Antonio on trial for bigotry or false accusations?
Alscher:	The answer to both those questions is yes.
Castel:	Well then, I submit, Your Honor, that the point that was made before about notice and an opportunity to be heard is highly relevant. These are not charges that are contained anywhere in any record.
Leval:	Shylock is certainly appealing from the forfeitures that were imposed on him, and the forced conversion.
Castel:	That's absolutely correct, and if I may—on the point of forced conversion, or the alleged forced conversion. My client is certainly not in this court or any other court seeking to enforce that. There is nothing in the record that suggests—
Leval:	But it was your client's idea.
Kissel:	It was your client who suggested it.
Castel:	It was my client who suggested it, there is no question. My client suggested it.
Alscher:	He didn't suggest it. He demanded it.
Ellerin:	Enforced by the court. The court decreed it, predicated on that suggestion.
Castel:	Your Honors, with all due respect. What happened, and I think the trial record was checked during Mr. Kornstein's argument, is that the duke said, "Well, agree to that or I'll revoke the pardon." But the fact of the matter is, those people in that courtroom that day were well versed in the fact that the pardon is irrevocable. A pardoner, a member of his cabinet, a member even of his family, that pardon, is, once made, final.
Leval:	I'd like to return to the issue of his principal on the loan, which Shylock was not permitted to recover. You, in your brief, cite a passage from the treatise *Corbin on Contracts* to the effect that when a contract has an unconscionable or unenforceable provision the entire contract is void and no part of it will be enforced, including the recovery of principal amount. All very well and good, but there is also a principle of the law called unjust enrichment or as they called it in ancient

Venice, *quantum meruit*, which provides that without need to resort to the express terms of the contract, one who conferred the benefit on the other may have it restored to him by the court. Even if your example from *Corbin* properly shows that under contract law Shylock cannot demand the performance of his contract including, for example, interest that he demanded thereon, why should the court not have awarded him, why should this court not require that what was his simply be returned to him.

Castel: Well, Your Honor, I think that is a salient question, and I just ask you to imagine the following hypothetical. Big Louie comes into court and he says, "You know, I lent a thousand dollars to this guy, and I said to him if you don't pay it by next Tuesday I'm going to break both of your legs. He hasn't paid it, and I want to be able to break his legs or at least get my money back." The law of the state of New York and every civilized jurisdiction I know is that where the parties are in a legal situation *in pari delicto*, the equitable maxim dictates that the court leave them where they are. They leave the status quo. The court will not dirty its hands with an illegal contract.

Leval: Let me ask you another hypothetical. Supposing that the one party goes to the other, begs for a loan for a million dollars, and the loan is made and payment is promised on a certain day, and the lovesick lender who loaned because of his love says one thing: "If you can't pay me back, you have to promise me a kiss." Does that man not get his principal back? Should the court refuse to give him his principal back because he demanded a condition that the court would not enforce?

Castel: Well, Your Honor, in that situation I certainly would see that as being perfectly appropriate to give him his principal back. That's not an illegal condition, that's not *malum in se*.

Leval: Suppose he asked for a little more than a kiss?

Castel: I know, for example, in New York in 1996, the General Obligation Law says that if you charge a usurious rate of interest you not only don't get the additional interest, you don't only not get interest at the legal rate, you forfeit your principal. And here, where you have a security for a loan that would be usurious, I

	think the result would be the same. Thank you very much.
Leval:	Five minutes for rebuttal.
Kornstein:	As I was listening to counsel, often I was reminded of a sentence or two in the trial record where one of the witnesses said, referring to Gratiano: "Counsel speaks an infinite deal of nothing. His reasons are bushels of chaff; You shall seek all day ere you find them, and when you have them, they are not worth the search."

A lot of points were brought up, but they don't bear scrutiny. About the delay, we filed a notice of appeal timely, within thirty days; the dockets have been clogged. As to the punishment meted out by the courts, the fact is that the courts took everything away from Shylock because what the duke says is, "If you're humble, maybe we'll remit the forfeiture of half your wealth to a fine," but Shylock, my client, is not the humblest of people, and as it is, now he has nothing. Antonio gets the use of the other half. It's not just the income, it's not just the income he gets to share. He can do whatever he wants with that half and then on Shylock's death, according to the severe judgment below, everything goes to this ungrateful child and her lover. Both. So these are some things that we have to focus on. Something the court hasn't mentioned yet but is relevant too. There was an adequate remedy at law here—damages—that the trial judge could have enforced. She could have given back the principal and substituted the interest. |
Ellerin:	Your client rejected that any number of times.
Kornstein:	He also accepted it twice.
Ellerin:	After putting the court through the trouble of the trial and what have you.
Kornstein:	The trial judge was having a good time. But that was after, as I said, we had been misled by the trial judge.
Leval:	I think you do injustice to the record because while it may be correct that after a certain period the simulated trial judge misled him to believe that he was going to prevail on his bond, previously she implored him to be merciful and take his principal thrice over, and he refused to do so. He said he would have nothing but his bond.
Kornstein:	He was upset. Had he time for calm reflection, had

he. . . . Remember he's the lone person there, and he didn't have an assistant. He certainly didn't have a lawyer, he didn't have anyone else. Everyone there was ganging up on him. You know, in essence, I'll say that this whole trial was a bias crime.

Gangel–Jacob: Counselor, let's go back to that bias that you talked a great deal about. If bias didn't exist, would you be making these other arguments for Mr. Shylock?

Kornstein: If I were at the trial level, I'd say, "Objection, speculative, calls for speculation by the witness," but we don't know. The truth is we don't know, because if that bias didn't exist, this trial might not have taken place, the issue may not have arisen. The bias so permeated—counsel used the word *permeated*—"Oh 'learned counsel.'" That's a good word—"a second Daniel"—permeated the transactions. Bias is what permeated the transaction.

Gangel–Jacob: Bias did not permeate the request for a loan. Shylock had to decide whether he would lend this lout the money. The bias seems to permeate the penalty that Shylock wants to extract in the event of default.

Kornstein: Well, let's look at it this way. Shylock had been the victim of bias his entire life. He tries to make amends. He wants to be friendly. He wants to show kindness, an interest–free loan of 3,000 ducats, no interest. He puts on this joke of a penalty clause that no one expected would ever happen. Bassanio has some foreboding when he says, "I like not fair terms and a villain's mind."

Gangel–Jacob: And then he goes after Antonio because he's so unhappy about his daughter. Whose bias was that? If it's right to play this religion card, let's look at who did what to whom?

Kornstein: I don't think it would be fair to interpret the record below as saying that Shylock, the powerful Shylock, so dominated society in Venice that he was imposing his will on the entire rest of the population. There-fore, the reality is Shylock was a minority member, and we can talk words about whose bias, but if the whole society is exercising that bias, then the victim, probably, would feel bias back.

Gangel–Jacob: Isn't Shylock really furious with his daughter, broken-hearted about his daughter, betrayed, he feels, by his daughter, and now he's going to take it out on

Antonio. Antonio isn't even the non–Jew who married his daughter.

Castel: Absolutely, and the court should take into account that disturbed emotional state.

Leval: All right, the court will take a five–minute recess.

RECESS

Leval: I'd like to report rapidly the vote of the court, and then each judge will speak for up to four minutes, no more, and in most cases probably less, and after that we will have an opportunity for members of the audience to be heard.

First of all, the question whether Shylock should be entitled to receive his pound of flesh. We had one vote yes. Four members of the court voted no and one dissenter, no pound of flesh.

As to whether Shylock should recover his loan with interest, all five members of the court were agreed that there should be no interest recovered. Four members of the court believe that Shylock should not recover his principal. One member of the court believes he should recover the principal of the loan.

As to whether the penalties should stand, first dealing with the monetary penalties, the forfeitures of Shylock's goods, three members of the court believe that the penalties should not stand; two members of the court voted in favor of having the penalties stand. And as to the conversion, whether the conversion should be reversed by the court and nullified, three members of the court believe that the conversion should not stand; it should be vacated by the court. One member of the court was contrary, and I think one vote I did not record, I'm not sure.

Now, each member of the court will have up to four minutes to speak on whatever subject they wish to address.

Kissel: I think perhaps one of the lessons that we will take away from this trial is the necessity of having lawyers. As a layperson I say that with some regret. However, the problems that arose from this trial arose from the fact that neither Shylock nor Antonio in the courtroom back in Venice 400 years ago brought in a lawyer. Shylock came with his knife and scale; Antonio came with nothing, because they were convinced that the law was in Shylock's favor, and it was not until Portia came in and pointed out this little minor detail about the Alien Statute.

My feeling, in general, was that by the laws of Venice at that time this was an entirely fair trial. Yes, Shylock was tricked, but the issue of anti–Semitism was raised. I think that was a very unfair issue to attach to something that took place at a time when anti–Semitism was the norm. Something that was omitted in the trial as a mistake here was Shylock's reference to the fact that he was as much entitled to his pound of flesh as the Venetians in this court were entitled to their slaves. Shylock does not say, "Oh slavery is wrong and illicit." He just said, "You have slaves, I'm entitled to my pound of flesh."

We look at it from a curious perspective. There was a play that was very badly done about ten years ago called *Death of the King's Horseman*. It was about a young man who had been educated at Cambridge or Oxford, and who comes back to the African tribe which he will lead because his father has died. Part of the tribal procedure is to kill the king's horseman so that he can accompany the king to the next world and serve him there as he did in this one. We are like that college, that Cambridge–or Oxford–educated son. We live in a world where for 200 years slavery has been an issue, where for some time anti–Semitism has been an issue. In this world of Venice, neither of those things was an issue. So we are bringing hindsight to bear on some things, and that is not entirely fair, but that is the artificiality of the situation.

Lastly, let me say that I think it is a very, very complicated play. I've always thought that as a work of art it perfectly exemplifies Marianne Moore's definition of poetry, that poetry is "imaginary gardens with real toads." For the most part this play is an imaginary garden, which goes on in Belmont where a wealthy girl's hand you get by guessing the correct casket. That's fairy–tale stuff. But in this play there is a very real tone against Shylock. On the question of anti–Semitism, one of the briefs, I think it was

Floyd Abrams's, quoted Harold Bloom as saying, "This is the most anti–Semitic play ever written." That is nonsense. I think Harold Bloom is following academic fashion. You can't join the gender–racist crusade in bringing up this.

The reason that we still get anxious about this play is not that it's anti–Semitic. If it were straight anti–Semitic like its model *Il Pecorone*, an Italian play, or even Christopher Marlowe's *The Jew of Malta*, there would be nothing at issue. The extraordinary thing is a world in which Jews are the killers of the savior. You have a speech like, "Hath not a Jew eyes?" That's what troubles us. It's not that Shakespeare is anti–Semitic. It's that he's philo–Semitic. That's all I have to say.

Alscher: It's a good thing that we are on opposite sides of the table here because I totally disagree with the remarks we just heard. Just for the record, if you just have a few minutes, I want to tell you, I want to put forward a theory for you to think about with regard to this play because I happen to be one who thinks, long before Harold Bloom said so, that the anti–Semitism is at the heart of the trial, and it's really why we're all here. We could all do with a trial in which somebody had to pay, you know, 50,000 ducats or 100,000 ducats. It's the forced conversion that bothers us because you won't find any other forced conversion in Shakespeare's other thirty–six plays.

I believe that in 1605 Shakespeare performed this play before King James. It was a command performance. It was the eighth play that he had commanded Shakespeare to do, and the unusual thing about it is that James wanted to see this play twice. I believe that the reason he wanted to see the play twice is because he didn't like the first presentation Shakespeare made. And just to be very brief, what James didn't like and the way Shakespeare presented it to him was a very pro–Semitic Shylock. A Shylock who made Antonio look like a loser, like a loser as Morroco and Aragon were losers in Belmont. They didn't give up and hazard all that they had. Antonio withheld from Shylock; he provoked Shylock; he abused him on the Rialto, and Shakespeare was an egalitarian Christian. So he took a tremendous chance, and he put forward a trial scene in which at the end, when Antonio says, "For this favor he must become a Christian," Portia intercedes without saying a word. But she went on to say, "No, I won't accept that ruling." She just said "No," and Antonio turned away, rebuffed and embarrassed, but nevertheless he will record a deed of guilt.

King James said to William—I'm theorizing here, but I'm just giving this for you to think about—King James said, "William, it's a wonderful play, marvelous scenes all of them, except for the trial. You had that Jew in your hands. Why didn't you convert him? For the sake of England, William come back here in two days with that Jew converted." And when under that pressure Shakespeare didn't change a word of his text. And King James, you remember James is the sponsor of the King James Bible. What we watched tonight was the King James version, and it can be played very effectively with Shakespeare refusing to let this conversion go through.

So it's been a tradition for hundreds of years to convert Shylock. And it provokes and makes us all very uncomfortable because he's a very real character. We can't believe that he would have accepted that condition. We know it's hypocritical on Antonio's part. After he has violated the only commandment of Christianity, which is to love your neighbor, all he does is hate his neighbor. So to ask him to become a Christian is to ask him to become someone who hates Jews. To ask Shylock to become someone who hates Jews, it just doesn't make any sense. It makes lots and lots of audiences very uncomfortable, and it's the reason why school systems won't touch this play. It's a good reason why they just don't want to get involved in it because they know it's nothing but controversy. Thank you.

Gangel–Jacob: Addressing first the question of whether Shylock should get his principal: As it was pointed out, even if it was an interest rate considered to be usurious, he would not be entitled to his principal, and this is the only way that the State can control people from doing this. If in fact, you simply say you don't get your interest if it's usurious, people will take a crack at it, right? They'll charge usurious interest rates. They either win or they lose, so that there has to be a penalty beyond that, and the penalty is you don't get your principal. The same thing is true, as a matter of fact, if your building contractor fails to get his license. You don't have to pay. He can't enforce the contract in court. If you pay him, you cannot get your money back. But if you don't pay him, and he has to come to court to collect, he will not be able to collect on his contract because he doesn't have a license to do construction work. And that's true of a whole variety of cases. So I think that surely forfeiture of principal is something that would obtain in New York State, in Venice, New York.

The other question that I would like to address is the Alien Statute. We don't need a description of what an alien is. We know the difference between a citizen and an alien. If you're not a citizen, you are an alien and under the laws of New York you can discriminate against aliens. There are certain classifications which are suspect if they don't get equal treatment such as Jews, religion, color—but aliens are not a suspect class. In fact, we have laws that say that an alien cannot be a policeman and an alien cannot be a corrections officer and an alien cannot be a school-teacher, and they have been upheld because they serve a purpose.

I think, truly, that what Shylock was confronted with was giving up all his money or saving part of it by conversion. It was a condition. He had a choice to make. The mere fact that the duke later said, "Well, he can't be pardoned, that is, I might consider putting you to death." That was not a judgment of the court; that was, I submit, an attempt by the court to get Shylock to agree. Holding up a threat like that sometimes effectuates an agreement. Shylock did not have to convert; he could have forfeited his money. The conversion, however, I think, from my point of view . . . I'm not sitting on an appellate court, normally I am sitting on a trial court, and so I feel very strongly that the trial court's decision should be upheld. I am not about to reverse a trial court lightly.

Ellerin: May I say, Phyllis, as an appellate judge, we do not reverse trial judges lightly either. But this trial judge, I think in certain respects, certainly deserved to be reversed. Our two nonjudges really pointed out the complexities of this play both as a play and as a human drama. So as a judge, however, I come at it in a little different direction. I took seriously the statements made that we were to interpret this in light of our current laws.

Well, clearly, a contract that requires one party to give up upon breach a pound of flesh is something that is so repugnant, I think, to our civilized society, that we would have to say that a contract of that sort is truly against public policy and can't be enforced. Notwithstanding that, as one of our speakers indicated, tremendously impressive emotional reasons explain why Shylock sought that kind of remedy, and we can sympathize with some of those reasons. In a civilized society, though, the contract would be abhorrent, so I was with the majority that Shylock should not be able to recover even the amount of the loan itself, let alone the interest.

However, once that was done with, to then suddenly subject him to criminal penalties without giving him even any notice of why a criminal statute should suddenly be engrafted in the proceedings is also in modern legal procedures anathema. And so I clearly would reverse the entire criminal proceedings. Now interestingly, Mr. Castel went along with the criminal proceeding not being before us. In fact he could have had an argument that this was really not a criminal proceeding. It was a civil forfeiture. Notwithstanding, I still would disagree that there was no statute that provided for that.

I disagree with Judge Gangel–Jacob on the alien aspect. What is an alien? In modern law because one is of a different religion doesn't take away one's citizenship. Here is somebody who lived in the community, who was a person who had a trade in the community. Why should he have been considered an alien? I mean that's really not relevant to the main reason why I am going for the reversal of the forfeiture and the conversion. Clearly in our modern society to force someone to undergo a religious conversion because he brought a civil suit is rather outrageous. So I was with the majority in that reversal as well. In other words, a modification confirming the nonrecovery on the bond itself in terms of damages and a reversal and dismissal of that part which made up the forfeiture and the conversion.

Leval:

I was the only member of the court who voted to give Shylock his principal back, and I'll say just a few words about why. I think the law and the courts are at their best when they seek to devise and enforce rules of general applicability, which time after time will give fair and just results. I think the courts are at their worst when they adopt a somewhat sanctimonious point of view trying to enforce morality in very, very broad strokes.

There has been talk, for example, about usurious rates of interest. My cojudges—all four who voted against me on this issue—are quite right that under normal legal proceedings the fact that someone does something in a contract that is said to be contrary to public policy results in a forfeiture of all rights with respect to that transaction. I'm not sure that should be the case. Usury laws are sanctimonious. Who says that a certain rate of interest should be the maximum, and when you go above it you're doing something wrong. Of course in Venice, at the time of Shylock, simply asking for interest on your money was immoral. It was a hateful thing. This was the big division between Shylock and Antonio.

In my view, although, of course, I feel as harshly as anyone about Shylock's effort to exact his pound of flesh. I don't see a comfortable principle in the law that should deny him the simple return of the money that he loaned. No interest, no benefits of the contract, but simply give him back what is his.

Moving on to the forfeitures, I was among the majority who thought that the forfeitures should be reversed by the court, both monetary and the conversion. My reasons were a little bit different from Judge Ellerin's reasons. I do not think so much that this was a matter of due process. Due process was very different in those days from what we have now. The world's a tough, cruel place. Nor was it an unconstitutional denial of equal rights. I can see no reason for that. Aliens are always treated more harshly under the law than citizens, but, furthermore, there were surely harsh measures that were applicable to Venetian citizens who sought to murder another citizen.

It was true that when Portia dealt with the issue of the bond, she was a brilliant lawyer. Her coming up with the notion: "Yes, you can have your pound of flesh, but you may not take a drop of blood because it's not in the contract. Nor may you take the smallest bit more or less than the pound of flesh, a just pound of flesh." This was a brilliant legal mind finding a way to do what judges today call a refusal to enforce a contract which is against public policy. I was filled with admiration for that part of Portia's performance.

However, when it came to the Alien Statute under which she commanded the forfeiture and the death of the duke's will of Shylock, this seemed to me to be where her legal talents went astray and were not under control, not properly applied. It seems to me that this statute that brings very very serious, harsh penalties, including death and forfeiture on an alien who seeks to take the life of a Venetian citizen applies to one who seeks to do murder, not to someone who comes into court and says "Look I've got a contract which calls for this. Tell me, does it get put into effect or not?" And so I thought that all of the forfeitures exacted on Shylock were illegally exacted under the statute.

17
Thoughts of a Literary Judge

Howard Kissel

For the layperson, our legal system, based as it is on adversary encounters, seems almost disturbingly aggressive and belligerent. For a layperson of a rather timid disposition to be on a panel of judges, even in a "literary" trial such as this one, is extremely odd because it means one must join the hostilities.

It will probably seem odd that someone who makes his living as a theater reviewer should shrink from being combative. Yes, my profession makes me tangentially a "judge," but the customary pose one takes sitting on the aisle is neutral. You are not supposed to indicate any emotional response, lest you later be accused of writing more negatively than you seemed to be responding. (No one is ever unhappy if you write more positively than you seemed to be responding).

Whatever notions I might have had of being a dispassionate observer evaporated very quickly as the actual judges on our panel began challenging the lawyers for Antonio and Shylock in a manner that struck me as peremptory if not downright condescending.

I had to remind myself that the idea of a legal trial developed in the Middle Ages alongside the idea of jousting as a form of entertainment. Though we may no longer accept the ideas behind trial be fire or trial by water, we still accept the notion that truth will emerge victorious from armed combat.

The challenges the real judges issued to the lawyers were based on contemporary legal precedents. Happily Daniel J. Kornstein, who was defending Shylock, made a literary analogy, which allowed me to join the fracas. He compared Shylock to another "outsider" who ran into trouble in Venice—Othello.

"Are you comparing a civil servant," I asked, in as sneering a tone as I could muster, "to a Jewish moneylender?" (Being Jewish, I hoped I didn't sound anti-Semitic.) Kornstein defended his analogy, but in effect withdrew it.

When we retired to "chambers" to debate whether or not to rescind Shylock's penalties, my mind had not been changed from my initial reading, which is that, given the circumstances of Venetian law, at least as Shakespeare presents them, Shylock had been treated as fairly as could be expected.

I have never even been offended by the demand on the part of the court that Shylock convert. It is true that Shakespeare takes a fairly dim view of the Christians he depicts in Venice. One of the most telling lines in the play was omitted in the presentation of the trial scene—Portia's first statement on entering the court, "Which is the merchant here and which the Jew?" Her confusion suggests limitations in costuming in Shakespeare's time, but it also implies that the difference between the Christian and the Jew was by no means self-evident.

For the most part we never have to make allowances for Shakespeare. He is invariably our contemporary. Nevertheless, there are times when it helps to see that his world was more different from ours than we generally imagine. I am reminded of Wole Soyinka's *Death and the King's Horseman*, in which a young African, in the early part of our century, is summoned back from Oxford when his father, the tribal chieftain, dies. The tribe intends to carry out its ancient ritual of killing his horseman, so that the latter can help him in the next world. The young man, with a Western education, knows this is barbaric, but to question it is to call into question the entire belief system of the community he must now lead.

We are sometimes in the position of that young man when we judge the past. The society in which Shylock demanded the terms of his bond was in no way pluralistic. It was a world in which Christianity and truth were synonymous. Although conversion was humiliating for Shylock, it was a way of bringing him to truth, maybe even salvation, which would have been impossible for him as a Jew.

What changes my mind about the proceedings and made me more lenient toward Shylock was Betty Weinberg Ellerin's assertion that the poor man had been subjected to a bait-and-switch operation. He arrives in court assuming he is there for a civil proceeding, which, under Venetian law, seems fairly cut and dried. Only halfway through the trial, Judge Ellerin noted, does Portia suddenly cite the Alien Statute, which suddenly turns the trial from civil to criminal. Shakespeare, of course, was not a lawyer. Nor was he a theologian, though only a generation earlier theater was still related to morality plays, and it is easy to see that Shylock, constantly invoking "the Law," represents the Old Testament; Portia, stressing "the quality of mercy," represents the New.

Shakespeare, of course, was not debating the merits of the two dispensations. His concerns were dramaturgical. He turns us against Shylock by having him fiercely reject any notion of mercy; so when Portia turns the tables on him, emotionally we can accept what follows. From a legal standpoint, however, the sudden reversion to criminal rather than civil codes is indeed unfair, and I was willing to go along with the majority's decisions to be kinder to Shylock than the duke had been.

What struck me as inescapable, looking at the trial from the perspective of law rather than theater, was that the playwright who, in recent years, has been celebrated for writing the line "First let's kill all the lawyers," was in this play, written a few years after the one in which that line occurs, stressing, albeit unconsciously, the absolute need for the legal profession.

Whenever I see the play from now on I will always be astonished that Antonio comes to court, knowing he may be murdered, but unarmed by legal counsel. Nor does Shylock, who comes to court intending to commit murder, think to defend his actions by hiring a mouthpiece. If he had done so, the lawyer would surely have pointed out his liability under the Alien Statute.

If at any point, from the signing of the "merry" bond to the invoking of it, either side had retained an attorney, of course, there would not have been all this anxiety. Nor would there have been a play.

18
Shylock on Appeal

Peter J. Alscher

It was a privilege and a joy to participate as an appellate judge in the 1996 Hofstra University School of Law symposium devoted to law and the arts in the special session on the case of *The Merchant of Venice: Shylock v. Antonio* on Appeal. This appeal case, held in the Hofstra Law School moot court room on October 31, 1996, was, I believe, the first of its kind. The format was modeled on U.S. appellate court procedures. Trial attorney Daniel J. Kornstein appealed (under New York State and U.S. law) on behalf of his "client" Shylock the "lower court" rulings of the Venetian Court of Justice, portrayed in act IV of Shakespeare's play *The Merchant of Venice*. Mr. Kevin Castel argued on behalf of his client, Antonio, to have the criminal and civil judgments against Shylock stand. Both lawyers are distinguished trial attorneys with considerable litigation experience in the areas of contracts, negotiations, issues of free speech and freedom of religion. Both lawyers were allotted twenty minutes to orally argue their case as presented in their briefs to the five appointed judges, with five minutes each for final rebuttal. Specifically, Kornstein petitioned vigorously that (1) the Alien Statute introduced by Portia against Shylock be overturned, (2) the coerced conversion to Christianity demanded by Antonio be vacated, and (3) Shylock's original principal, 3,000 ducats, be "returned" to him with interest, totaling roughly 109,000 ducats accumulated over a 390 year period.

The five judges hearing the arguments pro and contra did not come from academic backgrounds, as do the scholars, professors, or high school teachers who typically teach and interpret the Shakespeare play. Three of the Hofstra judges came from judicial backgrounds and are currently seated on the bench: Honorable Phyllis Gangel-Jacob, of the New York State Supreme Court; Honorable Betty Weinberg Ellerin, of the New York State Supreme Court, Appellate Division; and Honorable Pierre N. Leval, U.S. Court of Appeals for the Second

Circuit. Participating as judges with nonjudicial, but literary, backgrounds were Howard Kissel, theater critic for the *New York Daily News*, with expertise in Renaissance literature and contemporary theater; and Peter J. Alscher, a businessperson with a dissertation in English and Comparative Literature titled "Shakespeare's Merchant of Venice: Toward a Radical Reconciliation and a Final Solution to Venice's Jewish Problem" (Washington University, St. Louis, 1990).

This article serves as a background to the record of the judges' responses to briefs submitted by Mr. Kornstein and Mr. Floyd Abrams. I have been asked by Susan Tiefenbrun, the director of the Law and the Arts symposium and our moderator, Richard H. Weisberg, to play the role of "court reporter" (having no prior qualifications for that title!) and to record some of the significant areas of agreement and dissent reached by the judges in their interrogation of the advocates, in private chambers, and in public remarks from the bench. The five judges spoke extemporaneously, having read the briefs but having not otherwise prepared written responses to the oral arguments. (It should be noted that the original counsel on the brief for Antonio was the distinguished attorney Floyd Abrams, who could not participate at the last minute due to a conflict in trial scheduling. Thus Mr. Castel, Mr. Abrams's partner, generously agreed to take on the oral argument).

In this reporting I do not pretend to be "objective." Almost everyone reading or watching this highly emotional play tends to be pulled one way or the other, either "pro-Portia" and "pro-Antonio," on the one hand, or "pro-Shylock," on the other. It is extremely rare for contemporary theater audiences to come away from any production of this play with the same sense of joyful satisfaction at romantic resolutions and obstacles to marriage harmoniously overcome, felt from other major Shakespeare comedies as *Twelfth Night, Much Ado about Nothing* or *A Midsummer Night's Dream*. Nonetheless, having studied both sides of *The Merchant* conflict for many years, I certainly respect the perspective of those with whom I may disagree. I value the very fact that the play, despite and because of its controversy, continues to fascinate readers and audiences alike. Ultimately we all express our gratitude to, and admiration for, the extraordinary playwright whose comedies we will still be enjoying another 400 years from today (assuming we live that long). To help guide the reader through the intense oral arguments, and as a summary of what follows, I will state at the outset my own bias, indicating my own votes, and then do my best to record as much as possible of my fellow judges' reasoning in response to the two opposing lawyers.

On the two most substantial and controversial issues voted upon, that of reversing the Alien Statute and vacating the forced conversion, I voted with Judge Ellerin, and Chief Judge Leval, thus constituting a minimal majority in favor of Shylock. On the issue of whether Shylock was entitled to receive a pound of Antonio's flesh, I dissented from the 4–1 majority, who voted that he was not so entitled. (Thus I alone voted that Shylock was legally entitled to

Antonio's flesh, despite Portia's objection that there was no jot of blood mentioned in the bond. I did not argue that Shylock should have cut Antonio's heart out!)

On the question of whether Shylock should recover his initial 3,000 ducat loan with interest, we were unanimously agreed that he should not—but for different reasons, to be noted.

I voted with three other judges, Ellerin, Gangel-Jacob, and Kissel, that Shylock should not recover the original 3,000 ducat principal of his loan. Chief Judge Leval dissented, arguing publicly that Shylock should be awarded his loan, but without interest.

Before returning to the oral arguments between judges and lawyers, and our all too brief chamber deliberations and the individual judges' spoken opinions supporting their votes, I would like to put our proceedings in the context first of the Hofstra University School of Law event and then of the overall academic debate surrounding what is arguably for the twentieth century the most controversial of Shakespeare's fourteen comedies. I will occasionally draw attention to the engaging performance of excerpts of the play that we saw at Hofstra. The "sell-out crowd" of more than 150 had the benefit of watching a lively rendition of the crucial act I, scene 3 confrontation among Shylock, Bassanio, and Antonio where the conditions under which the terms of the "merry" bond are first exposed, followed by almost the whole of the famous "pound of flesh" act IV trial scene. For a daylong conference on the law and the arts, there could have been no more fitting denouement.

Let me indicate the parameters of the controversy surrounding the play. For most Shakespeare scholars and teachers—henceforward designated "the majority"—*The Merchant* is a fairly typical five-act Shakespearean comedy, with a fairy-tale background upon which Shakespeare embellishes. The majority might put it this way:

Once upon a time there lived a handsome Venetian gentleman Bassanio, who longed to marry the rich, beautiful and clever heiress Portia of Belmont. His kind, rich and generous godfather, Antonio, offered to give him the sea-fare as a gift, but first he had to borrow the sum from a greedy, spiteful and vengeful Jewish moneylender. The calculating Jew hated the good Antonio because he was a Christian and saved other Christians from the Jew's clutches. So the Jew plotted a deadly revenge against the unsuspecting Antonio.

Knowing in advance that the Jew will be summarily foiled, the majority urge that the play be read and enjoyed "unironically"—in the same spirit as other early and middle Shakespeare comedies. The main difference between *The Merchant* and the other comedies is the extended presence of a comic villain, whose bond threat temporarily threatens the completion of three love plots. For the majority, however, Shakespeare brilliantly succeeds in giving his bloodthirsty Jew his "day in court" by showing him the error of his vengeful ways. Instead of punishing him with death for demanding strict justice—when he himself is guilty of violating a Venetian statute—the court under Portia's merciful direction allows him gracefully to become a Christian himself, and thus enjoy the benefits of citizenship. For the majority, the trial scene is only an extended subplot, a necessary detour on the voyage to Belmont, making possible the resolution of all the other love plots in act V, where Shylock is conspicuously, and necessarily absent. With Shylock's conversion achieved, the tense, frightful atmosphere of impending death disappears, and harmony reigns in Belmont. Jessica, the Jew's daughter, and Lorenzo, her Christian husband, Nerissa and Gratiano, and Portia and Bassanio are now free to live "happily ever after."

For the majority, viewers should minimize "the problem of Shylock"—the only Jewish character in all of Shakespeare's thirty-seven plays—by accepting him as the unique comic villain he is, and also accept the Venetian trial scene as it is, at "face value." We should see in Shylock's admission of guilt and conversion to Christianity ("I am content") a projected rehabilitation and re-integration of the comic villain into Antonio's world, and thus into the beneficial world of Venetian citizens. Shylock, once a despised alien, becomes a welcomed citizen. Many "majority reporters" thus further see in the trial scene a symbolic or allegorical victory of its own. The scene represents, through Portia's "quality of mercy" speech, the triumph of the New Testament over the Old Testament; the victory of unstrained Grace over the self-destructive Law of the Old Testament, symbolized by Shylock's demand for bloodthirsty vengeance. For majority reporters, the conversion of Shylock is thus perceived as a positive blessing as Shakespeare's audience would have accepted it, while conceding that contemporary audiences, not trained in Elizabethan theology, have difficulty seeing it this way.

For purposes of this article let me say that the majority includes most, though not all, of published Shakespeare scholars, professors and high school teachers over the past many decades, even including the editor of the popular *Cliff Notes*, for lazy student readers. For these viewers, the dramatic focus of the play is not the Shylock-Antonio legal antagonism, although they concede the contract dispute provides an emotional and dramatic subplot, but only related thematically as a negative obstacle to Bassanio's quest for Portia's hand in marriage through the casket trials of Belmont, in act II and act III. Portia, they would claim, plays a kind of compelling judge's role both there and at the trial, through her obedience to her dead father's will. She must not reveal to any suitor which casket—gold, silver, or lead—contains her portrait, even when she is tempted to. Majority reporters note that only Bassanio makes the right choice, without Portia's interference, thus qualifying Portia to become the credible judge of the bond contract in Venice.

The effective climax of the casket trial awaits the solution of the "lost ring" plot in act V. This comes only after the legalistic plot is settled, dismissed and forgotten. This is the climax of the casket trial when Portia comes in Belmont and reveals the identity of the person to whom Bassano has lost his ring.

We may thus appreciate that counsel, Daniel J. Kornstein, in challenging Portia's credibility and bringing his brief on behalf of this "alien villain," was mounting a courageous counteroffensive in the face of an army of opposing critics! For the majority, Shylock remains, throughout the scenes in which he appears, the unredeemed "villain" whom Antonio initially categorizes: "an evil soul producing holy witness/ Is like a villain with a smiling cheek, a goodly apple rotten at the heart" (I.3.91-94). He is unrelenting and without conscience in plotting against Antonio, and turns himself into a bloodthirsty monster in court. He only gives up on murdering Antonio when confronted by a death sentence against himself. For the majority he is hopelessly legalistic, showing no mercy, and therefore bringing his own destruction upon himself. The only full-length *literary* commentary of our century on *The Merchant* is written from, and helps to define, this perspective: Lawrence Danson's 1979 study, significantly titled "The Harmonies of Merchant." Two of our judges, Gangel-Jacob and Howard Kissel, voting against Shylock on the two most contested issues, the applicability of the Alien Statute and Shylock's forced conversion, agree essentially with this Majority perspective.

(In fairness to "majority reporter" Kissel, while voting to uphold the lower Venetian court, and thus to reject Kornstein's appeal, he went out of his way to magnify what he saw as the surprising positive qualities of the "villain" Shylock, as we shall see).

Opposed to the academic majority report is the "minority report." The minority, while technically agreeing that *The Merchant* is a comedy—that is, it ends in multiple marriages and not in death—suggest that, nevertheless, in spirit the play is really a four-act tragedy, where Shylock, perceived as a dignified, highly ethical character, every bit Antonio's equal, if not his superior, is reduced to a nonperson, a speechless shell of a man, forced by hostile and even heartless Christians to convert to a shallow, hollow, and hypocritical Venetian norm of behavior. Thus, for most minority reporters the emotional climax of the play is reached not in act V, but at the end of act IV, when Shylock is cruelly prosecuted by the disguised Portia and her in-court ally, Antonio. Minority reporters suggest as well that Portia does interfere with Bassanio's casket choice in act III, thus "deceiving" her father's will. They argue a parallel deception in Venice, this time at Shylock's expense. It is argued that she at first deliberately lures the moneylender into believing his contract is valid, when she already knows she can and will prosecute him under the Alien Statute. Thus, some 1990s minority reporters still read the play as it was performed in many mid- and late-nineteenth-century English theaters: With Shylock's deliberate humiliation in court, the curtain came down! The audience lost interest in Bassanio and Portia, in Jessica and Lorenzo, and certainly in the "good" Antonio, whom they perceived as the source of the Jew's troubles in Venice. Without Shylock to air his grievances against the Christians on stage, the "play" was dead.

For other minority reporters, *The Merchant* retains its fifth act, but as in the rest of the play they see Shakespeare being pervasively ironic, perhaps more so than in any other single play, given the exclusively Christian audience for whom he was performing. The moderator of our panel, Richard H. Weisberg, has argued in *Poethics* that even though Shylock is defeated in court, Portia in act V begins living out, ironically enough, his Jewish principles of unmediated obligation and faithfulness in marriage by "prosecuting" Basssanio for giving away her ring. Again, writing for the minority, D. A. Moody (Shakespeare's *The Merchant*, 1964) sees the central attraction and challenge of the play for Shakespeare not in the Bassanio-Portia romance, where Moody in the casket trials also questions Portia's impartiality, but the confrontation between a dignified, ethical, "down-to-earth" Jewish moneylender, proud of his Jewish heritage, victimized by an arrogant, prejudicial Antonio, who contradicts Christian principles (particularly, love thy neighbor and thine enemy) while pretending to exemplify them. Minority reporters invert the "plotting" direction. It is not Shylock plotting vengeance against Antonio, but Antonio consistently provoking him beyond endurance. Yet the Christian, because he is a "majoritarian" and a citizen, always has the advantage over the "alien" Jew. Antonio is protected in his offensiveness by the Venetian statute.

Some minority reporters see the possibility of a friendship developing from the commercial loan, if only Antonio will cooperate. The minority sees "double vision" operating on Shakespeare's part, with the playwright subtly creating a pro-Jewish counter-fairy tale, virtually parallel to the pro-Christian fairy tale. The Jewish patriarch falls because he is ethical; the Christian paradigm succeeds while breaking his faith's central tenet. So for the minority, what emerges most glaringly from the ambivalent text is the "problem of Antonio." For some minority reporters, like Daniel J. Kornstein, this leads directly to "the problem with Portia," who so aggressively defends him. Others, like Weisberg, note that Portia specifically delegates Shylock's fate at the trial to Antonio, who is thus solely responsible for the cruelty that ensues.

To recapitulate, for the minority it is as though Shakespeare wrote not the comedy of the good merchant Antonio, but the unfortunate history of 1600 years of divisive Jewish-Christian relations, condensed and dramatized into two short hours. Christianity, for them, is not the winner.

Thus, when Judge Betty Weinberg Ellerin spoke out forcefully to overrule the conversion demand made by Antonio in court, dismissing it as "outrageous," while she spoke for a bare "majority" (3-2) she was reflecting a "minority" voice by academic standards. It seems to minority reporters that when Antonio exclaims:

> I am as
> like to call thee so again,
> To spit on thee again, to spurn thee too.
> If thou wilt lend this money, lend it not
> As to thy friends, for when did friendship take
> A breed for barren metal of his friend?
> But lend it rather to thine enemy,
> Who if he break, thou mayst with better face

Exact the penalty. (I.iii. 25-32)

He has virtually disqualified himself as a credible Christian and thus is in no position to demand conversion from Shylock.

Some majority reporters, like his defense counsel Kevin Castel, concede that Antonio is not, after all a saint! Among academic majority reporters and theater directors, the greatest objection to the minority report may be its challenge of Portia. If the minority report appears as "anti-Christian," and thus pro-Shylock, what becomes of Christian Portia's starring role in court? Is she not bound to save Antonio? Would we prefer it if his heart were cut out on center stage? The ultimate challenge for minority reporters is to discover how Shakespeare may have designed a truly egalitarian, nonprejudicial strategy whereby she persuades Shylock from killing Antonio, and at the same time refuses to let him be converted. Until such a performance can be realized on stage, minority reporters like Kornstein find the courage to speak articulately that Portia's court performance, as we have it, saves Antonio's life, but only at the expense of destroying Shylock's.

What follows is a transcript, not a word-for-word dictation, of the judges' questioning of trial lawyer Kornstein and lawyer Castel. The original dialogue is only available on audiovisual tape. It is recorded here for interested readers to appreciate the liveliness and seriousness with which all the judges treated the appeal. It should be remembered that the intent of the Symposium was to wrestle with the appeal in terms of twentieth-century constitutional law, not sixteenth-century Venetian or English law. Remarks in brackets are my own clarifications.

Both lawyers' briefs are available in separate publications. Daniel J. Kornstein's brief was based largely on his chapter 4, "Fie upon Your Law!" of his recent book, *"Kill All the Lawyers!" Shakespeare's Legal Appeal* (1994). Floyd Abrams's brief has been republished in the *New York Law Journal* (October 30, 1996).

Daniel J. Kornstein:	Your Honors, since my client waived specific performance [i.e., Shylock refused to claim the bond, to cut out Antonio's flesh], the Alien Statute penalties should be reversed. Further, he should receive his original principal [3,000 ducats].
Betty Weisberg Ellerin:	Your client waives forfeiture [of Antonio's flesh] now; can we ignore the pound of flesh claim as a noxious forfeit, against public policy? Does not this invalidate the [financial] agreement?
Kornstein:	Your Honor, look at the genesis of the bond. Shylock was not willing to make the loan at all. Look at the history of anti-Semitism. It was Antonio who put the penalty in. Shylock [treated it] as a joke. It was not until Shylock's daughter

eloped with a Christian. Shylock was distraught. He had no representation, no counsel. It is Antonio who made all the profit. [His three ships really were safe].

Pierre N. Leval: When a contract provides for an award that is unconscionable, the entire contract, is it then not susceptible to award?

Kornstein: Indicating that Leval's question is relevant, but denying unconscionability of the contract, he makes a joke of Shylock honing a blade in court. Your Honor, my client was only scraping off his shoe with a butter knife. [laughter from audience]

Ellerin: Your client was offered his principal three times in open court; he sought the court's good office to sanction a noxious penalty.

Kornstein: He was misled, your Honor, by the fake trial judge. She encouraged him: "You're going to win, don't worry." She was noxious! She talked about mercy, but she was the worst hypocrite in the history of law!

Phyllis Gangel-Jacob: Was she a judge? Was she not simply an expert? Was this a conference and a settlement?

Kornstein: Whatever my client consents to, it's not consent because it was under threat of death. The duke says, if you don't agree we take away your pardon; you die right now. So it's not negotiated!

Gangel-Jacob: But she does say to Shylock: "Are you content?"

Kornstein: When a fake trial judge says these words, she was spitting these words out, in sarcastic, nasty tones, knowing Shylock had no choice. . . .

Leval: On the Alien Statute being unconstitutional, how do you justify this claim? [In the play] there is nothing to compare it with. Surely if a Venetian citizen plotted murder with another Venetian citizen, there would be penalties for attempted murder. You haven't provided evidence from the play that an alien has been illegally discriminated against. If severe penalties exist for citizens, surely a severe penalty is justified for an alien who plots murder?

Kornstein: Not in Venice, New York. [laughter] No "citizen" law there. Why wasn't there one law for both?

Ellerin: Is there a definition [in the play] of what is an alien?

Kornstein:	It's a terrible law; alien is defined by religion, not foreign birth. Shylock is from Venice, he lives there; he works there. Consider my other client from Venice, Mr. Othello. [laughter] He is treated like a citizen, though foreign born.
Howard Kissel:	Are you suggesting an equation between a civil servant [General Othello] and a moneylender?
Kornstein:	Even the fake judge talked of the danger of precedent setting when discrimination appears. The message will go forth, when a minority is involved, that court can ride roughshod. . . . I haven't talked yet about forced coercion of religion; this can't be allowed. It has to be stopped, here and now . . . this is not a comedy, it is serious, it breeds intolerance.
Gangel-Jacob:	Where did the suggestion of conversion come from? Anyone in the court, or proposed from Antonio as a way out of losing all his wealth?
Kornstein:	Once the court endorsed it under the rule of *Shelly v. Kramer*, it became state action, government action. Yes, the court is involved in it. Remember the duke, "If you don't agree, I impose the death penalty; I lift the pardon."
Gangel-Jacob:	Oh, I don't think so. Doesn't the duke say, "Even without your plea for relief from the death penalty [I grant your pardon]?"
Kornstein:	I beg Your Honor's pardon. That's the first time. Let Your Honor check the trial transcript. First time: "I'll pardon your life before you ask," but just a few lines later, after Antonio proposes the hideous conversion, the duke says, "Thou shalt do this, or else I do recant the pardon I late pronounced here." Then Portia (that fake) says, "Jew what dost thou say?" Based on that, everything should be reversed.

The following is the questioning of counsel for Antonio, Kevin Castel:

Kevin Castel:	Antonio is a hard-working merchant. It has long been the law that when illegality permeates an agreement, the whole agreement is unenforceable.
Ellerin:	Why not let both [litigants, Antonio and Shylock] go home? Shylock lost, Antonio is richer by 3,000 ducats. Why did the Venice court go beyond that?

Would criminal sanctions have been there in the first place? Was Shylock familiar with criminal process before criminal trial? Wasn't Shylock converted to a defendant? Why was he given no opportunity to representation?

Castel: My client was the defendant. Shylock hunted him down on the streets of Venice. As for the claim that Shylock is entitled to some relief because he was not represented by counsel, the seventh amendment says you have the right to waive counsel, and it is inappropriate for the court to insist that litigants have one.

Leval: I am troubled by your arguments about the applicability of the Alien Statute. It provides that an alien who seeks the life of a Venetian citizen is subject to forfeitures. Yet these circumstances are not murder but an appeal to a court to grant relief. I'll give an example. If my wife is murdered, or if my daughter is murdered, I ask the court to impose a death penalty on the murderer. That husband, like Shylock, is asking a court to impose a legal sentence. If it is not appropriate under law, if Shylock's bond is contrary to the laws of Venice, then the court will not allow it. The duke says this bond cannot be enforced. End of matter. This is not a matter that falls under an essentially murder statute. How do you justify a murder statute?

Castel: There are exceptions to seeking relief. It was a vengeance attempt, with scales to measure the flesh, and knives—

Leval [interrupting]: It could be put. Here he asks for the court to adjudicate whether he is entitled to a pound of flesh or not? If Portia had said no, he would have gone home, perhaps unhappy.

Castel: There is a tort of abuse of process that says if a party seeks relief for extrajudicial purposes, then the rules are different. Why does he want flesh? "To bait fish with!" This is a revenge attempt.

Ellerin: Not if the court sanctions, as Judge Leval so aptly put it.

Castel: Well Your Honor, let's look at what's happening here. Is this man [Shylock] suffering under criminal law? You will recall that he was pardoned by the duke. Now my client Antonio has nothing to do with any criminal prosecution. He was pardoned, and as for the one half that was to go first to the duke, my client graciously urged the duke to allow Shylock to keep that half. The other half to go to Jessica and Lorenzo, whom Shylock was going to cut out of his will anyway, because of her conversion.

Leval: Antonio very generously "gave away" the part that was going to Venice! [laughter]"

Castel: Yes, I would call him a bright young man.

Ellerin: What authority can you point us to that would bring Shylock under the definition of "alien"? After all he's permitted to do business in a thriving commercial area; he is an active commercial person. Where in the statute is the word alien defincd?

Castel: Your Honor, the definition is not in the statute. The fact of the matter is at trial when Shylock is accused of being an alien, he did not say, "Oh no, I am not an alien here." He did not reserve that issue for appellate trial. [laughter]

Ellerin: To get back to due process, perhaps had he been on notice before he walked into that court, he would have consulted eminent counsel such as yourself, to indicate that the statute did not apply to him?

Castel: Well, I think Judge Leval raised a very important point in his questioning of counsel [Kornstein] here. What is the penalty for attempted murder of a citizen? We know in seventeenth-century England it would have been forfeiture of land and goods. So it may very well have been here. All of your goods go to the duke. In fact an alien in Venice might have been the recipient of more favorable treatment. The fact is, this is civil litigation. I would think there is a slight problem of statutory limitation to bring habeas corpus proceedings 400 years later. . . . I would be happy to address the "mistake point" raised by Mr. Kornstein, that is, the bond is not dependent on ships coming in; ships are not mentioned. There is an absolute obligation to pay within three months. If Shylock wanted to be a big sport about all this, he could have decided to forbear bringing litigation. He's the guy who

	declared a default. He went out of court. If he had waited and the ships came in, it would have been a different story. But this case must be adjudicated at the time of trial. Not on the basis of a subsequent happy discovery that the ships are not lost.
Alscher:	Counselor, isn't it true that the wording of the Alien Statute is: "If any alien attempt to take the life of a citizen"? Isn't it correct that it does not actually say, "attempt to murder a citizen?" It says, "take the life."
Leval:	It says "seek the life."
Castel:	Directly or indirectly.
Alscher:	Exactly. Isn't it correct that your client, on the Rialto, is reported by Shylock to have spit, kicked verbally abused, physically harassed and treated like a dog the moneylender? Is that not correct?
Castel:	I'm happy that you raised this very [relevant] question. [laughter]
Alscher:	I do want to know, did your client do those things?
Castel:	First of all, it's not in the trial record. This comes from Shylock's mouth.
Alscher:	Did your client deny the allegation that Shylock made, when he said, "On Wednesday last you called me misbeliever, cutthroat dog. How can you dare to ask me for moneys if I am only a stranger cur?" Did Antonio reply, "When did I say that, Shylock?"
Castel:	If you will give me an opportunity to respond I will do the best that I can for my client Antonio. I don't claim that my client is an angel. [laughter] Venice N.Y. was not a place without bigotry. I would like to show what more Shylock had to say when he first met Antonio. He was first introduced by Bassanio:
[Aside]	How like a fawning publican he looks. I hate him for he is a Christian, But more for his low simplicity, He lends out money gratis, And brings down the rate of usance Here with us in Venice [I.iii.38-49].
	It's apparent that Shylock is active and willing to participate in the ethnic bias that is prevalent in this town. It's wrong, but it has nothing to do with the adjudication of Shylock's claim against Antonio.

Alscher: It has a great deal to do with how we accept the credibility of the Venetian court. Because if it's true that Antonio was attempting to seek the life of the moneylender—not with a pointed knife to the heart—but [a slower death], with repeated kicks to the groin, abusive language. If your client is degrading the moneylender to the point that life is metaphorically being taken from him, and our moneylender is pleading: can't we come to some kind of truce, where we can [respect each other] . . . you will stop taking life from me—which your client refuses to consider; he cruelly swears "I'll spit on thee again." There is no apology from him. [He's supposed to be more kind than the Jew]. These grievances were brought by Shylock out of court [when he had no knife]. Antonio had a golden opportunity to say: "Shylock, I'm sorry, I won't do it again."

Castel: The question you ask is very relevant because we see it in the city of New York in 1996. Gangs are formed on the basis of ethnicity, racial taunts are everywhere. But the law is very clear. The fact that someone is taunted on the basis of race is a wrong act, but it never justifies murder or attempted murder. That is a pretty clear and important principle that this court upholds.

Alscher: In that case I would put it to you that there was no attempted murder in the courtroom. You tell me what evidence you have, since your client is very much alive [and no one forcibly resisted Shylock].

Castel: Your Honor, why are we here today? Are we here to review the criminal conviction of Shylock? Absolutely not. Is Antonio on trial for bigotry? Or false accusations?

Alscher: The answer to both questions is yes.

Castel: Then I submit the issue of notice and opportunity to be heard is relevant now. These charges are not contained anywhere in the record.

Leval: But Shylock is certainly appealing from forfeitures disposed of [by Alien Statute], including forced conversion.

Castel: Absolutely correct. On the point of forced conversion, my client is certainly not seeking to enforce in this court or any other court. Nothing in the

	record—
Kissel:	[reading text] Your client suggested—
Castel:	My client suggested—
Alscher:	[interrupting Kissel and Castel] He did not suggest it, he demanded it [as a condition of waiving the duke's fine]!
Ellerin:	It was enforced by the court. The court decreed it.
Castel:	Your Honor, with all due respect, what happened is that the duke agreed to that or, he said, "I'll revoke the pardon." But the fact is that everyone there knew that a pardon [from the duke] is irrevocable [laughter].
Leval:	To return to the principal of the loan. You cite reference that Shylock was not permitted to recover the principal when the contract has an unconscionable clause. The whole is unrecoverable. All well and good. But there is also the principle of unjust enrichment. Without need to resort to contract, one who confers benefit may have it restored. Even if under contract law, why not give him back what was his?

[Time expires.]

When we withdrew to our "chambers"/conference room to grapple with these conflicting issues, it was apparent we would not have—in ten minutes!—the time we wanted to sort through the volatile issues raised. A quick head count on the two most heated issues, the Alien Statute and forced conversion, showed we were at least divided, with no unanimous decision there. Before any further discussion or voting, I expressed my own immediate dismay at the audience hilarity that accompanied the performance of the trial scene. I mentioned that I had seen at least four public performances of *The Merchant* and the audiences had never laughed, especially not during such a crucial turning point as "Is that the law?" I pointed out that this was probably the most serious of Shakespeare's comedies, that high school teachers and college teachers, not to mention many theater directors avoided the play because of its potentially divisive anti-Semitism. I then asked if I could present to them quickly my "King James theory" of the play, which was my reconstruction of Shakespeare's original presentation of the play to the King James I, on February 10, 1605. Judge Leval, who was our "foreman," agreed.

I made several points before my time ran out: The 1605 trial staging was balanced. Portia reads "quality of mercy" to both men simultaneously. Portia was indebted to Shylock for lending the money at all, given Antonio's hostility. A dignified, outspoken Shylock repents of his oath to Abraham's God.

Otherwise, Antonio had no legal defense. Portia is relieved. She reads the Alien Statute to both Shylock and Antonio. She tries to get Antonio to tear up the Alien Statute with Shylock's dropped knife. Antonio refuses. He accepts the financial benefits of the Alien Statute, then demands the Jew's conversion. Portia refuses, defending Shylock's religion. The duke insists that Shylock sign the deed of the gift but not the conversion. Shylock loses financially but retains his dignity, his Jewish identity. Antonio wins financially but is shamed.

There was no time left to amplify or ponder this theory. I did say that the "original" staging could be performed today, but that it had not been, as of yet. Returning to the staging as we had just seen it, which was fairly typical of many contemporary performances where the Shylock character does not stand up to the Antonio character as an equal i.e., asking Antonio directly for an apology in the "Signior Antonio" speech but instead asks the audience to like him. Judge Leval took a head count on the Alien Statute and the conversion appeal. Judge Gangel-Jacob indicated she would not overrule on either of those issues, noting that Shylock voluntarily accepted Antonio's stipulation. Judge Ellerin registered immediate surprise and dismay at her colleague's conclusion. I made no comment. Judge Kissel joined with Gangel-Jacob, pointing out that anti-Semitism was "the norm" in Elizabethan England. Without further discussion, Leval, Ellerin, and I had voted for Kornstein's appeal, that is, for two reversals. Kissel and Gangel-Jacob voted to uphold the "lower court" judgments.

Judge Ellerin then suggested we vote on "principal and interest," as there might be greater agreement there. She reminded us that we were trying to think in terms of contemporary law and how such a case would be decided today. Here there was a 4–1 split in favor of not awarding Shylock his original principal when he asks, "Shall I not have barely my principal (IV.341)?" Judge Leval was the dissenter here, taking his allotted opinion time to defend his vote. I record that in the last section of this report. I initially asked to abstain on this issue because it was the least on my priority list and might seem misleading out of context. It might seem I wanted to penalize Shylock by not even granting him his mere principal back. My reasoning was the opposite of penalty. I believed Shylock never wanted just his principal from Antonio. He wanted far more: either the merchant's real friendship, or his "worthless" flesh. So awarding him his principal when Antonio denied the friendship would be just another slap in the face, beneath his dignity. That was why Shylock furiously turned 6,000 ducats down in open court. I thought this demand for 109,000 ducats or even 3,000 was the only weak part of Kornstein's argument.

Judge Ellerin expressed a different viewpoint when she stressed that having turned down more than the principal to ask the good offices of the court to sustain his bond claim, he could no longer expect what he said he did not want.

Leval asked us to vote whether Shylock was "entitled" to receive a pound of Antonio's flesh. Here we might surely have come to one unanimous decision, "no." Here I was again a lone dissenter. I confess I remained dedicated above all to the defense of William Shakespeare, as I read him, framing his Antonio not as the model, generous, heroic savior of the play, but as the arrogant obstacle to a reconciliatory ending. His excessive liberality at Shylock's expense almost brings disastrous grief upon Bassanio, not to mention anguish for Portia. I applaud Shylock for not endangering his own conscience before God by cutting out Antonio's heart, but I don't see Shakespeare providing Antonio with any credible legal defense given the reputation for strict reading of contracts to which Venice commits itself. If Shylock had been the vengeful, thirsty monster he was alleged to have been, Antonio would have been a dead man, just as Portia initially predicted. Antonio asked for the penalty. Shylock showed him mercy.

In light of our divergent responses to all the issues presented, Judge Leval decided we should each have five minutes *in open court* to speak to any issue we wanted. Checking his watch and multiplying five times five he quickly reduced that to four minutes each! In this last section I paraphrase my fellow Judge's spoken opinions, including my own minus what has already been reported. The actual order of presentation was: first, Kissel; second; Alscher; third, Gangel-Jacob; fourth, Ellerin; and last, Leval.

In her stated opinion on the Alien Statute and the conversion issue Judge Gangel-Jacob, though, aligned with the academic majority in refusing to over-turn the Venetian court ruling, and was in the minority in our court. She stressed that as a trial judge herself she did not like to be overruled on appeal. Laughter from the audience followed. Thus, she was voicing a parallel reasoning to most *The Merchant* teachers who also prefer not to radically "appeal" a character like Portia, whom they perceive as a consistent Shakespeare heroine, especially as "his spokesman" in the trial scene. The judge proposed that it was ultimately Shylock's choice to convert, in order to have the fine waived by the duke, on the one half of his wealth owed to the state. Against the objection of Kornstein that Shylock had no choice when Antonio made this conditional demand (for the favor of waiving the fine, he must presently become a Christian), because before Shylock had a second's opportunity to challenge Antonio, the duke retorted "You shall do this or I do recant the pardon," the judge insisted that the Venetian trial judge (the duke) was not being coercive, but "only persuasive." Laughter followed. He was "encouraging" Shylock to accept a good deal offered, not really threatening him with instant hanging if he refused Antonio's "offer," Judge Gangel-Jacob concluded.

Judge Ellerin responded immediately to this conservative opinion with a more sweeping liberal opinion upholding Kornstein's appeal. First, she pointed out affectionately and without any rancor that as an appellate judge she also did not like to overturn lower court judges "lightly." (Laughter from the audience followed). But in this case, she asserted the "lower" decision had to be overturned. Her major argument against the Venetian Alien Statute was that by contemporary standards, Shylock was definitely not an alien in Venice, because he lived there, worked in the city, engaged in legal trade there, and so by implication was Antonio's equal in this conflict. Just because he was Jewish was not sufficient reason to discriminate against him. Furthermore, she reasoned, the statute was brought wrongfully as a criminal punishment [because of its death penalty] in what was essentially a civil suit brought by Shylock.

Judge Leval later pointed out in support of this overruling, that the moneylender was not plotting private vengeance but openly asking the court's approval, in a deliberate legal manner, obeying all the rules, to claim a legally binding (as he saw it) contract forfeited.

Judge Ellerin developed her ruling thus: a modification of Shylock's bond, as against public policy; then a reversal of the criminal sanctions—the Alien Statute financial penalties; on conversion: "to force someone to undergo a religious conversion because he brought a civil suit is outrageous." In summary, Ellerin ruled, "for affirming the nonrecovery of the bond itself [no principal returned], with a reversal and dismissal of criminal sanctions (i.e., reversing all financial forfeitures against him and vacating the conversion stipulation)."

In explaining his sole dissenting opinion in favor of returning Shylock's principal to him, without interest, Judge Leval acknowledged that courts seek general applicability providing just results instead of enforcing morality. Normally, then, a contract that violates public policy forfeits all rights to claims. In this case it is claimed that Shylock's interest rate is generally usurious. But who can determine what are usurious interest rates? "Why not give Shylock what is his?" Leval asked the audience. "Portia is brilliant," Leval asserted, "in her judicial ruling: 'No jot of blood, no more and no less' [than a pound exactly], because here she is refusing to enforce a contract that is against public policy." "But then," Leval lamented, "her legal talents go astray." The Alien Statute is not necessarily unconstitutional, he maintained—aliens are always treated harsher than citizens—but it is harsh—the statute is antimurderers, not anti someone like Shylock seeking the court's permission. Therefore, the forfeitures were illegally exacted, so they should be reversed (in addition, his principal awarded).

Judge Howard Kissel, voting against our court's holding and sustaining the Venetian court on the issues of The Alien Statute and the conversion, made several passionate and insightful comments on the play as a whole. To the surprise of the largely lawyerly audience, he observed that Shakespeare ("Let's kill all the lawyers!") had ironically proved the "necessity for lawyers" through this play. (This drew laughter from the audience). Both men had gone to court without lawyers because they thought they wouldn't need one: Shylock, with his knife and scales because he thought he had Venetian law on his side; Antonio because he, too, believed Shylock would win. Kissel also pointed out that Shakespeare lived in an age where anti-Semitism was the norm, and that Shakespeare was far more evenhanded about Shylock than his contemporary Christopher Marlowe, who caricatured a Jewish financier in his popular hit play *The Jew of Malta*.

Judged by the laws of Venice at the time, Kissel felt that Shakespeare gave Shylock an entirely fair trial. He noted that the evening's performance omitted

Shylock's reference to slavery. He does not say that slavery is wrong, only that he is as much entitled to Antonio's flesh as the Venetians are to their slaves. Kissel observed that we look at the play from a curious perspective, in hindsight. Slavery was not an issue then nor was anti-Semitism. Both were accepted. There was an artificiality about our present discussion because of the advantage of our hindsight. He stressed that the play is very, very complicated. He said the play perfectly exemplified Marianne Moore's definition of poetry: "imaginary gardens with real toads." What goes on in Belmont when wealthy girls can marry because their suitor guesses the right casket—that's a fairy tale. But then there's a very real toad, and that's Shylock. On the question of anti-Semitism Kissel alluded disparagingly to critic Harold Bloom, whom lawyer Abrams quoted as saying that *The Merchant* was "the most anti-Semitic of all plays" referring to a Jew. "That is nonsense," Kissel retorted. "The reason that we still get anxious" he suggested, "is not that it's [the play] anti-Semitic. If it were straight anti-Semitic like its model, *Il Pecorone* . . . or even Christopher Marlowe's *The Jew of Malta*, there would be nothing at issue. The extraordinary thing is that in a world in which Jews are counted as the killers of the savior, you have incredible speeches like "Hath not a Jew eyes?"

In response to a later question from the audience Kissel emphasized again that Shakespeare gave his alleged "villain" some of the best lines in the play. Kissel reminded the audience of one. When Jessica suddenly elopes with the Christian Lorenzo, stealing his ducats, and selling his wedding ring for a pet monkey, the Jewish father is devastated by her thievery and her betrayal of him: "Out Tubal," Kissel recalled from memory, expressing Shylock's grief and shock at her betrayal, "That turquoise—I had it of Leah when I was a bachelor. I would not have given it for a wilderness of monkeys." "Shakespeare was no anti-Semite," Kissel closed. He was a philo-Semite!

In my public opinion (for the Kornstein appeal), I first replied that I disagreed strongly with Kissel and felt that anti-Semitism was very much an issue in the play while later agreeing on one subject of Shakespeare's philo-Semitism. I asserted that anti-Semitism was at the heart of the trial conflict, and why we as a group were here at Hofstra still engaged with it. I pointed out that one wouldn't find another forced conversion in any of Shakespeare's other thirty-seven plays, and that we wouldn't be concerned with a literary trial that was unjust only in its financial arbitration.

I suggested to the audience and judges a reconciliatory theory more favorable to Shakespeare. I related that on February 10, 1605, Shakespeare gave a command performance of *The Merchant* for King James. It was the sixth Shakespeare play the king had watched. The unique effect of *The Merchant* was that the king insisted on seeing it again. My theory is that James did not like the resolution of the trial scene he saw. Shylock's anguished repentance over his bond claim made Antonio look like a loser—just as Morocco and Aragon were losers in their Belmont casket trials. They did not give and hazard all from the heart, where Shylock had. So with Antonio. He had withheld from Shylock, he abused him instead. Shakespeare, I suggested, was an egalitarian Christian (i.e., not fundamentalist, not supercessionist, not triumphal theologically, where Jews were concerned). So Portia was speaking for Shakespeare when she interceded in defense of Shylock, against Antonio's demand that he convert. Antonio looks embarrassed, rebuffed. The king, I theorized, told Shakespeare, "It's a wonderful play, full of marvelous scenes, except for the trial: You had that villain Jew in the palm of your hands, why didn't you convert him?! For the sake of England, William, come back here in two days with that Jew converted. England will never forget that!"

Under that pressure, Shakespeare directed a second performance two days later on February 14 with Shylock converted. He did not have to change a single word of his script! (Remember King James I is the sponsor of the King James version of the Bible). In writing the "new" conversion, Shakespeare never included stage directions into his script. It has simply been the acting tradition for almost 400 years. No wonder we are confused and frustrated over that scene. Shylock (as Kissel emphasized) may be a toad, but a very real toad who gains our sympathies on many levels. We cannot believe he would accept those conditions, especially coming from Antonio. Since Antonio persistently shows contempt toward him and no love of neighbor, for Shylock to "become a Christian" means that he will, like Antonio, become a hater of other Jews. No wonder so many school systems throughout the world avoid teaching the play altogether.

I will close this report of the Hofstra *Merchant of Venice* trial appeal with one off-the-record example of what for me illustrates movingly Judge Kissel's Shakespearean philo-Semitism. In the recent 1996 Stratford Ontario production of *The Merchant*, director Marti Marden introduced a ground-breaking stage direction at the high point of tension in the trial scene. In most contemporary stage performances of the play, even when they deviate from the strict majority scenario, Portia is still shown tacitly approving of Antonio in his acceptance of the Alien Statute forfeitures and then again in his conversion demand. In Marden's direction, as though anticipating at least some of our own Hofstra deliberations in support of the Kornstein appeal, the Portia character, quite confident about defending Antonio up to the point that she convinces Shylock to drop his knife, has sudden second thoughts when Gratiano coolly knocks off Shylock's yarmulke, in preparation of his imminent conversion. With Shylock on his knees frightened and humiliated, actress Susan Coyne walks deliberately to center stage facing the audience. She hides her head with both hands. Shaking her head, she appears to cry over what is happening to Shylock. "How," she appears to be asking herself and the audience, "did it ever come to this?"

Part VI

Law and Art

19

Cass Gilberts's United States Supreme Court and the Comprehensive Planning Deal

Barbara S. Christen

American architect Cass Gilbert (1859–1934) is best known today for his designs of the beaux–arts inspired U.S. Custom House (1899–1907), his premiere New York skyscraper the Woolworth Building (1911–1913), and his contributions as consulting architect on the George Washington Bridge (1927–1931). In his own time, however, it was the Minnesota State Capitol (1896–1906) that established Gilbert as a nationally recognized architect. As a result of that particular work, he received commissions for a wide variety of government, civic, residential, and commercial projects. At the peak of his architectural career in the 1920s, Gilbert was commissioned to design a new building for the U.S. Supreme Court in Washington, D.C. This project represents one of Gilbert's grandest forays into the realm of civic architecture and also reflects the architect's familiarity with the classical antique architectural vocabulary at a time when modernism was moving rapidly into the mainstream of architectural expression.

Gilbert was particularly proud of the Supreme Court building and considered it to be among the most significant designs that he had produced during his fifty–year tenure as a leading architectural authority. As in other projects, Gilbert sought the highest quality materials and workmanship available. Ironically, this strategy included enlisting the aid of Italian Fascist leader, Benito Mussolini, to secure richly veined Sienese marble for the decoration of the central courtroom. Although Gilbert appears to have been impressed by *Il Duce's* dictatorial political skills, the architect's real concern was in creating the finest building possible.[1] The project even included a $200,000 budget for sumptuous and dignified furnishings, although the presiding justices insisted upon keeping their old courtroom seats that were valued at a total of $35.[2]

These anecdotes aside, the most significant feature of the U.S. Supreme Court is its placement within the urban fabric of Washington, D.C., which suggests Gilbert's long–standing interest in, and experience with, comprehensive planning. In fact, Gilbert considered himself to be as much a planner as an architect. By late in his career, Gilbert was producing works of vast public scale that differed greatly from those of a more modest scale and local context (such as his Shingle-style houses, and Renaissance- and Gothic-revival commercial buildings) that he had produced earlier. Gilbert's plans for the U.S. Supreme Court exemplify this shift in orientation—from an essentially local architect to that of a public planner—a transformation that is worthy of examination.

The project was Gilbert's last major endeavor. Completed posthumously, the $10 million building became the court's first permanent home after earlier structures had been located at various sites in New York, Philadelphia, and Washington, D.C. Ironically, though Gilbert had not been Chief Justice William Howard Taft's first choice as designer, Taft became the major proponent of Gilbert's design. Henry Bacon, the celebrated architect of the Lincoln Memorial, was initially Taft's choice, but when Bacon died unexpectedly in 1924, the chief justice contacted Gilbert to produce preliminary studies.[3] By 1928, with the formation of the Supreme Court Building Commission, progress on the new building had gathered momentum.

In this last project of his career, Gilbert elaborated on the formal and conceptual building arrangements that had captured his attention in earlier plans for Washington, D.C. (1900), St. Paul, Minnesota (1902), and New Haven, Connecticut (1908–1909). In each of these projects, Gilbert became involved with planning questions as an outgrowth of his contact with persuasive representatives of national and local institutional organizations. In the case of Gilbert's Washington, D.C., proposal, Glenn Brown, Secretary of the American Institute of Architects (AIA), effectively drew Gilbert into the public discussion of city planning issues for the first time in Gilbert's career by urging him to produce a plan for the reorganization of the core of the federal city.[4]

Gilbert's Washington, D.C. plan markedly influenced the later 1902 Senate Park Commission plan (also known as the McMillan plan) for the capital city. In his 1900 plan, Gilbert supplemented the ideas presented in Pierre Charles L'Enfant's 1792 plan for the capital city. Gilbert envisioned a balance between the Library of Congress and a similar (although then unidentified) building located just north of the library on East Capitol Street. These two buildings (of Gilbert's design) were meant to anchor the U.S. Capitol—the architectural symbol of democracy. The later Senate Park Commission report embellished this idea of surrounding the Capitol with a series of monumental buildings reserved for congressional and Supreme Court use.[5] In so doing, the commission recommended that "at no distant day" the Supreme Court should be built in the location where Gilbert had proposed his unidentified structure in 1900. This recommendation was carried out when the site was chosen over a quarter century later for the new court building.[6]

In sketches for the new building, Gilbert located the court and its corollary, the Library of Congress, as part of an approaches scheme similar to his 1902 Minnesota State Capitol Approaches Plan. As in his federal plan, Gilbert proposed a boldly simple yet symbolic building group that would anchor the capitol in St. Paul. Also as in his Washington, D.C. plan, Gilbert employed axial boulevards to connect the Minnesota State Capitol with the downtown of St. Paul. In his Supreme Court sketch (ca. 1929–1932), Gilbert proposed sweeping boulevards that extended radially from an unidentified area that was perhaps to include a park or monument. The U.S. Supreme Court, the congressional library, and the nation's capitol formed the mainstay of his plan. Gilbert thus revisited the formal features that he had proposed in both his 1900 and 1902 city plans.

Indeed, the use of a symbolic building group was a fundamental component of Gilbert's thinking. It was one that he had implemented in several campus and city plans during the peak of his career. In all of these designs, by following the beaux–arts formal principles and reform–oriented concerns of the City Beautiful ideal, Gilbert exhibited his strong interest in, and commitment to, creating environments that were more ordered, coherent, and appealing.

Cass Gilbert's campus and city plans (including those for the Minnesota State Capitol Approaches, New Haven, the University of Minnesota, the University of Texas, and Oberlin College) represent a significant chapter in American architectural and planning history. Gilbert was attuned to city planning questions initially through his beaux–arts oriented training at the Massachusetts Institute of Technology and his experience as a young draftsman between 1878 and 1880 at the New York firm of McKim, Mead & White. This experience was enhanced by his exposure to the visual and harmonious architectural order of the 1893 Chicago World's Columbian Exposition.

By 1900, Gilbert was ready to develop his own planning ideas. He did so by applying the visual and theoretical aspects associated with the City Beautiful movement which he had absorbed from his earlier experiences. Specifically, these aspects included the grand axial orientation of his plans, the architecturally bounded space enclosed by his building groups, the hierarchical arrangement of the component parts, as well as the belief that these ordered, classically–inspired spaces would elevate the human spirit by providing a noble and dignified living environment.

Examined as a group, these master plans illuminate Gilbert's contribution to the national application of such City Beautiful characteristics. This issue united late–nineteenth– and early–twentieth–century architects, planners, and designers alike in a common quest. Although Gilbert kept his distance from institutional groups such as the American Park and Outdoor Association and the American Civic Association—which championed the City Beautiful cause—his projects in St. Paul and Minneapolis, Minnesota; Austin, Texas; and Oberlin, Ohio reflect the visual and programmatic influence of beautification ideas.

Gilbert's work with the landscape architect, Frederick Law Olmsted, Jr., and their publication, *Report of the New Haven Civic Improvement Commission* (1910), represent the culmination of the architect's earlier experiments in master plans. In Gilbert's mind, the New Haven project represented a model for urban development. Gilbert came to this project after producing several station designs for the New York, New Haven, and Hartford Railroad, including those for Morris Park (1907), Pelham Manor (1907), Bartow (1909–1910), and Hunt's Point (1909–1910), all located in the Bronx, New York.[7] In late 1907, as president-elect of the AIA, Gilbert delivered at the Yale School of Art a lecture entitled, "The Grouping of Public Buildings," one of a series of six lectures that addressed the topic of civic improvement. In this talk, Gilbert revisited many of the same topics that he had addressed in his 1901 essay that had been published in association with his federal plan of 1900. These topics included questions about unity in composition; building scale, height, and proportion; and color and texture in materials. Most of all, he promoted the cause of beauty, while he did so with language stressing the need for economy and efficiency.

The New Haven plan, like Gilbert's St. Paul approaches plan, made use of a wide, axially oriented boulevard to connect key municipal centers.[8] Gilbert's 1908–1909 proposal for this grand boulevard would have connected two of the most vital areas of the city, the transportation and municipal centers. His proposals for the New Haven Railroad Station (1918–1919), the Ives Memorial Library (ca. 1908–1911), the Hall of Records, and the courthouse were all part of this master plan.[9]

Conceptually, Gilbert's national service on the Commission of Fine Arts (1910–1916) brought his ideas almost full circle. Along with such illustrious members as Daniel H. Burnham, Frederick Law Olmsted, Jr., Daniel Chester French, Francis D. Millett, Thomas Hastings, and Charles Moore, Gilbert was appointed to the first commission. This group was charged with reviewing the design and proposed location of all federal projects (including buildings, fountains, statues, monuments, and parks) that would affect the appearance of Washington, D.C.[10] In contrast to Gilbert's rather aloof attitude with respect to City Beautiful organizations, Gilbert was deeply committed to this position and prided himself on his active involvement in the commission.

The commission's first major project was to review the design and location of the Lincoln Memorial—the centerpiece of the 1902 Senate Park Commission plan. In 1911, the Commission of Fine Arts recommended that the Lincoln Memorial Commission follow the 1902 plan. Gilbert was so pleased with the Lincoln Memorial Commission's final recommendation to follow the 1902 plan that he called it "their greatest triumph." Gilbert's promotion of this influential earlier plan reflects his continuing interest in the ideas that he had broached in his own plan of 1900 for Washington. Thus, over a decade after his first forays in comprehensive planning, Gilbert was involved in the reemergence of these very same issues in discussions about the federal city. Then, over a decade after these early experiments, in the mid-1920s, Gilbert implemented these ideas in the design and construction of the U.S. Supreme Court.

Gilbert's plans for the U.S. Supreme Court constitute a potent reminder of the architect's varied experience with the questions of comprehensive planning. The architect's own experience, coupled with the general interest in, and excitement about, public design early in the century, caused Cass Gilbert to develop a unique planning rationale that he expressed in decades of architectural practice.

NOTES

1. As early as 1918, Gilbert admired the Italian leader from afar. Several years later, Gilbert tried to dissuade Mussolini from transforming Rome with the world's largest and tallest skyscraper—one that would dwarf St. Peter's. Gilbert first met Mussolini in 1927 (coincidentally on the same day that he had an audience with the king and queen of Italy) and again met the Duce in 1933. *See* correspondence and letter books, New York Historical Society and Library of Congress/Manuscripts Collection.

2. Cass Gilbert, Jr., *Courthouse*, 63 ARCHITECTURAL FORUM 11 (November 1935).

3. For reproductions of these studies, *see* Allan Greenberg & Stephen Kieran, *The United States Supreme Court Building, Washington, D.C.*, 128 ANTIQUES 760–69 (October 1985). Period photographs of the court are reproduced in Cass Gilbert, Jr., *The United States Supreme Court Building*, 72 ARCHITECTURE 300–34 (December 1935).

4. Cass Gilbert, *Grouping Buildings and Development of Washington, in* PAPERS RELATING TO THE IMPROVEMENT OF THE CITY OF WASHINGTON, DISTRICT OF COLUMBIA 78–82 (Glenn Brown ed., 1901). For a detailed discussion of Brown's contributions to the reshaping of the capital city, *see* William Brian Bushong, Glen Brown, the American Institute of Architects and the Development of the Civic Core of Washington, D.C. (1988) (unpublished Ph.D. dissertation, George Washington University) (on file with author). For an analysis of Gilbert's and Brown's relationship and also Gilbert's essay, *see* Barbara S. Christen, *Cass Gilbert and the Ideal of the City Beautiful: City and Campus Plans, 1900–1916*, Chapter 2 (1997) (unpublished Ph.D. dissertation, City University of New York) (on file with author).

5. JOHN REPS, MONUMENTAL WASHINGTON: THE PLANNING AND DEVELOPMENT OF THE CAPITAL CENTER 109, (1967).

6. *Id.* at 115.

7. Howard Frederick Koeper, The Gothic Skyscraper: A History of the Woolworth Building and Its Antecedents Appendix B (unpublished Ph.D. dissertation) (on file with author). *See also* Howard Frederick Koeper, *Along the "Harlem River Branch,"* 24 ARCHITECTURAL RECORD 417–29 (December 1908); and the Pelham Station as noted in Guy Kirkham, *Cass Gilbert: Master of Style*, 15 PENCIL POINTS 551 (November 1934); and photographs of the stations in the photo album, N.Y., N.H. & H.R.R. CO./THE SCHOOL OF INDUSTRIAL ART, TRENTON, N.J. (available at the Avery Art and Architectural Library).

8. This plan was published in THE RELATIONS OF RAILWAYS TO CITY DEVELOPMENT 48–49 (Glenn Brown, ed.).

9. For photographs of the Ives Memorial Library design, *see* photo album, IVES PUBLIC LIBRARY, NEW HAVEN/NEW HAVEN R.R. STATION (available at Avery Art and Architectural Library).

10. For general historical background on the Commission, *see* John W. Reps, MONUMENTAL WASHINGTON, THE PLANNING AND DEVELOPMENT OF THE CAPITOL CENTER 153–56 (1967); Sue A. Kohler, THE COMMISSION OF FINE ARTS: A BRIEF HISTORY, 1910–1976, WITH ADDITIONS 1977–1984, REV. ED., (1985); THE COMMISSION OF FINE ARTS, 1910–1963; A BRIEF HISTORY

BY H.P. CAEMMERER; SECRETARY OF THE COMMISSION, 1922–1954, WITH LATER REVISIONS AND ADDITIONS (1964); Sally Kress Tompkins, A QUEST FOR GRANDEUR: CHARLES MOORE AND THE FEDERAL TRIANGLE (1993); Glenn Brown, BILL FOR A NATIONAL ADVISORY BOARD ON CIVIC ART AND A PLEA SHOWING THE DEMAND AND NECESSITY FOR SUCH A BOARD (1906); Glenn Brown, THE DEVELOPMENT OF WASHINGTON; WITH SPECIAL REFERENCE TO THE LINCOLN MEMORIAL, (December 13, 1910 address); Cass Gilbert, *Roosevelt and the Fine Arts: A Forward*, 116 AMERICAN ARCHITECT 709–10 (December 10, 1919). For an in-depth study of the Lincoln Memorial, *see also* Christopher A. Thomas, *The Lincoln Memorial and Its Architect, Henry Bacon (1866–1924) (1990)* (unpublished Ph.D. dissertation, Yale University) (on file with author).

Index

About the Editor and Contributors

FLOYD ABRAMS is a partner at Cahill Gordon & Reindel in the general litigation department, a graduate of Yale Law School, and formerly a federal court clerk. He is considered to be one of the most famous and successful media lawyers in the United States, having won landmark First Amendment cases in the U.S. Supreme Court.

PETER J. ALSCHER is a Shakespeare scholar currently at work on a book about *The Merchant of Venice*. His unpublished dissertation is "Shakespeare's *Merchant of Venice:* Toward a Radical Reconciliation and a Final Solution to Venice's Jewish Problem."

NATHANIEL BERMAN is a professor of law at Northeastern University School of Law. His work focuses on nationalism and colonialism in the international legal imagination. He has written several studies on the cultural Modernist transformation of international law during the interwar period. His work deploys a range of disciplinary techniques, including those drawn from literary theory, art history, and postcolonial theory.

CHRISTIAN BIET is a professor of literature at the University of Paris X at Nanterre, and he focuses on history and theater at the Institute of Theatrical Studies. He has written several books about law and literature primarily of the classical period in France.

P. KEVIN CASTEL is a partner with the firm of Cahill Gordon & Reindel. He is former Chair of the Commercial and Federal Litigation Section of the New York State Bar Association. He serves as an officer and trustee of the Federal Bar Council and is a member of the Departmental Disciplinary Committee for the Appellate Division, First Department. He is a member of the Council on Judicial Administration for the Association of the Bar of the City of New York.

BARBARA S. CHRISTEN is executive director of Cass Gilbert Projects for the U.S. Courthouse and the Smithsonian Institution in New York. She has taught and lectured at the State University of New York at Stony Brook, the Whitney Museum of American Art, and several other institutions in the metropolitan area.

LAURA COHEN was born in France, and she is both an American and French citizen. She is currently a student at Sarah Lawrence College and is attending the British Academy of Dramatic Arts for her junior year. She has performed in both French and American productions.

SUSAN J. DRUCKER is an attorney and associate professor of speech communication and rhetorical studies at the Hofstra University School of Communication. Her primary interests include media law and the impact of laws on social interaction and interpersonal communication in public space. She is the author of many articles, and her current research centers on the implications of new technologies, social cohesion, and the field of legal geographies.

BETTY WEINBERG ELLERIN is an associate justice of the appellate division of the Supreme Court of the State of New York, First Department. She was the first woman appointed to that bench in March 1985, and she is chair of the New York State Judicial Committee on Women in the Courts.

HOWARD FAST is the author of many well-known novels, such as *Citizen Tom Paine* (1943), *Freedom Road* (1944), *Spartacus* (1952), and *Being Red* (1990). He is the recipient of many prestigious writing awards. He experienced years of hardship as a writer when he was placed on the black list during the McCarthy era.

DONALD FISHMAN is an associate professor in the Department of Communication at Boston College. His publications and reviews have appeared in many scholarly journals, and his research interests include libel, freedom of expression, and copyright. He is currently working on a book about censorship.

ERIC M. FREEDMAN is a professor of law at Hofstra University School of Law. His primary areas of interest are constitutional law and history with a special emphasis on First Amendment topics.

PHYLLIS GANGEL-JACOB is a justice of the New York State Supreme Court in New York county. Formerly a union organizer and social worker, she was elected a judge of the New York Civil Court in 1984 and a justice of the

New York Supreme Court in 1993.

WILLIAM R. GINSBERG is the Rivkin, Radler, & Kremer Distinguished Professor of Environmental Law at Hofstra University School of Law. Prior to joining the Hofstra faculty, Professor Ginsberg was a partner in a New York law firm and held appointive positions in New York City and state governments.

GARY GUMPERT is professor emeritus at Queens College, City University of New York, and the former chair of the Department of Communication Arts and Sciences at Queens College. He has published extensively, and his current research focuses on the relationship of new communication technologies and the use of public spaces.

LEANNE KATZ was executive director of the National Coalition Against Censorship since its formation in 1974. She was a consultant for Human Rights Watch, prepared papers for and led workshops at the Biennial Conference of the American Civil Liberties Union, and was consultant to a Task Force on Academic Freedom of the Modern Language Association. She delivered numerous public addresses and wrote widely on freedom of expression. She passed away on March 2, 1997.

DAVID KENNEDY is the Henry Shattuck Professor of Law at Harvard Law School where he teaches international law, international economic policy, legal theory, and contracts. He has practiced law with Cleary, Gottlieb, Steen and Hamilton in Brussels and worked with a variety of international institutions, including the United Nations and the Commission of the European Communities. He has been active in developing new approaches to international and comparative law among younger scholars, with a focus on the perspectives of women and scholars from the Third World.

DUNCAN KENNEDY has taught at Harvard Law School since 1971. He teaches property, contracts, torts, low-income housing law and policy, and the history of American legal thought. He was one of the founding members of the Conference on Critical Legal Studies. His most recent book is *A Critique of Adjudication (fin de siècle)* (1997).

LAWRENCE KESSLER is the Richard J. Cardali Distinguished Professor of Trial Advocacy at Hofstra University School of Law. Professor Kessler is a national expert in the field of trial advocacy training. He is a former senior trial attorney for the Legal Aid Society, Federal Court Branch, and has actively practiced law as a criminal defense attorney in the federal district courts for more than twenty-five years.

HOWARD KISSEL has been the drama critic of the *New York Daily News* since l986. Before that, he reviewed theater and films for *Women's Wear Daily* and *W*, where he was the arts editor for fifteen years. He is the author of "David Merrick: The Abominable Showman" and has written for *Vogue*, *Gentlemen's Quarterly*, *Playbill*, *Interview*, and other publications.

DANIEL J. KORNSTEIN is a practicing lawyer at Kornstein, Veisz & Wexler, LLP, in New York City. In addition to his busy litigation practice, he has published four books and hundreds of articles, essays, and book reviews. Much of his recent work has been in the law and literature field, and he was president of the Law and Humanities Institute from l991 to 1998. His interest in Shakespeare is exemplified in his book *Kill All the Lawyers? Shakespeare's Legal Appeal* (1994).

MITCHEL LASSER is an associate professor at the University of Utah College of Law, where he teaches comparative law, labor law, judicial process, and European Union law. His publications include "Judicial (Self-) Portraits: Judicial Discourse in the French Legal System" 104 *Yale Law Journal* 1325 (1995), and "'Lit. Theory' Put to the Test: A Comparative Literary Analysis of American Judicial Tests and French Judicial Discourse," in the *Harvard Law Review* (1998).

PIERRE N. LEVAL is a judge of the U.S. Court of Appeals for the Second Circuit, which sits in New York and covers the states of Connecticut, New York, and Vermont. He has been a judge for nineteen years, having served for three years on his present court and previously as a trial judge in the U.S. District Court for the Southern District of New York. Prior to his appointment to the bench, Judge Leval was a partner of the firm of Cleary, Gottlieb, Steen and Hamilton, where he specialized in international business transactions and was a federal and state prosecutor.

JASON O'CONNELL is a 1993 graduate of Hofstra University's theater program. He was born and raised in East Northport, Long Island, and he now lives in New York City where he has worked as an actor for the past four years. Mr. O'Connell has played a variety of Shakespearean roles from Hamlet to Falstaff, and he is also a stand-up comedian and freelance cartoonist.

STUART RABINOWITZ is dean and Andrew M. Boas and Mark L. Claster Distinguished Professor of Civil Procedure. He joined the Hofstra Law faculty in 1972 and has taught every class that has graduated from Hofstra Law School. His areas of special interest include communications law, civil procedure, federal courts, and conflict of laws.

SONDRA M. RUBENSTEIN is chair and associate professor of the Department of Journalism and Mass Media Studies in Hofstra University School of Communication. She has written extensively including articles on U.S. libel law and media violence.

PETER M. SANDER is chairman of the Hofstra University Department of Drama and Dance and a graduate of Carnegie-Mellon University. He is coauthor of *The Actor's Eye*. He is a professional actor and has appeared in New York and regional theater performances as well as film and TV shows. He played Shylock in the *Merchant of Venice* as a guest artist.

NORMAN SILBER is a professor of law at Hofstra University School of Law, and he specializes in consumer protection and regulation. He was law clerk to Judge Leonard I. Garth of the U.S. Court of Appeals for the Third Circuit and then practiced with the law firm of Patterson, Belknap, Webb & Tyler. He also taught history at Sarah Lawrence College and Yale University before becoming a law professor.

ARLENE STERNE is a professional actress and playwright. She was a broadcast journalist and talk-show host for TV and radio in Paris, Vienna, Addis Ababa, and Ottawa, Canada. She has appeared off-broadway, in regional theaters, dinner theaters, summer stock, film, and television. She wrote a one-woman play, *Final Curtain*, which premiered at Carnegie Hall in New York, and she has been performing it successfully in the United States and Europe. She played the role of Portia in *The Merchant of Venice* as a guest artist.

SUSAN TIEFENBRUN is the President of the Law & Humanities Institute, director of Hofstra's International Law Summer Program in Nice, France, administrative director of Hofstra's International Programs and LL.M. Program, and an adjunct professor of Law at Hofstra University School of Law where she teaches international business transactions and European Union law. She taught French literature at Columbia University and Sarah Lawrence College for more than twenty years before becoming a lawyer, and she has written extensively in the field of law and literature.

RICHARD H. WEISBERG is the recipient of the Walter Floersheimer Chair in Constitutional Law at the Benjamin N. Cardozo Law School of Yeshiva University. He was an editor of the Law Review at Columbia University. He is the author of three books in the field of law and literature, and he is the general editor of *Cardozo Studies in Law and Literature*.

ROBIN WEST is professor of law at Georgetown University Law Center. She teaches torts, feminist legal theory, jurisprudence, and law and literature at the Georgetown Law Center. She has written extensively in the field of law and literature.

ISBN 0-313-30805-5

EAN

9 780313 308055

HARDCOVER BAR CODE